Economic and Political Change after Crisis

The US government's accumulated national debt and unfunded liabilities in Social Security and Medicare could be pushing the country towards a fiscal crisis. How could such a crisis be avoided? If a crisis does strike, how might it be dealt with? What might be the long-term ramifications of experiencing a crisis? The contributors to *Economic and Political Change after Crisis* explore all of these questions and more.

The book begins by exploring how past crises have permanently increased the size and scope of government and how well the rule of law has been maintained during these crises. Chapters explore how these relationships might change in a future crisis and examine how the structure of the US government contributes to a tendency towards fiscal imbalance. In a provocative contribution, one author predicts a US government default on its debt. The book concludes by considering how a fiscal crisis might precipitate or interact with other forms of crises.

Social scientists from a variety of disciplines, public policy-makers and concerned members of the general public would all benefit from the contributions contained in this book. If the US is going to avoid a future crisis, or do as well as possible if a crisis occurs, the arguments in these chapters should be given serious consideration.

Stephen H. Balch is Director of the Institute for the Study of Western Civilization, Texas Tech University, USA.

Benjamin Powell is the Director of the Free Market Institute and a Professor of Economics in the Jerry S. Rawls College of Business Administration at Texas Tech University, USA.

Routledge Foundations of the Market Economy
Edited by Mario J. Rizzo, New York University,
and Lawrence H. White, George Mason University

A central theme in this series is the importance of understanding and assessing the market economy from a perspective broader than the static economics of perfect competition and Pareto optimality. Such a perspective sees markets as causal processes generated by the preferences, expectations and beliefs of economic agents. The creative acts of entrepreneurship that uncover new information about preferences, prices and technology are central to these processes with respect to their ability to promote the discovery and use of knowledge in society.

The market economy consists of a set of institutions that facilitate voluntary cooperation and exchange among individuals. These institutions include the legal and ethical framework as well as more narrowly 'economic' patterns of social interaction. Thus the law, legal institutions and cultural and ethical norms, as well as ordinary business practices and monetary phenomena, fall within the analytical domain of the economist.

For a full list of titles in this series, please visit www.routledge.com/series/ SE0104

30. Markets, Morals, and Policy-making
A new defence of free-market economics
Enrico Colombatto

31. Understanding the Culture of Markets
Virgil Storr

32. Producing Prosperity
An inquiry into the operation of the market process
Randall G. Holcombe

33. Austrian Economics Re-examined
The economics of time and ignorance
Mario Rizzo and Gerald P. O'Driscoll Jr

34. Economic and Political Change after Crisis
Prospects for government, liberty and the rule of law
Edited by Stephen H. Balch and Benjamin Powell

Economic and Political Change after Crisis

Prospects for government, liberty and the rule of law

Edited by Stephen H. Balch and Benjamin Powell

First published 2017
by Routledge
2 Park Square, Milton Park, Abingdon, Oxon OX14 4RN

and by Routledge
711 Third Avenue, New York, NY 10017

Routledge is an imprint of the Taylor & Francis Group, an informa business

© 2017 selection and editorial matter, Stephen H. Balch and Benjamin Powell; individual chapters, the contributors

The right of Stephen H. Balch and Benjamin Powell to be identified as the authors of the editorial material, and of the authors for their individual chapters, has been asserted in accordance with sections 77 and 78 of the Copyright, Designs and Patents Act 1988.

All rights reserved. No part of this book may be reprinted or reproduced or utilised in any form or by any electronic, mechanical, or other means, now known or hereafter invented, including photocopying and recording, or in any information storage or retrieval system, without permission in writing from the publishers.

Trademark notice: Product or corporate names may be trademarks or registered trademarks, and are used only for identification and explanation without intent to infringe.

British Library Cataloguing in Publication Data
A catalogue record for this book is available from the British Library

Library of Congress Cataloging in Publication Data
A catalog record for this book has been requested

ISBN: 978-1-138-20180-4 (hbk)
ISBN: 978-1-315-50569-5 (ebk)

Typeset in Times New Roman
by Cenveo Publisher Services

Printed and bound by CPI Group (UK) Ltd, Croydon, CR0 4YY

Contents

List of illustrations	viii
Notes on contributors	ix
Acknowledgements	xi

1	Introduction	1

STEPHEN H. BALCH AND BENJAMIN POWELL

PART I
Crisis and government power   **11**

2	Crisis without Leviathan?	13

ROBERT HIGGS

2.1 Introduction 13
2.2 Crisis as opportunity 15
2.3 Normality versus crisis 16
2.4 Opportunists' actions create the crisis ratchet effect 18
2.5 The crisis opportunist's priority list 25
2.6 Can anything be done? 28
2.7 Conclusion 32

3	The rule of law during times of economic crisis	36

TODD ZYWICKI

3.1 Introduction 36
3.2 Constitutional crises and constitutional opportunity 36
3.3 Maintaining the rule of law in times of crisis 39
  3.3.1 The rule of law and economic recovery 40
  3.3.2 The need to adhere to the rule of law 41
  3.3.3 Codifying short-term suspensions of the rule of law 43
  3.3.4 Moral hazard 47

vi *Contents*

3.4 *What determines whether constitutional crises*
lead to good or bad outcomes? 49
3.4.1 Accident 49
3.4.2 Elites 50
3.4.3 Popular ideology 53
3.4.4 Inevitability and the weakness of legal
constraints 56
3.5 *The rule of law and the next crisis 61*

PART II
Fiscal crisis   **71**

4 Fiscal crisis as a quality of progressivist democracy   73
RICHARD E. WAGNER

4.1 *Introduction 73*
4.2 *Public debt and contractual mythology 75*
4.3 *Public debt within a system of consensual democracy 77*
4.4 *Public debt within a system of factional democracy 79*
4.5 *Two forms of democratic budget tragedy: commons*
and factional 80
4.6 *Unfunded liabilities: more of the same 82*
4.7 *Time, democracy and political capital accounts 84*
4.8 *Expanding governmental scale and intensifying*
democratic oligarchy 87
4.9 *Liberty and democracy: towards constitutional*
reconciliation 89
4.10 *A closing peroration 91*

5 The consequences of a United States default
or repudiation   95
JEFFREY ROGERS HUMMEL

5.1 *Introduction 95*
5.2 *Why default or repudiation is the most likely outcome 97*
5.3 *The cascade into default 100*
5.4 *Short-run consequences 102*
5.5 *Long-run consequences 108*
5.6 *Historical case study 113*
5.7 *Conclusion 116*

Contents vii

PART III
Regime crisis **121**

6 The US military's role in national crises: past,
  present and future 123
  PAUL SPRINGER

  6.1 Introduction 123
  6.2 The military roles in war and peace 125
  6.3 The presidency in wartime 126
  6.4 The military during domestic crises 128
  6.5 The military and modern crises 136
  6.6 The military's role in future crises 138
      6.6.1 A succession crisis 138
      6.6.2 An environmental crisis 140
      6.6.3 An insurrection crisis 141
      6.6.4 An epidemic crisis 143
      6.6.5 A fiscal crisis 143
  6.7 Conclusion 145

7 The dark side of modernity: existential threats to
  life as we know it 150
  TEVI TROY

  7.1 Introduction 150
  7.2 Economic collapse 151
  7.3 The viral danger 155
  7.4 Grid collapse 158
  7.5 The dangers unchecked 163

Index 171

Illustrations

Figures

2.1	Total government spending as a per cent of GDP, United States, 1903–2012	14
2.2	Schematic representation of the ratchet effect	19
5.1	Federal outlays and receipts as a per cent of GDP, 1940–2012	99

Tables

5.1	How big is the national debt?	103
5.2	Holdings by sector of the outstanding national debt	104
5.3	Foreign holdings of Treasury securities	106
5.4	Treasury securities as a per cent of each sector's total financial assets	107

Contributors

Stephen H. Balch is the Director of the Institute for the Study of Western Civilization at Texas Tech University. Before joining Texas Tech University in 2012, Dr Balch served 25 years as founding president and chairman of the National Association of Scholars, an organization of higher education professionals dedicated to the traditional principles of liberal arts education. He earned his PhD in Political Science from the University of California at Berkeley.

Robert Higgs is Senior Fellow in Political Economy for the Independent Institute and Editor at Large of the Institute's quarterly journal *The Independent Review*. Dr Higgs is the author and editor of several books, a contributor to numerous scholarly volumes and author of more than 100 articles and reviews in academic journals. He earned his PhD in economics from Johns Hopkins University.

Jeffrey Rogers Hummel is a Professor of Economics at San Jose State University. He also serves as a Research Fellow at the Independent Institute. Professor Hummel is the author of *Emancipating Slaves, Enslaving Free Men: A History of the American Civil War* and a contributor to numerous scholarly volumes. He has published several peer-reviewed articles in the fields of economics and history. He earned his PhD in history from the University of Texas at Austin.

Benjamin Powell is the Director of the Free Market Institute and Professor of Economics in the Rawls College of Business at Texas Tech University. Professor Powell is the North American editor of the *Review of Austrian Economics*, past president of the Association of Private Enterprise Education and a Senior Fellow with the Independent Institute. He earned his PhD in Economics from George Mason University.

Paul Springer is an Associate Professor of Comparative Military History at the Air Command and Staff College, located at Maxwell Air Force Base, Alabama. Dr Springer is a Senior Fellow with the Foreign Policy Research Institute and the author of several books and articles in peer-reviewed academic journals. He earned his PhD in history from Texas A&M University.

x   *Contributors*

Tevi Troy is CEO of the American Health Policy Institute and a former Deputy Secretary of Health and senior White House aide. Parts of this chapter were excerpted from his book, *Shall We Wake the President? Two Centuries of Disaster Management from the Oval Office* (Guilford, CT: Lyons, 2016).

Richard E. Wagner is the Harris Professor of Economics and Director of Graduate Studies in the Department of Economics at George Mason University. Professor Wagner is the author and editor of several books and articles in peer-reviewed academic journals. He has served as editor of the scholarly journal *Constitutional Political Economy* and as a member of the editorial board for other academic journals. He earned his PhD in economics from the University of Virginia.

Todd Zywicki is George Mason University Foundation Professor of Law at George Mason University School of Law, Executive Director of the Law and Economics Center, Senior Scholar of the Mercatus Center at George Mason University and Senior Fellow at the F.A. Hayek Program for Advanced Study in Philosophy, Politics and Economics. Professor Zywicki is the author of more than 70 articles in leading law reviews and peer-reviewed economics journals. He earned his JD from the University of Virginia.

Acknowledgements

We are grateful for the research environment and support that Texas Tech University has provided us. This book resulted from a joint research project by the Free Market Institute (FMI) and the Institute for the Study of Western Civilization (ISWC), both at Texas Tech University. The chapters in this volume were presented as working papers at a one-day research conference hosted by our institutes in May 2015. As editors, we benefited greatly from the feedback that the contributors and our colleagues at Texas Tech provided on each of these chapters at the conference. A special thanks is due to FMI's Senior Administrator Charles Long, who was involved in every stage of the project. Thanks are also due to Audrey Redford, who was then a Research Assistant at FMI, and who did most of the work preparing the final manuscript, to James Dean, who aided in proofing the manuscript, and to Catherine Galley, Administrative Assistant at the ISWC, who made substantial contributions to the organization and management of the research conference.

We also thank the Bradley Foundation and the Earhart Foundation for the financial support that allowed our institutes to commission these chapters and host the conference.

Routledge has been a great publisher to work with to bring the final product together. Our thanks to two anonymous reviewers and Routledge's senior editor, Andy Humphries, who all provided valuable revision suggestions that improved this volume. We also thank Elanor Best, who helped to see this book through to completion at Routledge.

We are, of course, most grateful to the contributors to this volume. It was their diverse scholarly knowledge that ultimately made this book possible.

1 Introduction

Stephen H. Balch and Benjamin Powell

'You never want a serious crisis to go to waste. And what I mean by that is that it is an opportunity to do things that you think you could not do before.'[1] Those were the words Rahm Emanuel, chief of staff to the then President-Elect Barak Obama, spoke on television in 2009. Scholars have also long appreciated how crises can open up the opportunity for policy changes that were previously not possible. Writing in 1962, the future Nobel Laureate economist Milton Friedman stated, 'Only a crisis produces real change ... This, I believe, is our basic function: to develop alternatives to existing policies, to keep them alive and available until the politically impossible becomes the politically inevitable' (2002, xiv).

Friedman's observation provides the motivation behind this volume. We think that the United States is in danger of experiencing a crisis in the not too distant future. The most obvious candidate for the cause of the crisis is the unsustainable trajectory of federal government debt and the unfunded liabilities accumulating in the Social Security and Medicare programmes. If this crisis comes about it is crucial that we understand the policies, institutional arrangements and political incentives that led to the crisis and what reforms might help to avert future crises. It will be precisely at that moment of crisis that this understanding is most needed because that's the opportunity where major shifts in policies and institutions become possible.

Chapters 3 through 5 consider how a US fiscal crisis might come about and what might come in the wake of that crisis. Other types of crises are possible as well and may interact with, or stem from, a fiscal crisis. Chapters 6 and 7 examine the likelihood and reforms that might be needed in alternative forms of crisis or how an economic and fiscal crisis might precipitate or interact with other crises. But before proceeding to the future, the next chapter in this book examines how US policy has changed in response to past crises and what, if anything, might make policy respond differently in the future.

It is our hope that by examining some of these ideas now, before the crisis, we might help to start a dialogue to 'develop alternatives to existing policies and keep them alive and available', so that the United States might better respond to crises in the future than it has in the past. Before proceeding to that task, we should put into context some of the major changes in governance that have occurred throughout the world over the past 200 years and the role that crises have played to get a perspective of what is at stake.

2   *Stephen H. Balch and Benjamin Powell*

We sometimes think of the period 1776–1815 as the 'Age of Revolution'. It might better be thought of a revolutionary seedbed after which, throughout the Western world, political fundamentals could no longer be taken for granted. Europe, for centuries, had been home to a more varied ensemble of regimes than anywhere else in the world, but most of these regimes changed only slowly and rarely with reference to any ideological scheme. A political crisis might change the players but seldom the play. Indeed, historians often refer to the entire period before the French Revolution as the 'Ancien Régime'.

Since then regime collapse – the replacement of one constitutional arrangement by another, the new one purporting to learn from the mistakes, or overcome the ills and evils of its predecessors – has become commonplace. Thus, since 1789 France has known five republics, three kingdoms and two empires. Since 1870 Germany has had one empire, one dictatorship and three republics. Following the disappearance of a 400-year-old empire in 1917, Russia weathered three republics: pre-communist, communist and post-communist. Other European states have experienced similar overturns, as have – to an even greater extent – those in Latin America. By contrast, since the American founding period, the Anglosphere has been revolution-free, even if the amount of evolutionary political change in both the United Kingdom and the United States has been immense. Still, most Americans are apt to forget that the Constitution they have so long cherished is not their country's first but its second.

Viewed historically, regime change might be divided into three categories, each with typical causes, course and costs. Some might be described as 'pragmatic', in which underlying principles and ideology alter little, but regime design and fundamental policies change considerably; others might be termed 'radical', in that the basis of legitimacy changes, and there's a significant break in the continuity of institutions, but some of the underlying principles remain intact; still others can only be termed as 'revolutionary', wherein organizational and social structure, as well as principles of legitimation undergo a sea change, with the past condemned, repudiated and repressed.

Following this scheme, the replacement of the Fourth French Republic by the Fifth in 1958 would fall into the category of pragmatic change as would (though somewhat less so) the transition in the United States from the Articles of Confederation to our current Constitution. The grandfather of pragmatic changes was undoubtedly England's Glorious Revolution of 1688, which preserved the monarchy and parliament, while ousting the monarch and encumbering his successors with all sorts of important restrictions.

Examples of radical change would include the transition from Wilhelmine Germany to the Weimar Republic, both having parliamentary forms and the rule of law, but one a conservative, militaristic monarchy in which the emperor had considerable hereditary power and the other a fractious, civilianized republic. So too would the changes that occurred in some of Austria-Hungary's successor states after the Habsburg Empire's breakup at the close of World War I.

Revolutionary changes occurred when totalitarian regimes arose in Russia, Italy and Germany, and then again after they collapsed. (Though a case could be

Introduction 3

made that, given the relatively brief duration of fascistic totalitarianism in Germany and Italy, the reversion back to parliamentary governments had elements of a pragmatic character in Germany, and a radical one in Italy (where the monarchy was also eliminated).)

Regime crises are generally precipitated by a series of destabilizing events. The initial disaster, whatever its type, doesn't usually wreak its political havoc by itself or all at once. Rather, it produces a succession of shocks ripping away more and more of the confidence and institutional capability that bind a political system together. Fiscal breakdown thus often leads to economic depression and mass privation, mass privation to public disorder, public disorder to a loss of confidence and the spread of organized insurgency, etc. How far this progression proceeds influences the degree of change it produces and the costs society bears in undergoing it.

Pragmatic regime change has more deliberative qualities, involves less disorder, preserves more intact and often produces a regime more durable than the one it replaces. Its signature is the realization by a large portion of a governing elite that a continuation of the institutional or policy status-quo is intolerable and that they must reshape it or risk jeopardizing vital ideals or interests. The reshaping often occurs within the institutions of the faltering regime even as they lead to one that has a rather different architecture. The faster a looming regime crisis can be successfully resolved, and the less ramifying its economic and political damage, the more likely the outcome will be pragmatic.

Radical regime change typically occurs after an existing regime has largely or entirely ceased to function but enough of civil society remains for elements of its leadership to pick up some of the pieces and reassemble them in a form that has resemblance to earlier practices. Formal continuity is broken but a good deal of tradition survives – sometimes through the resurrection of what had been, for a time, abandoned. Radical change often overtakes a government whose legitimacy has from the start been tenuous, as with French regimes of the nineteenth century, or many Latin American states in both the nineteenth and twentieth centuries. Furthermore, it is generally marked by episodes of protracted civil disorder, military mutiny and other tumults either escaped or suppressed under circumstances of pragmatic regime change.

Revolutionary regime change requires the existence of contending, disparate ideologies together with rival elites, perhaps elites and 'counter-elites', who carry them. It generally also requires deep, long-term social divisions of a class or ethnic character. On the one hand, most revolutions have occurred after established regime, social and economic structures have been gravely damaged or demolished through invasion and/or civil war – the case, for instance, in Russian and China. They can also be imposed through conquest, as in Europe after World War II. Nazism, on the other hand, demonstrated that a genuinely revolutionary regime can sometimes come to power through constitutional, even democratic means. (One wonders whether something like this could be happening in parts of the contemporary West.) In any event, a sharp ideological contest preceding the event seems an essential prerequisite.

4 *Stephen H. Balch and Benjamin Powell*

The causes of regime collapse have been subject to exhaustive debate, particularly when historians and social scientists look for the deep, long-term economic, cultural, intellectual or institutional ones. Immediate triggers are somewhat easier to spot and less conjectural.[2] That they are immediate, however, doesn't mean they are casually unimportant. While long-term factors may dispose a polity towards regime change, the presence or absence of an adequate trigger can still determine whether revolution (or milder forms of regime change) will occur or be avoided – and there's no reason to think that a revolutionary opportunity avoided will necessarily come again. Sometimes one of the triggers is simply the presence of a politically gifted leader. Had Lenin been arrested after the Bolshevik's abortive July 1917 uprising, or had never reached Russia from his Swiss exile, the country might have escaped revolutionary regime change and developed as a constitutional republic. Similarly, without Hitler, there probably would not have been anything like a Nazi regime.

An examination of the full range of regime change causes and possibilities is beyond the scope of this book. As already noted our attention will be focused on several that seem most important, predictable and of greatest contemporary relevance to the United States (and many of the states of Europe). One of these, fiscal collapse, has frequently precipitated regime change, though usually after an extended period wherein governments dig themselves ever more deeply into financial holes. Others run the gamut of possibilities, some known since biblical times like pestilence and weather calamity, while still others, like grid breakdown, have a distinctly hypermodern quality.

Fiscal collapse, as the most predictable of our triggers, will be the main target of our analysis. Modern history contains some prominent examples of government insolvency playing a crucial role in political instability and breakdown. Fiscal collapse triggered the French Revolution in 1789 when, after almost two centuries of dormancy, the kingdom's Estates General convened to repair the finances of a debt-laden government but chose instead to begin overhauling its core constitutional structure. The result was a runaway process, politically mobilizing broad sectors of a long quiescent population, stoking a multitude of smouldering grievances, and evoking dramatically conflicting ideologies about the nature of political legitimacy and social class. Likewise, the spreading economic dislocations produced by the overuse of the printing press to fund its World War I efforts was the chief immediate cause of the Tsarist regime's February 1917 collapse. The subsequent disintegration of its army, the failure to provide a new fulcrum of legitimacy and the readiness of hardened revolutionary activists to exploit the resulting confusions transformed this initial radical change into a revolutionary one.

The German hyperinflation from 1920–3, resulting from reparations debt and resistance to foreign occupation, shook Weimar and launched National Socialism. By crippling commerce, weakening civilian morale and undermining state legitimacy the war-fed hyperinflation that wracked Nationalist China during the 1940s helped precipitate regime collapse. Greece's contemporary sovereign debt crisis has been accompanied by riot, protest and severe political polarization, stressing its own constitutional arrangements as well as those of the European Union.

Introduction 5

In none of these cases, however, do we have a fiscal crisis directly overwhelming one of the world's leading financial powers. Indeed, in some cases those powers were available for eventual bailout, rescheduling reparations and providing new credit lines. But should crisis move from the periphery to the centre the consequences would likely be more drastically systemic and much less manageable, threatening unprecedented dislocations and multidimensional instability. A great fiscal crisis come to America would be unmatched in its after-effects.

Apart from their intrinsic interest and under-researched status, we have, for this reason, included two final chapters dealing with reverberations: one considering the societal impact of widespread disorder, plague and famine, the three horsemen that have traditionally produced the fourth – massive mortality; and a second examining the roles the military might be called upon to perform in the face of these horrors. Obviously, chaos and destruction have historically had many causes other than fiscal, but with debt burdens and unfunded liabilities escalating in the United States and a number of other major nations, we believe the connections between fiscal peril and existential risk have become timely subjects for exploration.

Fiscal crises can be the direct result of a debt-caused inability to finance government operations, or a government's attempt to escape indebtedness by monetization, destroying privately held liquidities. In either case the regime's mismanagement reaches a point in which the confidence of its key supporters is lost, and/or those supporters become disorganized, demoralized and too disempowered to resist its enemies.

Economic crises can also occur in the private sector following financial bubbles and banking collapse. Inept government policies can set the stage for these bubbles, as with federal underwriting of sub-primes in 2008, or greatly exacerbate their consequences, as with the monetary contraction overseen by the Federal Reserve after the 1929 US stock market crash. But whether inept government intervention helps bring on a crisis, or aggravates it afterwards, the outcome – at least since the turn of the twentieth century in the United States, ironically – is often an expansion of government's reach and its capacity to do further economic and political mischief. The gradual building of an economically dysfunctional state of political affairs, as well as one increasingly hostile to liberty in general, has been one of the unfortunate concomitants of twentieth- and twenty-first-century fiscal and economic crises. Most of these, while falling short of themselves producing regime change, have nonetheless raised the odds that some sort of regime change would eventually occur. This story is told by Robert Higgs in Chapter 2 of this volume. Higgs concludes by considering how the growth of Leviathan after a crisis might be avoided in the future.

Fiscal and economic crises, by themselves, usually have the relative virtue of not destroying masses of people and infrastructure as other crisis phenomena may. The wheels of industry may slow, economic exchange may falter, but neither wholly disintegrates – the most basic everyday needs continue to be minimally satisfied. None of the fiscal and economic crises in the Western world during the twentieth and twenty-first centuries have, by themselves, brought on

6 *Stephen H. Balch and Benjamin Powell*

the disasters or mortality that normally accompany war, mass famine and widespread epidemics. In addition to considering economic crises, the last two chapters of this book also deal with disasters of these more death-dealing kinds, their consequences – which might well include regime change – and the things authorities can do beforehand to prevent or mitigate them.

In Chapter 6, Paul Springer documents the role that the military played in responding to various domestic crises throughout US history. He then speculates on the role the military might play in future fiscal, presidential succession, environmental, insurrection and epidemic crises and the desirability of the military playing these roles. In Chapter 7, Tevi Troy considers crises involving viral dangers and a grid collapse as well as an economic crisis, but broadens the focus beyond the military and asks more generally what could be done to minimize the risk of these types of crises and what might be done if, in fact, one or more of them occur.

There is a long record of famine and epidemics unsettling regimes. The inability of the Aztec and Inca empires to resist invasion by small bands of Spanish adventurers owed much the devastation wrought by the coincident import of Old World diseases like measles and smallpox. Protracted bad weather seems to have been associated with regime instability or collapse in many parts of seventeenth- and eighteenth-century Europe (Fagan 2002, 149–66). Nowadays, many might think that only regimes in the least developed states might face these dangers. But, paradoxically, high-tech societies have their own special vulnerabilities to these ancient scourges.

Pure food and water, and the efficient disposal of human and animal waste, together with antibiotics and other elements of scientific medicine are usually imagined as offering effective protection against epidemics. There are, however, countervailing factors. One which gave us a serious scare during West Africa's recent Ebola outbreak is the ease and volume of international travel. A second is the interest of contemporary terrorist groups and states in developing and weaponizing highly virulent infectious agents. A third involves lifestyle evolution with respect to factors like diet and sexual practice that can create heightened susceptibilities and new disease pools. A fourth lies in antibiotic use itself, which can select for especially resistant 'supergerms'. Both Ebola and AIDS have already endangered regime stability in parts of Africa, but the developed world is not immune to massive death-dealing contagions, especially if stressed by loss of economic or administrative capacity. A combination of these factors would certainly be regime endangering, all the advantages of modern technology notwithstanding.

But there are other postmodern ways in which a society and regime can become unglued. Perhaps the greatest single point of existential exposure, short of all-out nuclear war, would be the collapse of a modern economy's power grid. A systemic power, communications and IT failure of prolonged duration could create chaos in the ability of people to 'truck, barter and exchange' in the modern world. In less developed economies, closer to subsistence, basic survival skills – the ability to farm and maintain low-level technologies – are likely to be distributed more widely in a population, allowing more people to survive a temporary

Introduction 7

'state of nature'. By contrast, in today's societies, sustained by advanced and highly specialized technologies, this no longer holds. Contemporary society has some of the characteristics of a high-wire act, with a much longer distance to fall if the wire ever snaps. Apocalyptic novels and films rely on an implicit popular recognition of this fact.

Although civilian control of the armed forces is a deeply entrenched Anglo-American tradition, the possibilities of military government in name or essence following systemic collapse, or economic failure, cannot be discounted. Indeed, opinion polls show that while Americans are increasingly disenchanted with the performance of government's civilian branches, the military retains much more respect. George Washington and George McClellan were both urged by some of their colleagues to march on the nation's capital after the prestige of the civilian government had reached a low ebb. Britain, of course, had its Cromwell. By itself the discontinuity represented by even a temporary intervention of the military into American political life would constitute serious regime change. In the terra incognita of postmodernity the possibility can't be discounted.[3]

The Anglo-American political tradition is strongly liberty-centred. Its foundations rest on the ideals and practice of limited, representative government, the rule of law and the exercise of individual liberty and personal responsibility. Whatever else may befall our republic, we want to preserve these ideals and practices. We cannot, however, be complacent about their safety. The history of the US government in the twentieth century as described in the following chapter is, unfortunately, one of a steady expansion of government power, of the growth, if you will, of 'leviathan'. And leviathan is not just gigantic but, in most parts of the Western world, increasingly clumsy, suffocating, lawless and spendthrift. There are many signs that it is heading towards a fall, certainly towards the kind of crisis that will produce, probably compel, substantial changes in how America, and the entire West, continue to be governed. But the shape these regime changes take remains ours to determine.

Of the types of regime changes that can occur, pragmatic ones could solve the looming fiscal crisis with acceptable political and social cost. Pragmatic regime change tends to be the most rational, the least disruptive and most likely to preserve our heritage of existing institutions maximally intact. But for the more drastic alternatives to be avoided, our current elites need to recognize the perils of leviathan and take corrective actions while there is still time.

Right now there isn't much sign of this happening. Accumulating debt and unsustainable entitlements remain the third rails of American politics; few individual politicians are courageous enough to talk candidly about them, and have little collective stomach to pursue adequate remedies. The government also grows more routinely lawless, law-making increasingly devolved upon unelected bureaucrats, or hijacked through presidential or judicial degree in defiance of the plain language of statute and constitution. Such protests as occur among establishment politicians seem largely pro-forma.

Absent pragmatic reforms a fiscal crisis is inevitable. What will come then? In Chapter 3, Todd Zywicki argues for the necessity of maintaining the rule of law

8   *Stephen H. Balch and Benjamin Powell*

during times of economic crises and considers the factors that determine whether the rule of law is maintained during them or not. Unfortunately, he believes that today's political elites have little respect for the rule of law, especially during perceived 'emergencies', and sees little hope that civic education will cause the masses to realize that they should force the elites to respect it. Thus, Zywicki expects the pending fiscal crisis to further undermine the rule of law in the United States.

Richard Wagner also recognizes that a fiscal crisis is coming in Chapter 4. He argues that this crisis has been building for nearly a century and it stems from the American governance system morphing from a limited democracy to a progressive democracy, which encourages unsustainable growth in expenditures and people using politics to live at the expense of others. Rather than a policy error, Wagner sees the pending crisis as a feature of a system of government that requires an ongoing cycle of deficits, debt and debasement. He fears that the fiscal crisis will strengthen the progressive trend in politics but hopes the population will, instead, demand a return to a constitution of liberty that changes the fiscal rules of the game.

Jeffrey Rodgers Hummel, in Chapter 5, also predicts a fiscal crisis but he is more optimistic than the other authors. He predicts that the United States will default and/or repudiate its debt because politics-as-usual will prevent the spending cuts necessary to avert a crisis from being made. He argues that, relative to the other alternatives – such as hyperinflation – repudiation is the best way to deal with the crisis once it strikes and will have the added benefit of making it harder for the US government to borrow in the future. Thus, a repudiation might become a 'balanced budget amendment with teeth' that can help to limit government spending and to avert fiscal crises in the future – in effect, a pragmatic regime change.

When we look beyond current US politics we see the mixed role that financial crises have played in reform around the globe in recent years. In the previous 20 years, Ireland, New Zealand and India all experienced some form of financial crisis immediately prior to significant liberalizations (Powell 2008). There are those, more optimistic than our contributors, who see deepening fiscal problems as often likely to prompt market liberalization. Hans Pitlik and Steffen Wirth, for example, go so far as claim, 'A commonly shared wisdom among economists and political scientists is that crises promote the adoption of market-oriented reforms' (2003, 565). They reached this conclusion by examining how economic growth and inflation crises impacted a broad measure of economic freedom in 57 countries over five-year periods from 1970 through 2000, finding that they were significantly correlated with increases in economic freedom. Similarly, Jakob de Haan, Jan-Egbert Sturm and Eelco Zandberg (2009) found that banking crises are correlated with decreases in the size of government and, as Todd Zywicki documents in Chapter 3, there are instances of economic crises in the United States, such as the 1920 recession, that led to government retrenchment rather than government growth.

However, economists Jamie Bologna and Andrew Young (2015) give us reason to doubt financial crises are correlated with increased economic freedom. They examined 70 countries from 1966 through 2010 using five different types of financial crises (banking, currency, inflation, internal debt, external debt) to see how they impact five major areas of economic freedom (size of government, legal

Introduction 9

structure and property rights, sound currency, freedom to trade internationally and regulation) over five-, ten- and 40-year time periods. For the most part they found that crises were unrelated to economic liberalizations or growth in the size and scope of government.

It should be obvious that the following chapters, while informed by extensive scholarly research, are ultimately speculative. How the institutions of governance will evolve once a crisis strikes the United States will ultimately depend on the ideologies of the elite and mass public, and how crises interact with them.

Approaching crises sometimes succeed in concentrating society's mind. The 'Tea Party' movement has certainly reflected a deeply felt widespread concern about leviathan, and the impossibility of maintaining our current fiscal trajectory. And, as different from the 'Tea Party' as it has been, the 'Occupy Movement' has at least one thing in common with it, a perception of the unholy alliance between big government and big crony business interests. In this, perhaps, they draw upon converging currents of dissatisfaction that only await the appearance of a leadership that can effectively capitalize on them.

If this type of ideology comes to dominate political discourse, perhaps a future crisis will end the domination of big government and return the United States to a system more fully based on liberty, the rule of law and the protection of property rights. Some authors of this volume fear other more revolutionary regime changes could be ushered in during crisis and move us even farther from this form of governance. The record compiled by the more drastic episodes of regime change in recent Western history isn't particularly comforting. Their miseries have been many, and their direction has been, in general, towards authoritarian and statist solutions.

Whether pragmatic changes occur in time to prevent more radical or even revolutionary regime change yet remains to be seen. It is our hope that this volume will help contribute to an understanding of how a storeroom of future troubles is being built up by departures from the spirit of the American founding and how future rational reforms can move us in the direction of smaller, less intrusive government and greater individual liberty.

Notes

1   https://www.youtube.com/watch?v=1yeA_kHHLow
2   For a review and critique of some of the main alternative approaches, see Clifton B. Kroeber, 'Theory and History of Revolution'. *Journal of World History* 7, no. 1 (1996): 21–40.
3   http://www.gallup.com/poll/1597/confidence-institutions.aspx

References

Bologna, Jamie, and Andrew T. Young. 'Crises and Government: Some Empirical Evidence'. *SSRN Working Paper*, 2015. http://papers.ssrn.com/sol3/papers.cfm?abstract_id=2313846

De Haan, Jakob, Jan-Egbert Sturm and Eelco Zandberg. 'The Impact of Financial and Economic Crises on Economic Freedom'. In James Gwartney and Robert Lawson, eds, *Economic Freedom of the World 2009 Annual Report*. Vancouver, BC: Fraser Institute, 2009, pp. 25–36.

Fagan, Brian. *The Little Ice Age: How Climate Made History 1300–1855*. New York: Basic Books, 2002.

Friedman, Milton. *Capitalism and Freedom*. Chicago: University of Chicago Press, 2002.

Kroeber, Clifton B. 'Theory and History of Revolution'. *Journal of World History* 7, no. 1 (1996): 21–40.

Pitlik, Hans, and Steffen Wirth. 'Do Crises Promote the Extent of Economic Liberalization? An Empirical Test'. *European Journal of Political Economy* 19, no. 3 (2003): 565–81.

Powell, Benjamin, ed. *Making Poor Nations Rich: Entrepreneurship and the Process of Economic Development*. Stanford, CA: Stanford Economics and Finance, Stanford University Press, 2008.

Part I
Crisis and government power

2 Crisis without Leviathan?

Robert Higgs

2.1 Introduction

In 1801, when Thomas Jefferson became president of the United States, the national government was simple, small and limited. The only executive departments were Treasury, War, Navy, State and Post Office. A century later, when Theodore Roosevelt became president, the set of executive departments had been enlarged to include also Interior, Justice and Agriculture. Still another century later, when George W. Bush became president, the set of departments had been enlarged much further to include also Commerce, Labor, Defense (in lieu of the longstanding War and Navy departments), Health and Human Services, Housing and Urban Development, Transportation, Energy, Education and Veterans Affairs. In addition, during the twentieth century a number of cabinet-level positions had been created for a variety of new administrative and regulatory agencies, such as the Office of Management and Budget, the Council of Economic Advisers, the Small Business Administration and the Environmental Protection Agency.[1] The state and local governments likewise have expanded their fiscal, administrative and regulatory activities enormously since the nation's beginning, especially during the past century. As a result, very few areas of economic and social life now remain beyond the reach of government influence, management, or regulation and 'private' activities in general are subject to a great variety of such impact and control.

When Jefferson became president the national government had no regulatory functions and hence no regulatory agencies, independent or otherwise. A century later, not much had changed in this regard. There were only two such agencies: the Interstate Commerce Commission and, within the Department of the Treasury, the Office of the Comptroller of the Currency (to oversee the national banks, members of a system spawned during the War Between the States). There are now, however, so many such agencies and so much disagreement about their character and functions that no generally accepted list of them exists. Certainly hundreds of them exist at the federal level alone. Given the similar proliferation of administrative and regulatory activities at the local and state levels during the past century, it is probably fair to say that hundreds of thousands of distinct regulatory offices and agencies exist in the United State and the total number of their distinct rules, regulations, ordinances and other decrees is unimaginably gigantic, almost certainly in the millions.[2] Red tape, the USA is thy home and hearth.

To carry out the stupendously enlarged scope of its activities, the government has had to spend ever more money and – by taxation, borrowing, money creation and other means – to obtain the funds it expends. Probably the most commonly used index of the size of government is its total outlays as a percentage of the gross domestic product (GDP).[3] This measure indicates that, for more than a century, the national government scarcely grew at all except during major wars, after each of which a retrenchment to the *status quo ante bellum* occurred completely or almost completely. Beginning at some point in the early twentieth century, however, the trend tilted markedly upward. Thus, national, state and local governments that, except during wartime, had never spent altogether an amount equivalent to more than 7–8 per cent of GDP began to increase their aggregate rate of expenditure rapidly after 1914 – even more markedly, perhaps, after 1929. The upshot was that the government spending ratio rose almost six-fold after 1900 and now stands in the neighbourhood of 40 per cent.

A careful inspection of Figure 2.1 – and, even more clearly, an inspection of the underlying data – indicates that all of the large, abrupt, upward lurches in the spending ratio were associated with the onset of major national emergencies, especially the US engagement in the world wars, the Korean War, the Great Depression and the recent recession, which became most obvious during the financial debacle of late 2008 and the associated collapse of private employment

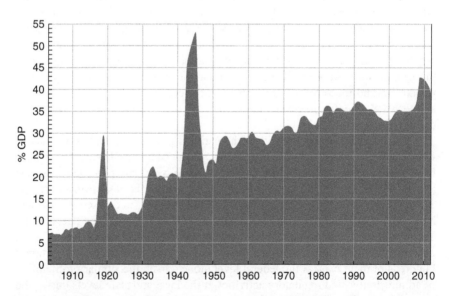

Figure 2.1 Total government spending as a per cent of GDP, United States, 1903–2012.

Source: usgovernmentspending.com

Crisis without Leviathan? 15

and income that continued into 2009. Careful historical research shows that other aspects of the growth of the government's size, scope and power have generally corresponded with national emergencies in the same fashion.[4]

None of these lurches was followed by a complete retrenchment to the pre-crisis status quo. Hence each of them represents an instantiation of the *ratchet effect*. This effect is best understood in terms of what I call *the political economy of crisis opportunism*.[5] If the continued growth of government is to be stopped, much less reversed, we must understand why the ratchet effect has occurred repeatedly during the past century in the United States (and in many other countries). This effect arises from certain definite factors under particular preconditions, which themselves may be subject to moderation or elimination. Indeed, unless such alterations are brought about, the ultimate result of the unchecked growth of government must ultimately be a breakdown of the politico-economic system with potentially devastating effects on economic and social life. It therefore behoves everyone who cares about the future to gain a deeper understanding of the matters discussed here and, for practical effect, to spread this understanding and thus help to bring about actions to halt and reverse the government's growth as soon as possible. Everyone's future freedom and prosperity hinge on the success of such efforts.

2.2 Crisis as opportunity

In personal life, no one relishes a crisis, but in political life, many people pray for a crisis as drought-stricken farmers pray for rain. For these people, a societal crisis promises to bring not extraordinary difficulties, dangers and challenges, but, rather, as many now frankly admit, enlarged opportunities. President Barack Obama's Chief of Staff Rahm Emanuel made no attempt to conceal his appreciation of such latent potential when he averred recently: 'You never want a serious crisis to go to waste. [T]his crisis provides the opportunity for us to do things that you could not do before.'[6] We need to understand how a crisis creates new opportunities for political actors and why it does so.

Politicians are not, however, the only ones who perceive opportunity in a crisis. Other types of actors also spring forth to exploit the economic, social and political changes that crisis brings. These opportunists include ideologues who have previously failed to augment their ranks or attain their programmatic objectives; economic-privilege seekers (now often called 'rent seekers') who have previously found themselves stymied by public hostility or political opposition; and militarists who see a new opening to promote their favourite foreign adventures and who sometimes tout military spending as a cure for economic malaise, and overseas military interventions as a tonic for depressed public morale and as an avenue to 'national greatness'. We must also understand how these various opportunists seek to exploit a crisis for the achievement of their particular ends and identify the conditions that promote or impede their designs.

The events of the past eight years illustrate clearly the political economy of crisis opportunism. After the financial crisis came to a head in the summer of

16   *Robert Higgs*

2008, the nation – and, to a large extent, the whole world – was buffeted by a tempest of unprecedented government measures ostensibly intended to save large financial firms from bankruptcy, to assist homeowners, businesses and others affected by the credit stringency, the housing bust and the deepening recession, and to brake the overall economic decline with huge infusions of 'stimulus' spending. By the end of November 2008, the government (including the Federal Reserve System) had committed $8.5 trillion – an amount equivalent to more than half the GDP – to an assortment of financial assistance measures, 'including loans and loan guarantees, asset purchases, equity investments in financial companies, tax breaks for banks, help for struggling homeowners and a currency stabilization fund' (Pender 2008). The snowball continued to roll, becoming ever larger during the following six months. On 15 June 2009, the *Wall Street Journal* reported:

> Since the onset of the financial crisis nine months ago, the government has become the nation's biggest mortgage lender, guaranteed nearly $3 trillion in money-market mutual-fund assets, commandeered and restructured two car companies, taken equity stakes in nearly 600 banks, lent more than $300 billion to blue-chip companies, supported the life-insurance industry and become a credit source for buyers of cars, tractors and even weapons for hunting.
>
> Government spending as a share of the economy has climbed to levels not seen since World War II. The geyser of money has turned Washington into an essential destination for more and more businesses. Spending on lobbying is up, as are luxury hotel bookings in the capital.
>
> (Davis and Hilsenrath 2009)

We may debate whether the actual economic conditions warranted such extreme government reactions – in my judgement they did not – but there is little doubt that government officials, politicians, media commentators and substantial elements of the public viewed the economic events of 2008 and 2009 as the onset of a national emergency. Moreover, they believed that these extraordinary events warranted extraordinary government measures.

2.3 Normality versus crisis

During normal times in a modern representative democracy, political life involves much pulling and hauling with relatively little to show for all the efforts. Many individuals and interest groups seek to attain their political ends, but the legislature can attend to relatively few of these matters at the same time, and many proposals must perforce be rejected or set aside for the time being. Moreover, as a rule (analogous to Newton's Third Law of Motion), for every political action there is an equal and opposite reaction. Virtually every proposal of much importance has both organized supporters and organized opponents, and in the great majority of cases the opponents are strong enough to block a proposal's adoption or to weaken it substantially.

Crisis without Leviathan? 17

It's not as though nothing gets done, however. Even a 'do-nothing' Congress may enact hundreds of bills in a session; the regulatory agencies churn out several thousand new or revised regulations each year at the federal level alone; and the courts decide a multitude of cases. But most of these actions are fairly inconsequential. The public swallows them without choking, if indeed it has any awareness of them. Lawyers rewrite some contracts; payroll administrators and accountants tweak their software. Life goes on, altered, to be sure, but not altered greatly. As Jefferson famously remarked, 'The natural progress of things is for liberty to yield and government to gain ground,'[7] but in normal times, liberty does not yield greatly and government does not gain much ground.

We may liken Jefferson's 'natural progress of things' to a river's current, which flows invariably towards the sea. Most of the time this current is slow and predictable, and the river stays within its banks. The trees that loggers cut, trim and shove into the river for transportation downstream we may liken to the proposals and cases that interested parties push onto the legislatures, the regulatory agencies and the courts. The floating logs are usually so numerous that when the river's current and water level are normal, logjams form, impeding the passage of nearly all them. Occasionally, a log may break away and continue downstream, or the loggers, risking life and limb, may go onto the floating jumble and undertake to loosen the mass of logs and set some of them free to continue downstream.

In politics, the natural flow consists of an ideological current. Especially since the ascendancy of progressivism, more than a century ago, Americans (and Western Europeans and many others as well) have viewed the government as the institution of first resort for the solution of perceived social and economic problems. This progressive inclination, however, is not the same as a yearning for totalitarianism. Most people, including most progressives, continue to believe that in normal times the government should be limited, though they disagree about where the limits should be placed. People are normally disposed to appreciate that a private sphere ought to be preserved and that, especially in economic life, the invisible hand of market relations can accomplish much good and ought not to be smashed to pieces by the visible fist of the state.

A crisis, however, alters the fundamental conditions of political life. Like a river suddenly swollen by the collapse of an upstream dam, the ideological current becomes bloated by the public's fear of impending harm and its heightened uncertainty about future developments. Bewildered people turn to the government to resolve the situation, demanding that government officials 'do something' to repair the damage already done and to prevent further harm. The public's cry, for the most part, is not for any particular government action, because in truth few members of the public have a definite idea of what should be done. Nevertheless, the people demand that the government do something, trusting that public officials will react to the situation intelligently and effectively. In sum, *under modern ideological conditions*, the onset of a crisis is marked by heightened deference to public officials, increased trust in their judgement and greater willingness to grant them considerable discretion in selecting and implementing a course of action (Higgs 2007).

18 *Robert Higgs*

In shaping a response to this public outcry, government officials draw from three major reservoirs. The first consists of plans and programmes the government was already seeking to implement that had been blocked by public or interest-group opposition (e.g. the USA PATRIOT Act of 2001, for the most part a collection of provisions long sought by the Department of Justice). These policies are already sitting, as it were, on the government's shelf, and government officials need only take them down, whisk off the dust and put them into operation as soon as they receive formal authority to do so. The second source of crisis actions consists of proposals put forth by organized interest-group advocates (e.g. the Agricultural Adjustment Act of 1933, for the most part a collection of subsidy schemes long sought by agricultural lobbies and financially related interest groups). Like the government's own off-the-shelf policies, these plans and programmes may have languished for a long time without political success. Finally, the government and the interest groups may bring forward fresh proposals that they have formulated quickly as the crisis has developed – attempts, so to speak, to 'strike while the iron is hot' (e.g. proposals to raise the prices of agricultural exports in 1933 by abandonment of the gold standard and the resulting devaluation of the dollar in international exchange).

All of these proposals, under normal conditions, would serve only to clog the policy logjam even tighter, but, in a crisis, they actually have a much greater chance of adoption. This enhanced potential arises in part from the public's fear-driven insistence that the government 'do something' extraordinary to restore peace, order, security, or prosperity. Government officials perceive that adoption of a slew of new laws and regulations will be widely and favourably viewed as 'doing something'. In addition, the government and the interest groups may dynamite the logjam, so to speak, by an implicit agreement that every important group may get its most desired policies adopted now, if only each group will set aside its normal objection to the other groups' most desired policies. Thus, what political scientists would call a huge 'log roll' (i.e. a collection of self-serving vote trades) breaks what I have called the normally prevailing policy logjam. Crisis therefore produces a virtual free-for-all adoption and implementation of policies, programmes and plans that expand the government's power in new directions and strengthen it where it previously existed in a weaker form.

2.4 Opportunists' actions create the crisis ratchet effect

In analysing the crisis-driven growth of government, it is useful to think in terms of a stylized *ratchet effect*. This shows schematically how such episodes pass through five distinct phases, the net effect of which is to lift the trend line of the government's growth to a higher level. We may identify these phases as follows: I, pre-crisis normality; II, expansion; III, maturity; IV, retrenchment; and V, post-crisis normality. The most important aspect of this representation is that the retrenchment phase is insufficient to return 'the true size of government' (conceived as a composite index of the government's size, scope and power) to the level that would have been attained if the government had simply continued

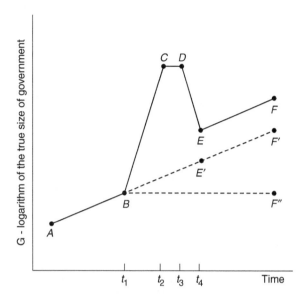

Figure 2.2 Schematic representation of the ratchet effect.

Source: Higgs (1987, 60)

along the path of its growth during the phase of pre-crisis normality. Thus, although the government does surrender ground during the retrenchment phase, it does not lose enough to compensate fully for the ground gained during the expansion. It has a net gain, not only as compared with its pre-crisis size, but also as compared with the position it would have attained had it continued to grow as it was growing before the onset of the crisis (Higgs 1987, 57–74).

Opportunists, both inside and outside the formal state apparatus, play distinctive roles during each of these phases. Indeed, it is fair to say that their actions create the ratchet effect, although, to repeat, this entire phenomenon presupposes an essential precondition – a dominant ideology of progressivism or something akin to it, which disposes the public at large to regard the government as the saviour of first resort in a perceived national emergency.

During normal periods, organized interest groups, politically ambitious individuals and ideological entrepreneurs work assiduously in politics as usual, seeking to gain marginal improvements in their positions, yet understanding that because of the mutually blocking logjam of competing proposals and counterproposals jostling for executive, legislative and judicial attention and action, they will probably have to be satisfied with a half loaf, if indeed they have any success at all. These supplicants and schemers understand, however, that when a crisis comes along, their prospects will brighten substantially and that success will be more likely to the extent that they have prepared themselves for fast action and cultivated the relevant ground well in advance.

20   *Robert Higgs*

Therefore, the various individuals, lobbyists and group representatives occupy themselves in formulating and refining desired executive, legislative and judicial actions that are more expansive than present conditions will accommodate. As they do so, they devote resources to publicizing and promoting their ideas, to 'soften up' opinion leaders and the mass public so that when the propitious day finally comes people will not react strongly against a scheme that might strike them as unnecessary or excessive if they had never encountered arguments for it in the past. Thus, for example, if people had never heard proposals for nationalizing health insurance, they might be startled by political attempts to enact such a plan during an economic emergency, such as the recent financial debacle and economic recession ('On Healthcare' 2009). Having softened up the public by promoting this scheme for years, however, the interest groups and ideological entrepreneurs who favour it stand a much better chance of gaining its approval during a crisis than they otherwise would have had.

Therefore, even in normal periods, when nothing extraordinary seems to be happening in politics, many individuals and groups are working hard to lay the groundwork for future gains, appreciating that ultimate success is unlikely except in a crisis, when a general weakening of offsetting political blockages will occur as the quickening current of 'do something' sentiment alters the calculations of the president, the bureaucrats, the legislators and even the judges. It was no mere coincidence, for example, that the Supreme Court revolution of 1937 took place in the midst of the nation's greatest peacetime emergency. Judges, too, feel the pressure and feel compelled to yield to it. Justice Owen J. Roberts, the 'swing man' who, more than anyone else, bore responsibility for the Court's constitutional turnaround in 1937, later observed: 'Looking back, it is difficult to see how the Court could have resisted the popular urge.' He referred obliquely to 'the tremendous strain and the threat to the existing Court, of which I was fully conscious'.[8] During normal periods, interest groups are looking ahead to the crisis-driven emergence of, among other things, the next swing man (or woman) on the Supreme Court. Lawyers are honing their arguments for future briefs aimed at him (or her).

When a crisis occurs, time becomes all-important and each actor who seeks to exploit the occasion rushes to get his nose under the policy tent ahead of others. Raymond Moley, the most important member of the Franklin D. Roosevelt's so-called Brains Trust, recalled that, immediately after Roosevelt took office as president in 1933, 'Washington became a mecca for the old Socialists, single-taxers, utility reformers, Civil Service reformers and goo-goos of all types' (Moley 1939, 128). As the president's 'unofficial sieve on policy', Moley spent hours each afternoon in appointments with 'a choice variety of panacea artists'. He received, for example, 'literally dozens' of 'plans for industrial rehabilitation'. 'Official Washington', he wrote, 'was in the grip of a war psychology as surely as it had been in 1917' (ibid., 167, 185, 191).

In the mad scramble, even powerful interest-group advocates may get lost in the crowd. The decisive advantage rests with the executive branch of government, especially with the president and the few people who have immediate access to him or can exert substantial influence on him. At such times the president's autonomy and discretion reach a maximum, and hence his capacity for shaping events to suit his own desires also peaks. In the spring of 1933, wrote Moley, 'Congress was in the mood to give [President Roosevelt] power as great as that of any other President in history' (ibid., 221). But not even the president's extraordinary power will last indefinitely, and if he does not move quickly, opponents of his favoured measures may succeed in marshalling enough counterforce to foil him. Hence, all delays, even those required for gathering and assessing the most important facts about the crisis, must be avoided in favour of 'action, and action now', as Roosevelt expressed it in his first inaugural address in March 1933. It therefore came as no surprise when President Barack Obama declared on 5 February 2009: 'The time for talk is over. The time for action is now, because we know that if we do not act, a bad situation will become dramatically worse. Crisis could turn into catastrophe for families and businesses across the country.'[9]

Like President Obama, proponents of particular government actions after the onset of a crisis generally claim that the proposed action is imperative: unless it is taken quickly, they insist, horrible consequences will ensue. Therefore, they assert that delays to weigh their proposal's costs against its benefits, studies to identify adverse longer-term effects and careful considerations of who will gain and who will lose are all intolerable. They urge that the government must act immediately. In such a frenzied atmosphere, the usual efforts to deliberate, to listen to the views of opponents or sceptics, to adhere to procedural due process and to attend to due diligence before making great expenditures are likely to be set aside in favour of hasty action. In the recent financial debacle, for example, trillions of dollars in loans, loan guarantees, capital infusions and other forms of financial aid were committed without the knowledge even of members of Congress. Senator Byron Dorgan complained on the floor of the Senate on 3 February 2009: 'We've seen money go out the back door of this government unlike any time in the history of our country. Nobody knows what went out of the Federal Reserve Board, to whom and for what purpose. How much from the FDIC? How much from TARP? When? Why?'[10]

Because this situation strongly favours political insiders, especially the president and those closest to him, it is no coincidence that crisis has been associated not only with the abrupt growth of government, but also with the centralization of government power and control of the government's financial resources. A crisis is a president's time in the sun. As Jimmy Carter wrote to an adviser, 'When a president has authority to act unilaterally (as in a crisis), his leadership can be exerted. Otherwise, compromise, delay and confusion are more likely.'[11] All modern presidents understand this reality, and most of them strive to exploit it to the maximum. The so-called imperial presidency has grown for the most part out of 'bold' presidential actions during national emergencies and from the subsequent institutionalization of such crisis-time precedents.

As the president and others closest to the pinnacle of political power act, they undertake to rationalize and marshal mass support for their actions. Hence, they typically mount unusual efforts to propagandize the public, to intimidate

22   Robert Higgs

opponents by branding them as 'slackers' or as otherwise lacking in patriotism and, in extreme cases, by jailing dissidents or expelling them from the country. To ensure that opponents do not undermine the chosen emergency policies, the government usually undertakes to place many more people under surveillance, often justifying this action as an effort to ferret out spies, saboteurs and terrorists, even though such surveillance invariably extends much more widely and often targets completely peaceful persons and groups, such as pacifists and people who oppose the government's actions on religious grounds. As more and more people fall under the government's watchful eye, some who might have spoken out or organized others in opposition to the government's emergency measures are intimidated into silence, and such effective muzzling helps the government create the impression that no real opposition exists except for that of traitors, subversives and 'wreckers'.[12] The surveillance state that has assumed frightening proportions in the wake of the 9/11 attacks has had a significant chilling effect on the behaviour of many Americans and, in particular, on their willingness to exercise freedoms supposedly protected by the First Amendment (Lerner 2014). According to a recent study by Human Rights Watch and the American Civil Liberties Union, 'Many existing surveillance programs are indiscriminate or overbroad, and threaten freedom of expression, the right to counsel, and the public's ability to hold its government to account' (Human Rights Watch 2014). The government may also organize the mass public to turn them into de facto informants, putting even greater pressure on opponents of its programme to keep silent, lest they expose themselves to malicious reports by unfriendly neighbours or acquaintances.

Meanwhile, the government paints the sacrifices and burdens entailed by its chosen emergency policies as patriotic, beneficial and even heroic. Policies that may bring benefits to only a chosen few are depicted as required by the 'public interest' or by pressing economic, social, or national-security necessity. Proponents invite those who remain hostile to the chosen policies to shut up unless they have 'something better' to propose or 'something constructive' to say. Such combative debating tactics help to quieten critics and, again, to create the impression that the government's crisis policies enjoy near-universal public approval.

During the third, or maturity, phase of the ratchet phenomenon, the government has implemented an array of emergency plans and programmes and occupies itself primarily in making them work passably well while the crisis persists. Calling this phase 'maturity' does not imply, however, that the government's actions have settled into a fixed pattern or mode of operation; indeed, constant changes, adjustments, reversals and accommodations of various sorts always occur. The welter of exemptions, deadline deferrals and other changes the government has made to the Patient Protection and Affordable Care Act (Obamacare) since its enactment in 2010 provides an apt example. This flux reflects the 'disequilibrium' that the government has created by imposing its power on a population disposed to act differently. If, for example, the government imposes price controls, it will have to devise ways to placate persons placed at a disadvantage by such controls, to make

Crisis without Leviathan? 23

exceptions to its rules in cases where they are proving especially counterproductive to the government's own purposes and to refine the programme's substantive details and its administrative setup.[13]

In this phase, the opportunists who have succeeded in gaining implementation of their favoured plans and programmes occupy themselves in defending their schemes against critics (many of them insiders operating elsewhere, perhaps somewhat competitively, within the government), consolidating their newly gained powers, enlarging their budgets and generally striving to entrench their operations within the government and the overall society. In a sense, these actions take place within a crisis setting that has itself, for the time being, become the 'normal' condition for the government's operations. So, to some extent, logjams similar to those that characterize the pre-crisis normal period may develop, although they will differ in their details, reflecting the way in which the crisis has brought forth an assortment of emergency programmes to deal with the prevailing situation. Thus, for example, even at the peak of a war, inter-service rivalry characterizes the military budgeting process just as it did before the war began, only now its dimensions will be greatly enlarged – the army, navy and air force may be fighting over the division of 10 or 20 per cent of GDP, rather than 3 per cent.

As the crisis continues, the emergency programmes will benefit from the general public's accommodation to the new realities of the government's enlarged role. People not only will learn how to avoid the new arrangements' worst disadvantages, but, more generally, will to some extent accommodate their thinking to those arrangements, as well. To people who had not been subject to military conscription (e.g. Americans between 1919 and 1939), the initiation of a draft may seem to be an outrageous assault on their liberties. Once this system of involuntary military service has operated for years, however, people may come to regard it much as they regard destructive weather – an act of nature that must be endured in the event that it happens.

When the crisis ends or at least wanes significantly, many people will naturally expect that some, if not all, of the government's extraordinary measures adopted ostensibly in response to the crisis will be terminated or greatly scaled back. After all, one invariant aspect of the government's actions during the expansion phase of the ratchet phenomenon is that significant new burdens are placed on the general public. Even if people have accepted the government's measures as desirable or regrettably necessary in response to the crisis, their enthusiasm for them will eventually wear thin, especially when the measures' rationale seems to have evaporated. At this point, the government will feel itself under pressure to 'return to normalcy', as Warren G. Harding expressed the idea during his campaign for the presidency in 1920. Now, as we enter the fourth, or retrenchment, phase of the ratchet phenomenon, the opportunists who gained so much ground in the second phase and successfully defended it during the third phase will be placed unavoidably on the defensive.

Although some emergency-programme managers may themselves be keen for a return to normal conditions, many others will not be. During the crisis, a variety of new 'iron triangles', as political scientists call them, will have been created or

24   *Robert Higgs*

strengthened. Each of them consists of government oversight and appropriations committees in the legislature, a government bureau responsible for making purchases or administering regulations or controls and a set of private-sector beneficiaries who have profited somehow from the emergency programme's operation during the crisis. The leaders of these three groups, and to a lesser extent their rank and file as well, stand to lose positions of substantial value in the event that the programme is abolished or greatly scaled back. They are, therefore, likely to search for and find reasons why such retrenchment should not be made at all or at least should not be carried out on a drastic scale.

One time-honoured tactic is to redefine the threat against which their crisis-time operations presumably were directed. So, for example, after the surrender of German and Japanese forces in 1945, the US armed forces, which had grown spectacularly between 1940 and 1944, faced the prospect of returning to a budget of 1 per cent of GDP (approximately the amount spent on the military in fiscal year 1940), after having reached a level of more than 40 per cent of GDP at the peak of the war effort (Higgs 1990, xvii). Not only would the military's cash flow be squeezed to a relative trickle, but – not to be ignored in this context – the number of required flag officers would be diminished commensurately, which would mean the involuntary retirement of hundreds of generals and admirals who had only recently attained these high levels of command. Is it any surprise, then, that the leaders of the armed forces immediately perceived a need to maintain an armed force much larger than the one the nation had maintained in 1940, in order to allay the threat allegedly posed by the Soviet Union?[14]

Another tactic is to shift mission categories while keeping the emergency agency or powers intact. So, for example, after the Armistice in 1918 and the peace treaty in 1919, the US War Finance Corporation, which had operated during the war to steer financial capital to enterprises given high priority by the government's economic mobilization plans, was retained when Eugene Meyer, its wartime managing director and others perceived that it could be used to finance US exports, especially agricultural exports, to Europe at a time when the European purchasers were hard pressed to arrange their own financing (Higgs 1987, 153–4). Similarly, the Emergency Fleet Corporation, created to build merchant ships to carry US supplies to Europe during World War I, continued to build ships after the Armistice, and under the Merchant Marine Act of 1920 the agency, now called the Merchant Fleet Corporation, put the ships to use by transforming itself into a government-owned general shipping line in competition with private shipping suppliers (ibid., 153).

Attempts to eliminate or diminish emergency programmes run up against a fundamental principle of political action: people will fight harder to keep an established benefit than they will fight to obtain an identical benefit in the first place.[15] This asymmetry assists every effort to hang onto iron triangles created or enlarged during a crisis. Legislators do not enjoy visibly taking benefits away from constituents; doing so may cost them votes down the line. Political actors thrive on the creation of programmes with concentrated benefits and dispersed costs. By the same token, they try to avoid actions that entail dispersed benefits and concentrated costs because those on whom the concentrated losses will fall are certain to howl and to deploy every resource they can command to avoid the loss. After a crisis has clearly ended, it is not possible for beneficiaries of crisis-oriented programmes to hang onto everything they have gained during the emergency, but often they can stage an organized retreat that allows them to retain some of the ground they occupied previously under the pretext of emergency necessity.

When the dust of the retrenchment fights has settled, the politico-economic system finds itself endowed with an altered dynamic. Some emergency agencies (perhaps renamed or repositioned as offices in permanent government departments) remain in operation; some emergency laws remain in force; some court decisions reached during the crisis stand as precedents for future decisions, including decisions in cases arising in normal times. Above all, the population goes forward with its political sensibilities altered from their pre-crisis configuration. If the government's crisis management can be plausibly represented as having been successful, which it often can be, then people may be more likely to trust the government to take on more tasks or to grapple with old problems more energetically than it did previously. Which is to say, the experience gained by having passed more or less successfully (or so people believe) through a crisis in which the government took a variety of extraordinary actions is likely to shift the dominant ideology to a more favourable stance towards new, perhaps quite different kinds of government initiatives in the future. We may think of this sort of change as ideological learning from experience (and from related propaganda), and thus as a form of path dependency.

Of course, such learning will not be left for people to carry out on their own. The crisis-programme managers are virtually certain to write memoirs recounting their heroic emergency performance and proclaiming the virtues of the extraordinary government activities they oversaw during the crisis. Ideologues who prefer bigger, more powerful government in any event will seize on the apparent lessons to be drawn from the just-concluded crisis and the surge of government action that came forth in response to it. Many progressives in particular will seek to use wartime actions as springboards for similar, permanent government activities.

2.5 The crisis opportunist's priority list

As we have seen, the opportunists who emerge to exploit a national emergency have a variety of options at their disposal. Some of these options serve their purposes better than others, even if they pursue simultaneously all feasible avenues to achieve their ends. The general ordering of these options, in increasing order of potency, is as follows:

- new (or additional) government funding, including funds to pay subsidies
- new government personnel
- new government policies
- new government agencies

26   *Robert Higgs*

- new authorizing statutes
- new court decisions, especially Supreme Court decisions.

Another option, difficult to rank because it may take a multitude of specific forms, consists of new precedents in government action, responses to problems created by crisis policies and accommodation of opponents and other aggrieved parties – all of which, generally speaking, amount to new precedents for dealing with the negative feedback that crisis-spawned government actions may generate. If new government actions are to succeed, the government must somehow sooth the people who are especially irate about its actions. Simply telling them 'We've got the guns and you haven't' only stimulates opponents to work harder to oppose, evade, cripple and terminate the offending actions.

A well-known political aphorism informs us that 'personnel is policy'. Even if the laws, regulations and judicial precedents have not changed, new officeholders can move the substance of the government's policy substantially in new directions by choosing to ignore certain issues or, conversely, to pour more resources into them. Benign neglect of enforcement, for example, is a time-honoured way for regulators to nullify a regulation, even though it remains formally in force. Alternatively, regulators or judges may begin to come down hard on violators of rules that no one was bothering to enforce previously.

So, the first, and usually the easiest, thing government officials (backed, as usual, by their supporting coalition of interest groups inside and outside the government) can do in a crisis, aside from gaining increased funding, is to replace existing officeholders with 'our people'. Within the federal executive branch, this sort of replacement goes back at least to Andrew Jackson's Administration, with its forthright embrace of the spoils system. The federal civil service system eventually reined in such replacements for the bulk of the executive branch's personnel, but in the upper echelons officeholders continue to serve at the president's pleasure, and every president begins his term(s) in office with a thorough 'housecleaning' and an installation of his own appointees. The onset of a national emergency often calls for another housecleaning, sometimes as a gesture of national unity (e.g. Franklin D. Roosevelt's appointment of leading Republicans Henry Stimson and Frank Knox to head the War and Navy departments in 1940, when the president was striving to win over Republicans in general and Republican industrialists in particular to support his preparation for war).

Even better than replacing personnel at the outset of a crisis is the alteration of policies. To some extent, such changes, even when highly important, require nothing but executive orders as authorization. Indeed, many policies can be changed without any formal proceedings at all; department heads simply tell their subordinates that henceforth they should handle certain matters differently. Policy changes are likely to be more durable than personnel changes because policies that remain in place for some time create vested interests in their preservation – new sets of beneficiaries who stand to lose power, jobs, contracts, subsidies, or other privileges if the most recently implemented policy should be abandoned. Such vested interests will have a strong incentive to work hard to prevent a policy reversal in the future,

Crisis without Leviathan? 27

and therefore they will help to ensure that the emergency policy, perhaps with some repackaging of its public rationale, continues after the emergency has passed. For example, on 21 May 2009, the *Wall Street Journal* reported that although some big banks were seeking to repay TARP funds to the government, 'many of the other emergency measures created to prop up the financial system are developing an air of permanence' ('US Rescue Aid' 2009). Sure enough, the Fed's payment of interest on commercial bank reserves, which began as an emergency measure late in 2008, remains the policy as I write more than six years later. Given that reserves as of 18 March 2015, were $2,783 billion, even the interest rate of 0.25 per cent entails a Fed payment to the banks at a rate of almost $7 billion per year.

For a crisis opportunist, even better than a new policy is a new government agency, especially one with a new, designated function that effectively institutionalises support for an interest-group agenda inside the apparatus of government itself. Such agencies may be created by executive order, as Woodrow Wilson created the War Industries Board during World War I. Agencies first created by a mere presidential order may then proceed more easily to acquire statutory authority. Thus, the Federal Energy Office, created unilaterally by President Richard Nixon to deal with the energy crisis in 1973, became the statutorily authorized Federal Energy Administration in 1974 and, ultimately, the Department of Energy in 1977.

Although such a progression may appear in retrospect to have developed sequentially in response to an ongoing series of events, crisis opportunists sometimes foresee and work to bring about this kind of permanent institutionalization from the very beginning. Thus, as Broadus Mitchell writes, 'though the framers of the [Agricultural Adjustment Act of 1933], to overcome congressional objections, presented it as an emergency measure, there is abundant evidence that all along they intended it to be the basis of long-time policy' (Mitchell 1969, 187). Although the Agricultural Adjustment Administration, which administered the act's provisions during the 1930s, was later eliminated (and the 1933 act itself was overturned by the Supreme Court in 1936), its functions were folded into the Department of Agriculture (USDA) and – under authority of statutes enacted in 1936, 1938 and later years – the USDA has continued to administer a system of direct and indirect agricultural income and price supports since the 1930s.

For a crisis opportunist, even better than a new agency is a new law. Once a policy and its administrative agency have received statutory authority, the burden of discontinuing the policy rests heavily on the policy's opponents. In Congress, it is much easier to pass a new statute than to repeal an existing one. Legislative procedures give the defenders an advantage (e.g. single senatorial objection to a bill, traditional filibuster, etc.). Vested interests invariably lobby to retain their statutory privileges. Only rarely does the general public take much interest in a law's repeal, and public apathy fosters greater legislative inertia in regard to potential repeal. Laws often remain on the books long after they have become completely obsolete and even absurd. Ronald Reagan famously quipped that 'nothing is as permanent as a temporary government program'. He might well have added, 'especially if it rests on statutory authority'.

28   *Robert Higgs*

For a crisis opportunist, even better than a new statute is a new court decision, especially one by the Supreme Court. Statutes avail their supporters nothing if the courts of appeal declare them unconstitutional. During a crisis, of course, the courts are likely to be especially accommodating to the government's programmes: *Inter arma enim silent leges.*[16] Although the courts may not become completely mute or totally submissive during a peacetime crisis, as the great court fight of the mid-1930s illustrates, they are always more likely to concede extraordinary powers to the government during a perceived national emergency than they would be in normal times. Once the court has rendered an obliging decision, however, that decision remains on the record and may serve as a precedent for arguments in subsequent cases in which the government's power is contested during normal times. If statutes are difficult to overturn, Supreme Court decisions are even more difficult. Constitutional revolutions occur only at long intervals. For this reason, crisis opportunists especially prize their court victories during episodes of national emergency. To this day, for example, the Supreme Court's favourable decisions on rent control and military conscription during World War I continue to carry weight in court cases.

Finally, crisis opportunists may value, above everything else they achieve during a national emergency, the lessons they learn about how to manage new powers so that opponents do not obstruct their operation or somehow nullify them. Crisis managers learn how to deal with dissent: some opponents may be clapped in prison or deported; others may be silenced by vaguely worded warnings against unpatriotic obstructionism. Thus, in December 2001, Attorney General John Ashcroft wasted no words on nuance when he declared: 'To those who . . . scare peace-loving people with phantoms of lost liberty, my message is this: Your tactics only aid terrorists for they erode our national unity and diminish our resolve' ('Ashcroft: Critics' 2001). Each time the crisis managers navigate through a new storm, they learn more about where the rocks are and how to avoid them or blow them out of the water.

During World War II, for example, the government strictly censored news from the battlefields and, for most of the war, even forbade the publication of photographs of dead American servicemen. In Vietnam, in contrast, the reporters got into the thick of the fighting and sent back gory, unsettling videotape that, being shown regularly on the nightly television news programmes, helped to expose the usual lies and distortions being distributed by the military authorities. Taking this lesson to heart, the armed forces in the US attack on Iraq in 2003 put into effect a system of 'embedding' reporters in military units, thereby effectively preventing them from going where they might need to go to find out about the most important developments in the area and helping to ensure that they would bond with their de facto protectors and report the news from these soldiers' point of view.[17]

2.6 Can anything be done?

Having recognized the dangers that inhere in the government's (and the public's) responses to perceived national emergencies, we might well ponder whether

Crisis without Leviathan? 29

anything can be done to prevent or moderate the harms they cause. Although an ironclad guarantee against such harms is inconceivable, apart from the dissolution of the government that causes them, we can imagine several ways in which the government's worst crisis-born excesses might be prevented or reined in.

First, we must recognize that virtually all modern, large-scale, socio-economic emergencies result from actions by the government itself, which are usually actions the government represents as entirely innocent, highly recommended by experts and aimed exclusively at promotion of the general public welfare. Notwithstanding such soothing representations, the reality remains: only the government has the power and the resources to bring about pervasive, national, socio-economic crises. To cite the two most important examples, both wars and steep business contractions result from ill-chosen government policies: in the former case, bad foreign policies, for the most part; and in the latter case, bad fiscal and monetary policies, in particular. Anything the public can do to limit the government's reach will tend to operate as an insurance measure against the disasters that arise from the government's overreaching – an overreaching that is rarely if ever as public-spirited as it is represented to be and is commonly aimed primarily at aggrandizing high government officials and enriching the powerful persons and special interests with which these political kingpins are entangled and for whom they frequently serve as de facto mouthpieces and errand runners. Keeping the government as limited as possible is not only beneficial in an immediate sense, but even more beneficial by restraining the government's desire and capacity to 'do something' during national emergencies – this 'something' commonly serving only to exacerbate and prolong the dire conditions that the government's actions have brought about in the first place.

By restraining the government's responses to perceived national emergencies, the magnitude of its expansion during phase II of the ratchet effect is minimized; therefore, if it turns out later that little or nothing can be done to increase the government's retrenchment in phase IV, the episode's overall effect in fostering the long-term growth of government will still be diminished. People who cherish the restoration of a free society might well do everything within their power to teach their fellows about the benefits and glories of 'do-nothing' government and to disabuse them of the ideological conviction that governments have either the knowledge or the incentive to intervene in ways that benefit the general public and should do so especially during perceived national emergencies. This conviction is an ideological superstition, not a scientifically or historically established truth, and the sooner the general public recognizes it as a superstition, the sooner the government's destructive actions will be resisted and curtailed. By far the best policy for coping with quicksand is never to venture into it in the first place.

Given the progressive ideological background condition, the public's support for all crisis policy-making springs fundamentally from widespread fear and even panic, and little can be done to prevent such hysteria except by challenging the inaccurate news reports that feed it and the government propaganda that exploits it. Such mainstream news-media reports and government statements should always be viewed with scepticism. Until a variety of independent private sources

30 *Robert Higgs*

has confirmed the reality of the alleged emergency conditions, one should withhold judgement in regard to any action proposed to deal with them. Government excuses that, notwithstanding the absence of a demonstrated ability to deal productively with an alleged emergency, it must 'do something' immediately should be rejected out of hand and ridiculed as a foolhardy response to conditions. The idea that it is better for the government to act now even if its actions are likely to be stupid and counterproductive is worse than a superstition. It is sheer, wilful folly. The only ones who stand to gain from such ill-advised government actions are the government officials who will wield the new powers that people fearfully and hastily place in their hands in a crisis.

Although efforts to rein in the government's overreaching must concentrate, first, on affecting the public's thinking about how the government ought to act during an emergency, efforts might also be productively devoted to changing the machinery of government so that ill-considered or poorly justified measures cannot be adopted so easily. In short, protective efforts may be directed, first, towards policy education and ideological change and, second, towards institutional change.

Policy education might well seek to reveal the great extent to which past government emergency measures have proved counterproductive at the time of their implementation and, even worse, when they persisted after the emergency had passed. Analysts might well emphasize the extent to which these policies have been driven by special interests posing as friends of the general public interest, often by advancing transparently fallacious arguments and by making false or unrepresentative declarations of fact. Studies might well focus on the distribution of benefits and costs. A showing that some group, perhaps even a seemingly large one, benefited from a crisis-driven policy should never be accepted as a sufficient justification for the policy's adoption: analysts should reveal the policy's full costs, the distribution of these costs across the entire population and the various pecuniary and nonpecuniary forms the costs took; and they should trace how these aspects of the policy changed over the entire period in which the policy remained in effect or continued to have discernible consequences. To a large extent, these efforts amount to little more than systematically fleshing out Frédéric Bastiat's teachings about taking into account both the seen and the unseen, along with Henry Hazlitt's insistence that economic analysis, properly performed, must attend to how an action affects not simply some, but all groups, and not simply the immediate situation, but the long-run future as well.

Above all, the government should never be given a pass merely because, in someone's estimation, government officials 'cared' about the people even as they acted in ways that harmed the very people about whom they claimed to care. Franklin D. Roosevelt and the New Deal constitute the classic case of this sort of faulty evaluation by historians and other policy analysts. Giving government officials credit for caring, rather than for actually promoting the general public interest, encourages emotional posturing and the public shedding of crocodile tears instead of the implementation of public policies that actually benefit the people as a whole (e.g. protection of private property rights, enforcement of voluntary private contracts, noninterference with domestic and international

Crisis without Leviathan? 31

trade, maintenance of sound money or, better, relinquishment of monetary matters to the private sector).

In reforming government institutions to guard against harmful government actions during a crisis, anything done to restore the classic institutional protections related to federalism and the separation of powers – fundamental aspects of US constitutional design that have eroded dangerously over the ages – will prove helpful. Many of the mistakes the government makes during a national emergency spring from excessively hasty action and from the excessive discretion ceded to the executive branch by the other branches of government. One may grant that emergencies may justify quicker government action, yet still insist that even in such circumstances, actions may be taken *too* hastily. What is the point of acting very quickly if the government can do so only in a biased, ill-considered and ultimately, all things being considered, harmful way? Gridlock is not an altogether bad thing, even in a crisis, and it is certainly not the worst thing possible. By allowing time for competing points of view to be heard and for potentially adversely affected interests to mount and voice opposition, more balanced and better justified measures may be designed before bad policy provisions become locked in place, perhaps forever.

Finally, all emergency measures should have sunset provisions, lest special interests and other opportunists use the pretext of crisis to get a permanent foot in the door. If the government's crisis measures have explicitly stated dates of expiration in the near future (say, in two years or less), special interests will have less incentive to push for them because their long-term duration will be less certain and because the necessity of having to obtain their future reauthorization, probably under calmer conditions, will lower the special interests' prospective benefits and increase their prospective costs.

Even those who believe, as I do, that the foregoing suggested measures have little chance of success can take heart from the knowledge that, ultimately, the government will attain such bloated size and scope that its own survival on such a scale will no longer be possible, and it will implode, as the Soviet Union and other similarly overreaching politico-economic orders have imploded. Governments that grow and grow eventually find that their predation becomes greater than their prey can support, at which point such predators are doomed. Foreign lenders will then decline to prop up the government, and it will no longer be able to sustain itself on its existing scale absent serious reconfiguration of its institutions and policies. Such a day of reckoning has come about for several governments in recent decades (e.g. New Zealand in the 1980s). For now, we can say only that the present system of government in the United States (and in many others) contains the seeds of its own destruction, even if those of us who abhor it cannot stop or slow its continued growth in the near term. Some of the younger people among us may live long enough to help in picking up the pieces and beginning anew. One hopes that the new beginning will rest on a less coercive, more voluntary basis than the present system. Otherwise, it will be destined to retrace the same path of predatory rise that the present system has followed and to arrive at the same self-destruction that ultimately awaits our own politico-economic order.

32 Robert Higgs

We might well recognize, however, that in recent decades some governments have successfully reversed course, some seemingly permanently and others long enough at least to pull themselves away from the precipice of complete economic destruction. For example, the British government under Margaret Thatcher made enough reforms of the country's postwar economic regime to revitalize the UK economy, at least relative to its prior performance and relative to the nearly stagnant economies of most Western European countries. Shortly afterward, also in the 1980s, New Zealand and Ireland made similar turnarounds with even more impressive results. Ireland later faltered and suffered greatly from the housing boom and bust of the early twenty-first century. New Zealand, however, despite some backsliding in more recent times, remains one of the world's freest economies. During the past 30 years or so, India has successfully removed many of the self-imposed obstacles to entrepreneurship, investment, international trade and economic growth that its decades-long postwar experiment in economic dirigisme had created. Of course, the formerly centrally planned economies, especially China and a few of the smaller Eastern European countries, have made major reversals of their previous policies and performance trends. All of these examples and others show that complete economic ruin is not predestined, that it can be averted or responded to in productive ways.

Whether the United States and the major countries of Western Europe can make similar alterations, of course, remains doubtful at this time. In these countries the welfare state has become so deeply entrenched and anti-economic regulations so pervasive and widely supported that it is difficult to see how the political barriers to successful reconfiguration of the political-economic regimes can be overcome. This is not, however, to say that it cannot be. The barriers are almost entirely political and ideological, and ideological change can occur, as it has in the past. If such change should be brought about on a wide scale either by persuasion and education or by force of events, it would almost certainly bring about in its train major political changes. With sufficient restoration of economic freedom in the US and Western European economies, they could easily move into a higher gear for technological, organizational and economic developments that would tilt upward substantially the trajectory of their economic growth. The odds of such reformation are, in my judgement, slight, but, to repeat, such changes are certainly conceivable, and they are goals towards which freedom-loving people might well direct their efforts while there is still time to avert disaster.

2.7 Conclusion

Crisis brings opportunists running, both from inside and from outside the government, because crisis alters the fundamental forces that impel and constrain political action. It thereby creates unusual opportunities for extraordinary government actions, plans and programmes to be implemented. That crisis has this effect is widely understood by political actors inside and outside the government. Opportunism is therefore to be expected and ought to be guarded against – especially by the general public, which is likely to be saddled most heavily with the crisis programmes' burdens and injustices. Throughout US history, national emergencies have served as outstanding occasions for the ratcheting loss of economic and social liberties. If government is, by its very nature, an institution that allows some people to plunder the wealth that others have created, then national emergency creates the context in which this nature becomes expressed to the maximum. Of course, the crisis opportunists invariably claim that every move they make actually serves the broad public interest – sensible people would scarcely expect them to say anything else. But these reassurances ring hollow when contrasted with the political logic and the historical facts that pertain to national emergencies. Everyone understands that a crisis, virtually by definition, is a time of unusual danger, but too few understand that the greatest danger often resides not in the perceived threat but in the government's ostensible measures to allay it. The public needs a greater understanding that in a crisis not all the barbarians are outside the walls. Until such an understanding develops, it is unlikely that anyone can do much to avert the ultimate catastrophe, and we can only await the final crackup, hoping that those who rebuild on the rubble will have greater wisdom and love of liberty than their forebears had.

Notes

1 For the administrative and regulatory agencies that currently publicize their rule-making in the *Federal Register*, see the rather overwhelming list at 'Agency List'. See also 'List of Federal Agencies'.
2 Here is a conservative, back-of-an-envelope calculation. The 20,000 cities, with 500 distinct enforced rules each, yield a total of 10 million rules; the 17,000 townships, with 100 distinct enforced rules each, yield a total of 1.7 million rules; the 3,000 counties, with 1,000 distinct enforced rules each, yield a total of 3 million rules; the 50 states, with 10,000 distinct enforced rules each, yield a total of 500,000 rules; and US government adds at least 100,000 distinct enforced rules. Under the foregoing assumptions, the grand total is at least 15.3 million distinct enforced rules in the entire country.
3 This measure, though the most commonly used, is not the best one, however. For a recent discussion of alternative measures, see Higgs (2015).
4 See, for example, the evidence presented in Higgs (1987) and Higgs (2012), esp. pp. 242–68, on the most recent crisis.
5 See Higgs (2009). In the following exposition, I draw heavily on this paper and attempt to extend it by giving more attention to how the ratchet effect on the growth of government might be moderated or eliminated.
6 Quoted in Krauthammer (2009).
7 Jefferson to Edward Carrington, 4 August 1787, printed in Jefferson (1900), Entry No. 4683.
8 Quoted in Leonard (1971, 144, 155). More recently, one might view in a similar light Chief Justice Roberts's bizarre ruling in a case challenging the constitutionality of the Patient Protection and Affordable Care Act of 2010, *National Federation of Independent Business v. Sibelius*, 132 S.Ct. 2566. On this decision, see Hoff (2013).
9 Quoted in Niskanen (2009).
10 Quoted in Pittman and Ivry (2009).
11 Carter, as quoted in Gerson (2009). Note that the parenthetical phrase '(as in a crisis)' is part of Carter's original statement.
12 The actions described in this paragraph were most notable during the War Between the States and the two world wars, but the government also took similar egregious actions more recently under the COINTELPRO rubric between 1956 and the early 1970s. For a

34 *Robert Higgs*

well-documented survey, see Linfield (1990). See also Higgs (2007, 1–22), which gives evidence running up to the present 'war on terror'. Peacetime emergencies brought forth less of this kind of government action, but by no means a complete absence of it. During the early New Deal, for example, the government strove to whip up mass support for the National Industrial Recovery Act, stigmatizing those who declined to cooperate with this national cartelization scheme as 'slackers' and 'chiselers'. See Higgs (1987, 179) and sources cited there.

13 See, for example, Shultz and Dam (1977, 65–85).
14 I say 'allegedly posed', not because I take a benign view of the Soviets or minimize the genuine threat they posed to many Europeans and Asians, but because the threat they posed to *US* national security in the late 1940s was a much more problematic matter. The literature on the origins of the Cold War is immense, but with special relevance to the 'switching missions' point I am making here, see Lazarowitz (2005).
15 This behaviour reflects a more basic psychological preference for loss avoidance relative to a gain of the same amount. See Kahneman, Knetsch and Thaler (1991) for more on loss aversion.
16 Translation: In times of war, the laws fall silent.
17 See, for example, Center for Media and Democracy n.d. and 'Embedded Journalism'.

References

'Agency List.' *Federal Register.* https://www.federalregister.gov/agencies

'Ashcroft: Critics of New Terror Measures Undermine Effort.' *CNN News*, 7 December 2001. http://archives.cnn.com/2001/US/12/06/inv.ashcroft.hearing/

Center for Media and Democracy. 'Embedded.' *SourceWatch*. http://www.sourcewatch.org/index.php?title=Embedded

Davis, Bob, and Jon Hilsenrath. 'Federal Intervention Pits "Gets" vs "Get-Nots." *Wall Street Journal*, 15 June 2009. http://www.wsj.com/articles/SB124501974568613573

'Embedded Journalism.' Wikipedia. Last updated 3 March 2016. http://en.wikipedia.org/wiki/Embedded_journalism

Gerson, Michael. 'Obama's Crisis: Credibility.' *Washington Post*, 9 September 2009. http://www.washingtonpost.com/wp-dyn/content/article/2009/09/08/AR2009090802958.html

Higgs, Robert. *Crisis and Leviathan: Critical Episodes in the Growth of American Government.* New York: Oxford University Press, 1987.

Higgs, Robert. 'Introduction: Fifty Years of Arms, Politics, and the Economy.' In Higgs, ed., *Arms, Politics, and the Economy: Historical and Contemporary Perspectives.* New York: Holmes and Meier, 1990, pp. xv–xxxii.

Higgs, Robert. *Neither Liberty nor Safety: Fear, Ideology, and the Growth of Government.* Oakland, CA: Independent Institute, 2007.

Higgs, Robert. 'The Political Economy of Crisis Opportunism.' *Mercatus Policy Series, Policy Primer No. 11*, October 2009.

Higgs, Robert. *Delusions of Power: New Explorations of the State, War, and Economy.* Oakland, CA: Independent Institute, 2012.

Higgs, Robert. 'How Big Is Government in the United States?' *The Beacon*, 20 March 2015. http://blog.independent.org/2015/03/20/how-big-is-government-in-the-united-states

Hoff, John S. 'Obamacare: Chief Justice Roberts's Political Dodge.' *The Independent Review* 18, no. 1 (Summer 2013): 5–20.

Human Rights Watch. 'US: Surveillance Harming Journalism, Law, Democracy: Government Spying Undermines Media Freedom and Right to Counsel.' 28 July 2014. https://www.hrw.org/news/2014/07/28/us-surveillance-harming-journalism-law-democracy

Jefferson, Thomas. *The Jeffersonian Cyclopedia*. New York: Funk and Wagnalls, 1900.

Kahneman, Daniel, Jack L. Knetsch and Richard H. Thaler. 'Anomalies: The Endowment Effect, Loss Aversion, and Status Quo Bias.' *Journal of Economic Perspectives* 5, no. 1 (1991): 193–206.

Krauthammer, Charles. 'Deception at Core of Obama Plans.' *Real Clear Politics*, 6 March 2009. http://www.realclearpolitics.com/articles/2009/03/a_dishonest_gimmicky_budget.html

Lazarowitz, Arlene. 'Promoting Air Power: The Influence of the US Air Force on the Creation of the National Security State.' *The Independent Review* 9, no. 4 (Spring 2005): 477–99.

Leonard, Charles A. *A Search for a Judicial Philosophy: Mr Justice Roberts and the Constitutional Revolution of 1937*. Port Washington, NY: Kennikat Press, 1971.

Lerner, Mark. 'The Chilling Effect of Domestic Spying.' *American Policy Center*, 5 August 2014. http://americanpolicy.org/2014/08/05/the-chilling-effect-of-domestic-spying

Linfield, Michael. *Freedom under Fire: US Civil Liberties in Times of War*. Boston: South End Press, 1990.

'List of Federal Agencies in the United States.' Wikipedia. Last updated 16 March 2016. http://en.wikipedia.org/wiki/List_of_federal_agencies_in_the_United_States

'Loss Aversion.' Wikipedia. Last updated 10 March 2016. http://en.wikipedia.org/wiki/Loss_aversion

Mitchell, Broadus. *Depression Decade: From New Era through New Deal, 1929–1941*. New York: Harper Torchbooks, 1969.

Moley, Raymond. *After Seven Years*. New York: Harper and Brothers, 1939.

Niskanen, William A. 'slow Down the Political Response to a Perceived Crisis.' *Cato Institute*, 9 February 2009. http://www.cato.org/pub_display.php?pub_id=9951

'On Healthcare, Obama Pushes for Fast Action.' *Boston Globe*, 29 May 2009.

'Operation TIPS.' Wikipedia. Last updated 10 February 2016. http://en.wikipedia.org/wiki/Operation_TIPS

Pender, Kathleen. 'Government Bailout Hits $8.5 Trillion.' *San Francisco Chronicle*, 26 November 2008.

Pittman, Mark, and Bob Ivry. 'US Taxpayers Risk $9.7 Trillion on Bailout Programs (Update1).' *Bloomberg.com*, 9 February 2009. http://www.bloomberg.com/apps/news%3Fpid%3Dwashingtonstory%26sid%3DaGq2B3XeGKok

Shultz, George P., and Kenneth W. Dam. 'The Life Cycle of Wage and Price Controls.' In George P. Shultz and Kenneth W. Dam, eds, *Economic Policy beyond the Headlines*. New York: Norton, 1977, pp. 65–85.

'US Rescue Aid Entrenches Itself.' *Wall Street Journal*, 21 May 2009.

3 The rule of law during times of economic crisis

Todd Zywicki

3.1 Introduction

Our next constitutional crisis is likely to differ from those that have come before. Although prior crises have been caused by economic dislocations (the period under the Articles of Confederation, the Great Depression and the 2008 financial crisis) or national security concerns (the Civil War and the War on Terror) the next crisis will likely result from collapse from the accumulated expense and debt of the welfare state. Although the causes of the next crisis will be novel, prior crises provide a window on the rule of law and constitutional change in times of crisis. Why is it that, in some instances, crises produce a strengthened constitutional order and in others they do not?

This chapter explores the rule of law in times of economic crisis. First, it develops the case for why adherence to the rule of law is important during times of crisis: because it is useful to create economic stabilization during the crisis, but also because deviations from the rule of law are typically ratified not reversed after the crisis abates. Second, I turn to the question of what factors determine whether the rule of law and constitutional government survive during a period of crisis. Finally, I conclude with some thoughts on the applications of these lessons to anticipate the constitutional consequences of our looming fiscal crisis.

3.2 Constitutional crises and constitutional opportunity

Moments of constitutional crisis can also be moments of constitutional opportunity. In the crucible of crisis, constitutions can emerge strengthened or weakened.

Although some would challenge the claim, America's first two constitutional crises are generally regarded to have produced beneficial results from a constitutional perspective. In 1787, faced with concerns about rising economic chaos at home and continued foreign threats, the Founders scrapped the Articles of Confederation and replaced it with the Constitution. The purpose of the Constitution was to 'provide for the common defense' and create the institutional conditions to build a modern commercial society. In particular, the Constitution aimed at two interrelated principles: first, to promote individual liberty and, second, to frustrate the power of factions (i.e. interest groups) that might seek to

The rule of law 37

commandeer the power of government to promote their private interests rather than the 'public interest', however vaguely defined.

The Framers sought to attain these goals through the erection and maintenance of certain 'auxiliary precautions', namely separation of powers, checks and balances, and federalism, later backed by the adoption of a Bill of Rights to enumerate protected individual rights. For example, the Constitution composed the various branches of individuals selected by different constituency bases – the House of Representatives directly by the people (eventually via districts) for two-year terms, the Senate was elected by state legislatures via staggered six-year terms, the president indirectly via the novel arrangement of the Electoral College for a four-year term and the Judiciary was appointed by the president subject to the advice and consent of the Senate to serve for 'good behaviour'. In addition, the election of senators by state legislatures (rather than by the people) was thought to be a necessary and sufficient institutional protection for federalism (Zywicki 1997). As a result, while the Supreme Court adopted a fairly expansive definition of the Constitution's grant of federal powers in its early cases, prior to the enactment of the 17th Amendment in 1913 Congress rarely pushed its exercise of federal power to its constitutionally permitted limits.

And, in fact, aside from the obvious and unforgivable exception of slavery the original Constitution succeeded admirably in achieving its stated goals of preserving individual liberty, building a robust interstate market and frustrating faction. Although tested at times, the Constitution also proved adequate to respond to foreign threats in times of war. Moreover, the scope of the federal government remained relatively constrained and while interest groups frequently succeeded in obtaining favourable tariff legislation, they largely failed to capture the federal government to their advantage. Most notably, the federal judiciary provided a firm hand on the tiller, defending and strengthening the Contracts clause, protecting federal commerce against state protectionism and preserving the rule of law against populist pressures. For example, through Justice Story's far-seeing decision in *Swift v. Tyson*, the federal judiciary created a modern system of commercial law in the federal courts that facilitated not only interstate commerce, but international commerce as well, providing security for foreigners that invested in the United States.

Inevitably, however, the issue of slavery had to be resolved, which it finally was with the Civil War. And although the Civil War marked an expansion of the federal government, it did so by aiming to expand individual liberty and by reducing the ability of majoritarian factions at the state and local level to exploit minorities. In that sense, the constitutional structure that emerged from the Civil War can be seen as an extension of the principles of the original Constitution and an application of those principles, even if those changes also had many unintended consequences. In particular, the grotesque institution of slavery and the treatment of blacks generally reflected Madison's particular concern in 'Federalist No. 10' regarding the power of majority factions to oppress permanent minorities. At the same time, of course, the constitutional structure and ideology that emerged from the Civil War contained the seeds of the subsequent expansion of

38 Todd Zywicki

power by the federal government and the later ability of factions to commandeer the central government for their advantage.

As railways and other improvements in transportation and information technology promoted the growth of national markets, local special interests became increasingly aggressive in trying to erect new barriers to interstate competition from more efficient producers and to favour local interests at the expense of out-of-staters. As Michael Greve demonstrates, the role of the federal judiciary was especially important during this period to police these protectionist impulses at the state and local level (Greve 2012). Through aggressive and relentless oversight, the federal courts struck down state protectionism and facilitated the growth of national markets and economic dynamism.

On other fronts, however, the federal judiciary acquitted itself less admirably. In particular, the Supreme Court's unfortunate decision in the *Slaughter-House Cases* eliminated the most powerful tool for freed slaves and others to challenge protectionist legislation at the local and state level. Thus, much of the promise of the 14th Amendment to enable individuals to challenge rent-seeking legislation at the state and local level was swept aside by the Supreme Court.

Still, the Supreme Court found other tools for protecting individual liberty from the predations of interest groups at the state level, as best exemplified in the case of *Lochner v. New York*. As shown first by Bernard Siegan (2006) and more recently shown in much more elaborate detail by David Bernstein (2011), the law in *Lochner* that regulated the working hours and conditions of bakers appears to have been a classic 'Bootleggers and Baptists' law, combining the well-intentioned efforts of public health reformers for more sanitary working conditions and product safety with the narrow economic self-interest of large corporate bakeries and their unionized workforce to stifle competition from small, family-owned, Eastern European immigrant bakeries. While Bernstein argues that, in fact, the *Lochner* court was not a roving commission self-deputized to strike down rent-seeking laws wherever they were found, their advocacy in favour of liberty of contract had the effect of limiting the ability of interest groups to capture state legislatures and regulators for their private benefit. Meanwhile, at the national level, while rent-seeking existed, it was largely contained.

The onset of the Great Depression, however, created a new constitutional crisis. The foundations of the new constitutional order were actually laid during the Progressive era and World War I. For example, 1913 saw the enactment of the 16th Amendment permitting a federal income tax and the 17th Amendment providing for direct election of senators. While the 16th Amendment unleashed the taxing power of the federal government, the 17th Amendment eroded one of the most important institutional bulwarks of federalism and bicameralism in the original constitutional structure. More important, while the 17th Amendment stripped the states of their only institutional protection for federalism (which, had in any event been attenuated as a protection for federalism by that time anyway due to the piecemeal adoption of de facto direct election and the rise of national political parties that came to dominate local elections [Schleicher 2013]), no new institutional protection for federalism was added to take its place. The combined effect of the Progressive era constitutional amendments was to weaken the 'auxiliary precautions' for federalism that the Framers had seen as protecting individual liberty and restraining special-interest faction. And while the political leadership of the Harding and Coolidge years and the general ideological resistance to the centralizing tendencies of the national government restrained the working out of these principles to their logical effect, there was, even during that period, a creeping growth in rent-seeking legislation at the national level. As is well known, the defining characteristic of administrative agencies is the combining of legislative, executive and judicial powers in one body, and the supposed substitution of non-political agency expertise for political decision-making. In short, whereas the Framers saw the structures of the separation of powers and federalism as the institutional safeguards of individual liberty and good government, Progressive thinkers and politicians saw them as obstacles to achieving their political goals.

With the constitutional foundations thus weakened, the transformation of the Constitution during the Great Depression and New Deal was little more than a mopping up operation. While the Supreme Court half-heartedly tried to hold the line against more egregious rent-seeking such as the National Recovery Act, the judicial gavel proved little resistance to the presidential pen. Eventually, judicial resistance collapsed, opening the door to an unprecedented assertion of power by the federal government over the economy but also the acceleration of the rise of the administrative state that had begun during the Progressive era. Moreover, political favouritism for particular firms and industries and other powerful interest groups (such as labour unions) were woven into the political and regulatory structure and thereby implicitly into the constitutional structure.

As Mancur Olson (1982) has shown, this political bargain between the government and powerful interest groups grew during the post-war era until the political and economic systems were choking on rent-seeking legislation and regulation. And while the Reagan era, like the earlier Harding–Coolidge era, pared back some of the political excesses of post-war era, it did little to restore the underlying constitutional foundations. Thus, by the time of national security emergency during the War on Terror hit in 2001 and the financial crisis of 2008, the government response followed the pattern established during the New Deal – massive executive discretion, followed by promises to create constitutional rules that would constrain executive discretion in future crises. In fact, as detailed below, legislation adopted in the wake of the financial crisis has done nothing to restrain future executive decision-making and, in fact, has essentially just codified and expanded the vast range of discretion seized by presidents Bush and Obama and the Federal Reserve during that period.[1]

3.3 Maintaining the rule of law in times of crisis

Because the history of the financial crisis is so recent, understanding its dynamics provides a useful framework for anticipating future similar crises and their constitutional stresses. Yet a close examination of the most recent crisis as well as those of the past reveals the exact opposite truth: adherence to the rule of law is actually

40 *Todd Zywicki*

more important during periods of economic crisis, both to restore short-term economic prosperity during the crisis and for the long-term systemic impact.

There are four reasons why this is so. First, adherence to the rule of law is necessary for economic prosperity in general, but even more so during economic crisis. Second, adherence to the rule of law is necessary to restrain the opportunism of politicians and special interests that use the opportunity presented by the crisis to piggyback their own narrow interests, often with no relationship to the real problems. Third, once discretion is unleashed during the crisis, history tells us that the dissipation of the crisis does not promote a return to the rule of law – in fact, there is a 'ratchet effect' (see Chapter 2, this volume) of government discretion as the post-crisis period brings about a consolidation of governmental discretion rather than new limits on it. And, finally, the mere potential for discretionary action promotes moral hazard, thereby creating the conditions for still further rounds of intervention. Thus, while little is lost in the short run by tying the government's hands from discretion, more importantly the only way to promote long-term economic growth and preserve freedom in the long run, and to avoid precisely the circumstances that then justify future government intervention, is to constrain government discretion in the short run. Consider each in turn.

3.3.1 The rule of law and economic recovery

First, adherence to the rule of law is necessary for long-term economic growth; indeed, this was the feature that animated the 1787 Constitutional Convention. Established rules of contract, property, bankruptcy, corporate law and the like provide the institutional infrastructure for economic growth. It is a trite and obvious statement that the modern global economy is an incredibly complex system. But that should still not distract us from how miraculous it is that milk appears in supermarkets when we want it. The economy is a system in constant flux. From missed planes in Toledo to hail storms in Oslo, the underlying conditions of economic prosperity are in constant flux and of bewildering complexity. As Hayek noted, the miracle of the modern economy is the ability of individuals to coordinate their affairs amid this constant system of flux and uncertainty. The backbone of that system is the rule of law, which enables parties to coordinate their affairs by enabling them to predict how *others* will act. Thus, it is little wonder that economists have identified the presence of the rule of law as one of the key determinants of economic prosperity in the developing world.

But this also means that adherence to the rule of law is even more important during periods of economic dislocation. It is precisely because other variables of the economic system are in even greater flux than usual that adherence to the bedrock predictability of the rule of law takes on special institutional significance. Yet many believe exactly the opposite – that the government's discretion and arbitrary power should be greater, rather than lesser, during periods of economic dislocation.

I suspect that this justification rests, in part, on an intellectual error that confuses the appropriate responses to a national security emergency with that of an economic crisis. In a national security emergency, centralized government discretion may be necessary in order to anticipate and respond to idiosyncratic threats from particular state and human actors and to seize tactical opportunities swiftly and decisively. But that is *not* what is needed following an economic crisis. What is necessary is to re-establish coordination among billions of decentralized decision-makers, not a centralized response to highly specific threats. Political uncertainty about the integrity of contracts and future regulatory policy undermines investor confidence and raises interest rates. Thus, for every job supposedly saved through arbitrary intervention there may be many others that are never created as a result of the uncertainty created by government intervention in the economy.

Thus, for example, scholars have argued (convincingly, in my mind) that the depth and duration of the Great Depression were worsened by the constant, erratic economic interventions promulgated by the government and supposedly intended to fight the crisis (Higgs 1987). It has been similarly argued that the chaotic and pell-mell nature of the government's interventions during the 2008 financial crisis slowed recovery from the banking panic (Koppl 2015).

Most notably, the government's unprincipled decision-making as to whether to bail out particular financial institutions bred unpredictability and moral hazard about government policy which made the financial crisis much worse than it would have been had the government acted according to a principled approach. For example, in the period preceding the bankruptcy of Lehman Brothers the bank had the opportunity to merge with other banks that could have saved Lehman (Skeel 2011). Yet Lehman rejected those offers as insufficiently generous. Why did it do so? Because just months earlier the Bush–Paulson team had bailed out Bear Stearns, a much smaller and systemically less-important bank, leading Lehman to assume that it would be bailed out too. Because discretionary decisions enter into individual's expectations about future policy-making, erratic, discretionary and politically tinged policy-making turned out to have much worse results than had the government not bailed out Bear to begin with.

3.3.2 The need to adhere to the rule of law

Second, adherence to the rule of law is especially important during periods of crisis because that is when potential for political opportunism by politicians and interest groups to pervert government power for their private ends is most dangerous. In focusing on the potential for government intervention to do good things, Pollyanna-ish political analysts ignore the potential of politicians and interest groups to abuse the target-rich environment presented by the crisis to further their own self-interests. President Obama's then chief of staff summed up the mentality when he observed that you should 'Never let a serious crisis go to waste,' a mantra which the President invoked in order to ram through a number of unrelated pieces of legislation and pet political projects. Indeed, every act taken by the Obama Administration in response to the financial crisis, from the initial $1 trillion stimulus, to the Dodd-Frank financial reform legislation and the auto bailouts, evidences

42 *Todd Zywicki*

this theme of piggybacking special interest and other provisions on the back of the purported crisis.

In the auto bailouts, for example, the Administration used the narrow excuse that the reduced availability of debtor-in-possession financing as a result of the continued impact of the financial crisis on lending markets justified government support for post-petition financing.[2] But even if that is true, it hardly justifies the government's heavy-handed and arbitrary intervention in the process, including the plundering of secured creditors in Chrysler, the massive wealth transfers to the United Auto Workers, the rigged bidding processes that foreclosed rival plans and the political interference with General Motor's business decisions and operations while under government ownership (Zywicki 2011). None of those activities in any way contributed to the rehabilitation of the auto companies and, indeed, they were largely adverse to that goal (Zywicki 2014).

In addition, the government used its leverage during the auto bailouts to further its political agenda of promoting the manufacture of 'green cars', supposedly environmentally friendly alternative fuel-powered vehicles and those that get higher gas mileage. For example, one special incentive provided to Fiat as part of its sweetheart acquisition of Chrysler was a special financial incentive that bene-fited Fiat if its total fleet reached a certain miles-per-gallon level by a particular date (Skeel 2011). Ironically, while Chrysler and General Motors have returned to profitability since emerging from bankruptcy, they have done so *despite* the government's incentives to produce fuel-efficient cars, not because of it. In partic-ular, while American car-makers continue to lag in sales of small cars, they have experienced a massive surge in demand for light trucks and other similar larger vehicles (Zywicki 2014). There is no guarantee, given the high union-imposed labour costs in the United States, that the US can ever profitably manufacture and market small cars and compete with lower-wage countries, nor does it seem even to be desirable to do so.

More to the current point, all of this government pushing and prodding was done completely 'off the books' with no formal regulatory action or the like. In short, like the housing government-sponsored enterprises (GSEs) (Fannie Mae and Freddie Mac), which melted down in part because of government pressure to engage in affordable housing policies without the government directly bearing responsibility for them, the government, essentially, used Chrysler and GM as quasi-GSEs to promote its preferred environmental policies.

The allocation of bailout funds from the Troubled Asset Relief Fund (TARP) also illustrates the confluence of special-interest favour-seeking and political provision during times of crisis. Studies of how the government distributed TARP funds consistently and strongly show that political connections and campaign contributions were crucially important factors in determining which banks received bailout funds.

Couch *et al.* (2011) found that campaign contributions from the financial services sector played a significant role in explaining which politicians voted for the taxpayer-funded bailouts. They argue that the funds were not directed in a way consistent with increasing liquidity but rather were funnelled 'to financial

The rule of law   43

institutions with political clout'. Similarly, Dorsch (2011) found that contributions from the financial services sector had a significant impact on the probability that legislators supported the bailout, on average.

Duchin and Sosyura (2010) examined the role of political connections in determining which firms received bailout funds from the Capital Purchase Program (CPP). The authors found that, controlling for other factors, banks with an executive on the board at the Federal Reserve were 31 per cent more likely to receive CPP funds, and a bank's connection to a House member on a key finance committee was associated with a 26 per cent increase. The authors also found that these effects were strongest for the banks with lower liquidity and poorer performance, suggesting that 'political ties shift capital allocation toward underperforming institutions' (ibid., 6).

Igan *et al.* (2011, 220) examined the relationship between financial institution lobbying and firm performance using an event study, and found that higher levels of lobbying were associated with more risk-taking by firms before the crisis and worse performance after. Firms that lobbied more intensively also experienced positive abnormal returns after TARP was announced, 'implying that the market anticipated lobbying lenders to be more connected to the policymakers and have higher chances of benefiting from the bailout'.

Duchin and Sosyura (2012) used data on firms' applications for TARP funds to test the role of banks' political influence on how TARP funds were distributed. The authors found that, controlling for other factors, banks employing a director who worked at the Treasury or one of the banking regulators were 9 percentage points more likely to be approved for government funds. Firms headquartered in the election districts of House members on key finance committees were 6 percentage points more likely to be approved. The authors also found that the politically connected banks that received bailouts underperformed other TARP recipients that were not similarly connected.

Blau *et al.* (2013) examined the role of both lobbying and political connections on a firm's likelihood to receive TARP support. The authors estimated that firms that lobbied Congress were 42 per cent more likely to receive a bailout than firms that did not lobby, while politically connected banks had a 29 per cent higher chance of receiving TARP support than non-connected firms. Similarly, the authors found that firms that lobbied and politically connected firms received larger bailouts than non-lobbying and unconnected peers. The authors estimate that, 'for every dollar spent on lobbying during the 5 years prior to TARP, firms received between \$486 and \$586 in TARP support'.

Thus, as these examples demonstrate, once discretion is unleashed in the midst of a crisis, it is almost inevitable that it will be used to benefit and enrich favoured interest groups and by politicians to gain political support, not for the purported public purposes for which power ostensibly was granted.

3.3.3 Codifying short-term suspensions of the rule of law

Third, the cessation of the crisis does not produce a retrenchment from the discretion that accompanied it. Instead, the post-crisis period produces a codification

44   *Todd Zywicki*

and consolidation of the government's discretion, making it a long-term element of the economy. The massive, 2,400-page Dodd-Frank legislation, for example, entrenches much of the lawless and discretionary activity taken by the President and Federal Reserve during the financial crisis, although vesting it in other authorities. For example, it gives the government virtually unreviewable authority to seize what the government considers to be failing financial institutions and to deem certain institutions but not others to be 'systemically risky' – although it nowhere defines the criteria that distinguish such institutions as such (Dodd-Frank Wall Street Reform and Consumer Protection Act 2010). Indeed, under the statute, a firm may not even challenge a designation that it is a systemically risky institution. Similarly, the law places strict limits on the ability of a bank to challenge a conclusion by regulators that it is insolvent, essentially depriving the bank of effective judicial review to challenge the judgment of regulators.

In addition, once constitutional constraints and the rule of law are overridden, the new regime creates clear winners and losers, and the winners have little incentive to support a return to the rule of law. It is often overlooked that the value of the rule of law is to benefit ordinary citizens. Wealthy, powerful special interests can hire the lawyers and lobbyists that enable them to thrive in a system defined by loopholes and arbitrary government decision-making. Ordinary citizens, however, are excluded from these back-room deals. Thus, this post-crisis period reinforces the dynamics that emerge during the crisis.

Despite the reality that large multinational banks and investment banks provided the catalyst for the financial crisis, one ironic legacy of the subsequent legislative response is that smaller banks have borne the brunt of the new regulatory costs imposed by Dodd-Frank and the other regulatory responses to the financial crisis. Empirical studies of the impact of Dodd-Frank have found that the costs of its regulations have fallen proportionally more heavily on small banks than larger banks, reflecting the well-known fact that many costs of regulatory compliance (such as paperwork obligations) are not related in a linear manner to the size or output of the regulated firm; or, in other words, there are economies of scale in regulatory compliance such that many of the costs of regulation can be borne relatively more cheaply by larger firms than by smaller ones (Pashigian 1982). Thus, while regulation may raise the costs of all firms in an industry, it may disproportionately impact some firms as compared to others, providing larger firms with a competitive advantage.

Dodd-Frank appears to be consistent with this understanding of regulation. While Dodd-Frank has raised the regulatory compliance costs of all firms, it has raised costs proportionally more on community banks than larger banks. A study by scholars at the Kennedy School of Government found that, in the period since Dodd-Frank was enacted, the asset bases of smaller banks has shrunk twice as fast as large banks, a result that they attribute to the comparatively high regulatory costs imposed by Dodd-Frank on small banks relative to larger banks (Lux and Greene 2015). A survey by the Mercatus Center study of the impact of Dodd-Frank on smaller banks has found that the law has imposed huge compliance costs on small banks and that they have been relatively less able to bear those costs than large banks (Pierce *et al.* 2014). As a result, small banks are reducing their product offerings (such as exiting the home mortgage market) to reduce their regulatory compliance costs or considering merging into larger banks.

Indeed, big banks have acknowledged that Dodd-Frank improved their competitive position. For example, JP Morgan Chase CEO Jamie Dimon observed that the aggregate costs of complying with all of the rules, regulations and capital costs associated with Dodd-Frank has enabled the bank to build a 'bigger moat' against competition from smaller institutions (Rouan 2013). Goldman Sachs's Lloyd Blankfein announced in 2010 that the bank would be 'among the biggest beneficiaries' of Dodd-Frank as its regulatory costs and regulatory-created profit opportunities would be especially advantageous to large banks that could bear those costs more easily (Carney 2015).

Moreover, despite all of these regulatory costs, there is little reason to believe that Dodd-Frank actually eliminated the 'too big to fail' (TBTF) problem and the problem of bank bailouts, but more likely actually entrenched it. The problem of TBTF institutions is not just the risk of having to invest taxpayer money in bailing out large banks. It is also that the implicit government guarantee given to TBTF institutions reduces the risk of lending to such firms, thereby enabling them to access capital markets at relatively less expense than smaller firms.

The existence of a TBTF subsidy prior to the enactment of Dodd-Frank is well established. Kelly *et al.* (2012) compare risk-adjusted crash insurance prices at US financial institutions and found that the insurance premiums for large banks were significantly lower than for smaller banks during the 2007–9 financial crisis. The authors attribute this divergence to an implicit government bailout guarantee that favoured equity holders of the 90 largest financial institutions in the US. They estimate the value of this crash insurance subsidy at an average of $50 billion during the financial crisis (ibid., 37).

Acharya *et al.* (2014) compared the risk profiles of US financial institutions and the credit spreads on their bonds, and found that between 1990 and 2012 the risk-to-spread relationship was significantly weaker for the largest US institutions than for small and medium-sized firms. The authors attribute this distortion to the perceived subsidy provided to TBTF institutions, allowing them to borrow at more favourable rates. The authors estimate an average funding cost advantage for the largest institutions of about 30 basis points per year from 1990–2012, which they value about $30 billion per year on average during that period. Balasubramanian and Cyree (2012) estimated a TBTF subsidy of 133 basis points in the period preceding the financial crisis (Lester and Kumar 2014; estimating 100 basis point TBTF subsidy prior to Dodd-Frank).

Evidence remains mixed as to whether Dodd-Frank actually eliminated the TBTF subsidy. A report by the Government Accountability Office, for example, concluded that while Dodd-Frank may have reduced the size of the so-called 'TBTF subsidy' for large banks, it probably did not eliminate it, indicating that large banks still retain an implicit government guarantee. Similarly, a study by the International Monetary Fund concluded that the subsidy to TBTF banks in the United States amounts to some $70 billion per year in lower capital costs and that,

46 *Todd Zywicki*

in turn, the existence of an implicit government guarantee promotes the moral hazard problem of greater risk-taking by large banks (International Monetary Fund 2014). By contrast, other studies have concluded that the TBTF subsidy has shrunk substantially (Lester and Kumar 2014)[3] or has been eliminated (Balasubramanian and Cyree 2012).[4]

On the other hand, it is possible to have political opportunism in the form of rent-extraction by politicians without any direct special-interest rent-seeking behaviour (McChesney 1997). For example, big pharmaceutical companies received harsh criticism in the *Wall Street Journal* and elsewhere for their outspoken advocacy in support of the Affordable Care Act (ACA, aka, Obamacare) ('Obamacare's Secret History' 2012). It is easy to offer a hypothesis as to why they would support the law, in that increasing access to Medicaid and health insurance would presumably increase demand for prescription drugs. According to an industry insider with whom I spoke, however, the support of the pharmaceutical industry for the ACA came despite the fact that, in the industry's assessment, the law would be harmful to the industry overall. Nevertheless, he argued, the industry was presented with the choice between a version of the law and regulations that would impose some losses on the industry or another version that would impose large losses on the industry. He argued that, in order to suffer smaller losses, the industry had to support the bill in a public way, and thus it was a rent-extraction scheme. In fact, it appears, on the one hand, that the name-brand pharmaceutical industry benefited from the enactment of the ACA (Ababneh and Tang 2013).[5] On the other hand, it also appears that the industry's initial expectation that it would benefit has turned out to be incorrect as the Obama Administration reportedly 'reneged' on a deal that it had cut with the industry to avoid price controls on its drugs ('Big Pharma's Obamacare Reward' 2015).

In addition, once the premise is established during the crisis of arbitrarily picking winners and losers, those habits persist after the abatement of the crisis. Consider also the so-called Durbin Amendment to Dodd-Frank, named after its primary sponsor, Democratic Illinois Senator Dick Durbin (Zywicki *et al.* 2014). Added at the last moment to Dodd-Frank as a floor amendment with no hearings and little discussion, the Durbin Amendment imposed price controls on the interchange fees of debit cards issued by banks with more than $10 billion in assets, requiring that those fees be 'reasonable and proportional' to the incremental cost of processing debit card transactions. Under the terms of the Federal Reserve's rule implementing the Durbin Amendment, the average interchange fee charged on debit cards issued by covered banks was slashed in half. It is estimated that, once implemented, the Durbin Amendment will reduce interchange fee revenues for covered banks by approximately $6 billion per year.

Although there are many theories about the causes of the financial crisis, the idea that it resulted from overuse of *debit* cards is not one of them. Nor does it seem likely that sucking $6 billion out of the revenue stream of banks is likely to actually increase their financial stability and help them to avoid future crises. Why then was the Durbin Amendment inserted into the Dodd-Frank financial legislation? At the lobbying of Walgreen's and other big box retailers that saw an

The rule of law   47

opportunity to reduce the amounts that they were paying on payment card processing fees (they failed, however, to impose price controls on credit cards). Empirical studies indicate that the Durbin Amendment will save big box retailers some \$1–\$3 billion annually in debit card interchange fees. And while economic theory predicts that some of these savings eventually should be partially passed on to their customers in the form of lower prices or higher quality, after two-and-a-half years there was still no evidence of any pass-through, meaning that big box retailers and their shareholders have pocketed the windfall. Meanwhile, at that time, there was no indication that smaller businesses had received any reduction in costs and some merchants actually saw their fees increase. Overall, however, one study estimated that over its expected lifespan the Durbin Amendment would result in a net transfer of some \$20 billion to big box retailers and their shareholders (Evans *et al.* 2013).

Forced to offset this loss in revenues, banks responded by raising banking fees for customers and reducing access to free current accounts. The percentage of bank accounts eligible for free cheques fell by half, from 76 per cent to 38 per cent of all accounts, over just three years after the Durbin Amendment was enacted (Zywicki *et al.* 2014). For those accounts charged a monthly maintenance fee, the average size of the fee doubled, other fees increased as well, and the minimum average balance necessary to be eligible for a free current account increased as well. Not only did bank customers pay more and get less as a result of the Durbin Amendment, but also those who were unable to afford the higher fees were driven out of the mainstream banking system completely, as the number of unbanked Americans rose by about 1 million between 2009 and 2011. Although there are several possible explanations for these fee increases and increased numbers of unbanked individuals, the Durbin Amendment and the increased bank fees that it led to for consumers were important factors – indeed, the decline in access to free current accounts occurred *only* at large banks that were subjected to the Durbin Amendment; smaller banks demonstrated no reduction in access to free current accounts – which suggests the crucial role of the Durbin Amendment in leading to higher bank fees for consumers.

Did 'high' interchange fees charged to big box retailers have anything to do with the financial crisis or the systemic risk issues or the consumer protection concerns that spawned Dodd-Frank? Of course not. Yet, given the feeding frenzy of anti-bank sentiment in the air following the financial crisis, politicians and organized interest groups saw in the Dodd-Frank legislation an opportunity to attach their wish list for financial services regulation to the law. Like free-riders hitching on a freight train as it roars through town, politicians and their interest-group supporters saw an opportunity to use the legislation as a vehicle for their own rent-seeking legislation.

3.3.4 Moral hazard

Finally, discretion invariably produces problems of moral hazard and the inevitable production of the conditions for further future interventions. Precisely because

48   *Todd Zywicki*

the government *can* exercise discretion when it believes necessary, this creates an incentive to force the government to exercise discretion by foreclosing alternatives. For example, one reason the bankruptcy of Lehman Brothers was so catastrophic and disruptive was because Lehman Brothers rejected government efforts to broker a bargain to save it in the anticipation of holding out for a better bargain, or alternatively, a Bear Stearns-style bailout. Similarly, when General Motors was spiralling towards insolvency, management refused to make plans for a bankruptcy filing, thereby effectively guaranteeing the self-fulfilling prophecy of a disorderly bankruptcy unless the government acquiesced to a bailout.

Moreover, now that President Obama has touted the auto bailouts as a successful exercise of governmental industrial policy, this will likely embolden still more moral hazard. For example, several states face impending financial calamities as the result of overly generous salary and benefit plans for state employees. In light of the political success that Obama claims for the auto bailouts, there will be little incentive for states such as California facing massive budget shortfalls to repair their fiscal houses rather than to career towards a fiscal cliff in the hope that the Obama Administration will bail them out on the basis that the state is 'too big to fail'.

The only way to preserve the rule of law in the long run is to also preserve the rule of law in the short run. Short-run expedients in the midst of a financial crisis rarely assist in addressing the crisis and open the floodgates to future arbitrary governmental action. One fears, however, that the opposite lesson has been absorbed by the public and the political class, with dire consequences for the nation.

For example, it has been found that bailing out banks or creating an implicit government guarantee for certain banks will promote moral hazard by the benefited interests. For example, Duchin and Sosyura (2014) examined the behaviour of banks that received TARP money and found that there was a 'robust increase' in risk-taking by banks approved for government assistance. TARP recipients originated 5.4 percentage points more higher-risk mortgages (defined by the loan-to-income ratio) than banks that were denied federal assistance. And while the authors admit that the increase in risk-taking at government-supported banks is attributable to a number of factors, they conclude that moral hazard likely contributed to that increase. They also observed that bailout recipients shifted towards higher-yield retail and corporate loans, rather than expanding credit volume.

Black and Hazelwood examined the average risk ratings on commercial and industrial (C&I) loans originated at banks after the bailouts and identified a relationship between reception of TARP funds and bank risk-taking (Black and Hazelwood 2013). But the results differed by bank size: the average risk rating for loans originated at large TARP recipients increased relative to large non-TARP banks, while the average risk rating of C&I loans at small TARP recipients did not. The authors also note that loans outstanding at large TARP banks decreased relative to non-TARP banks, suggesting that the increase in risk-taking 'did not correspond to expanded lending'.

3.4 What determines whether constitutional crises lead to good or bad outcomes?

The government response during and after the 2008 financial crisis paints a picture similar to that which occurred during the New Deal: a major political crisis that was also a constitutional crisis, testing the boundaries of the structural protections of the Constitution and the Bill of Rights. In 1787 and following the Civil War, the constitutional order emerged strengthened by the crucible of the crisis. During and following the New Deal and most recent financial crisis, by contrast, the Constitution and the rule of law emerged permanently damaged, crystallizing the special-interest preferences that emerged during the crisis and consolidating rather than reversing the infringements on the constitutional order. What explains the different outcomes of these different eras?

3.4.1 Accident

One possible explanation is merely the exigencies of chance and character. In establishing the first Constitution, the United States had the inestimable blessing of being led by George Washington. Although social scientists often ascribe great social outcomes to patterns and generalizable forces, it is impossible to discount the unique role of George Washington in consolidating the original Constitution – not only in how he governed as president but, probably more important, his willingness to walk away after just two terms rather than establishing himself as a *de facto* king. He thereby established the important precedent of *de facto* two-term limit on the president, a precedent that held until Franklin Roosevelt. Similarly, although it can never be known what Lincoln would have done had he lived, his succession by the weak President Andrew Johnson had the incidental effect of re-establishing the balance of power between Congress and the president. While a mixed blessing in the short run, the ascendancy of congressional power relative to the president tends to have the effect of dispersing decision-making and decentralizing power, especially in the pre-17th Amendment era.

By contrast, Roosevelt was presented with the twin crises of the Great Depression followed by the outbreak of World War II. In his hands, both crises proved centralizing factors that reinforced one another in terms of promoting greater executive discretion and authority and seeing the Constitution as little more than a nuisance. At the same time, of course, Roosevelt lacked Washington's commitment to republican self-discipline – Washington stepped away after two terms in office, Roosevelt persisted in being elected four times before dying in office. The government's response to the 2008 crisis reflected this same confluence of factors, simply in reverse order: a national security emergency (the War on Terror) followed by the financial crisis. Thus, although I am aware of no direct evidence that would support this claim, it seems plausible that the extraordinary and unprecedented actions that President Bush took during the War on Terror provided the context and milieu for the extraordinary and unprecedented actions he later took during the financial crisis, including legally questionable bailouts of

50 *Todd Zywicki*

banks in the first place, followed by legally dubious use of TARP funds to recapitalize banks (rather than buying 'troubled assets' as authorized under the statute), to the illegal diversion of TARP funds to fund the auto bailouts (Zywicki 2011). Would President Bush have been so cavalier about the legality of his actions during the financial crisis had he not become accustomed to exercising extreme discretion in fighting the War on Terror? It is not clear, but it is at least plausible that both he and others became comfortable with extreme executive discretion that provided a foundation for later actions. And, of course, Barack Obama has subsequently extended executive power and arbitrary discretion beyond breaking point, despite numerous reversals in the Supreme Court ranging from his abuse of the recess appointments clause to particular regulatory initiatives.

Thus, it may be that there is little that can be generalized from these earlier instances and that no lessons can be learned for future crises. Still it is worth considering alternative explanations that do not rest on good luck or the fluke of coincidence.

3.4.2 Elites

Scholars who have examined the resiliency of constitutions to crises have argued that the most important factor in determining how a Constitution withstands a crisis hinges not on the institutional details of the Constitution but the faith of societal elites in it (Burton *et al.* 1992). Under this theory, the contours of constitutional and political order are established by the prevailing consensus of opinion among elites as to the appropriate processes for resolving crises as they arise. Typically theories of elite governance of institutions rest on the premise that the framework of *de jure* formal rules, such as constitutional structures, do not determine the processes by which conflicts are resolved; rather it is the *de facto* informal processes of consensus and negotiation among elites. On the one hand, while elites might converge on agreement that formal constitutional processes should be followed in resolving crises, it is the underlying extra-legal commitment to formal legal processes that matters, not the formal existence of constitutional rules themselves. Thus, where elites believe in and are committed to supporting and operating within the established constitutional order, this belief system reinforces the order itself and constrains those who would like to act outside of legally sanctioned structures. On the other hand, where elites lack faith in the formal rules, they will instead move to extra-legal mechanisms for resolution of crises. The peculiar role played by elites in sustaining constitutional government has been particularly studied in the context of countries that are transitioning *to* democratic self-government after periods of totalitarianism or dictatorship, but the lessons are equally applicable to countries such as the United States that are in the process of transitioning *from* democratic self-government to governance by executive *fiat*, or what can be now referred to as 'pen and phone' lawmaking in the terminology advanced by President Barack Obama (Zywicki 2015a).

The positive role that elites can play in using crises to sustain the rule of law are evidenced in the constitutional crises in 1787 and 1865. Gathering in

The rule of law 51

Philadelphia in 1787, the delegates to the Constitutional Convention were aware of the need to create institutions that would protect contracts, property rights and internal free trade against the populism of the masses. Elite opinion recognized that the United States would not be taken seriously on the world stage without a system of laws and courts that was forceful enough to protect the necessary conditions for commerce and to defend the country from external threats. As such, a primary purpose of the Constitution was to protect propertied interests from the populist redistributive impulses of democratic excess. Similarly, the post-Civil War constitutional system rooted in formal legal equality for freed slaves reflected the views of political elites in providing for equality and the extension of legal rights of citizenship to freed slaves.

The important role of elites in shaping the response to crisis is illustrated in the disciplined response of the federal government to banking panics and other economic crises during the nineteenth century, often in the face of strong populist demands for a more active government response. Although the record in almost every case contains some blemishes, elites of the nineteenth century responded to economic crises by supporting the rule of law and focusing on the need to promote long-term recovery rather than taking panicked short-term actions that would slow and weaken the eventual recovery. Equally important, the Supreme Court did not hesitate to uphold the Constitution and the rule of law, thereby preserving the conditions necessary for economic recovery and restraining the opportunities for rent-seeking and political opportunism.

For example, consider the Panic of 1819 and subsequent recession, which resulted in the wake of the monetary expansion and other economic distortions associated with the War of 1812 (Rothbard 1962). Although state legislatures frequently succumbed to popular demands for debtor relief where possible, President Monroe and the national government generally resisted calls for monetary expansion and higher protective tariffs in response to the recession, attacking the economic downturn through a policy of government economy and resistance to new policy innovations. While it is difficult to determine to what extent the federal government's decision to resist monetary expansionism and other activism at the national level was consistent with underlying popular support, the success of the programme in promoting swift and strong recovery seemed to strengthen popular support for the maintenance of the rule of law during times of crisis.[6]

The federal government's response to the Panic of 1837 was similarly muted, largely because of the strong elite consensus that supported maintenance of the rule of law and spending restraint in response to economic downturn (Hummel 1999). Faced with the Panic of 1837 there was growing pressure for monetary expansionism to confront the crisis. Martin Van Buren responded not just by calling for a programme of government belt-tightening, but also by calling for a clearer separation of government from the banking and currency system so as to eliminate the temptation for future monetary meddling. Van Buren's refusal to inflate the currency allowed for flexible price adjustments, creating 'a nearly full-employment deflation' as prices were permitted to fall 'fast and far enough to restore market equilibrium quickly', in contrast to the Great Depression (for example) when

52 Todd Zywicki

government efforts to prop up prices exacerbated the length and depth of the Depression (ibid., 269). In addition, the federal government's refusal to bail out financially overextended state governments imposed discipline on them and avoided the moral hazard problems associated with bailouts. As economist Jeffrey Hummel observes, 'The refusal to bail out defaulting state governments produced a widening ripple of salutary effects, not the least of which was to make more difficult any future squandering of state money on public works and government-owned railroads' (ibid., 270). As Hummel concludes, 'The domestic policies of the Van Buren presidency, however, did more than bequeath a superior financial regime. They also thwarted all attempts to use economic depression as an excuse for expanding government's role' (ibid., 267).

Examining the depression of 1893, Robert Higgs identifies a similar dynamic at work in President Grover Cleveland's commitment to maintaining the rule of law in response to economic crisis (Higgs 1987). In 1893, real GNP per capita fell by 7 per cent and investment spending fell by over 20 per cent (ibid., 84). The year 1894 witnessed another 5 per cent drop in GNP per capita and an unemployment rate that hit 18 per cent. Labourers demanded public works projects to alleviate unemployment and farmers demanded inflationary policies to raise prices, stricter regulation of rail shipping rates and below-market loans (ibid., 86–7). Yet Cleveland, seemingly backed by public opinion, rejected these calls for monetary inflation and to give in to labour unrest. Cleveland also sought to lower tariffs, but faced a demand within his own party for the imposition of an income tax to offset the reduction in tariff revenues (ibid., 98). Despite his lack of enthusiasm for an income tax, Cleveland allowed the bill to become law without his signature.

Following a convoluted and controversial process, in 1895 the Supreme Court struck down the income tax legislation as unconstitutional (ibid., 102). This action came on the heels of the Supreme Court affirming the power of the government to enjoin the illegal Pullman railway workers' strike. As Higgs puts it, the Supreme Court of the era 'acted in accordance with three ideological imperatives: the rule of law, private property rights and, above all, public peace' (ibid., 104–5). During this period, the Supreme Court played an assertive role in resisting populist pressures. Thus, while much of Cleveland's programme had broad-based public support, the Supreme Court's intervention was still necessary to protect private property rights and the rule of law. Indeed, upon Cleveland's exit from the White House, the Democratic Party turned to easy money populist William Jennings Bryan, sweeping away much of Cleveland's ideology of restraint within the party.

A final example of government restraint in the face of economic crisis is the federal government's limited response to the 1920 depression that followed in the wake of the winding down of World War I and post-war inflation (Grant 2014). Nominal GNP fell 24 per cent and real GNP fell 9 per cent from 1920–1. In response to the downturn, the government 'implemented settled doctrine, as governments usually do' (ibid., 72). According to Grant, 'In 1920–21, this meant balancing the federal budget, raising interest rates to protect the Federal Reserve's gold position and allowing prices and wages to find a new lower level' (ibid.). Equally important, President Harding and his sage Secretary of the Treasury

The rule of law   53

Andrew Mellon rejected the grandiose plans of hyperactive Secretary of Commerce Herbert Hoover to implement the types of grandiose plans to prop up nominal wages and prices that Hoover would impose so disastrously a decade later as president. As Grant observes, despite the depth of the economic contraction in 1920, 'For this reason, not least, no one would wind up affixing the label "great" on the depression of 1920–21' (ibid., 72). Instead, the downturn ended after 18 months as wages and prices re-established equilibrium levels.

An open question raised by these case studies is the relative influence of elites versus public opinion in shaping government response to crises. In each case there were agitators – farmers, labourers, business leaders – who sought greater government activity to respond to the crisis. But lacking modern polling data, it is difficult to determine how widespread or forceful these views were at the time. Still more, even if public opinion was aligned against interventionism, it begs the question as to the degree to which elites shape public opinion or are constrained by it. Moreover, the range of activity available to politicians to respond to crises and the political pressures they generate is constrained by the prevailing attitude of the Supreme Court, a prototypical elite institution. To the extent that the Supreme Court is seen as limiting the range of action available to political actors, this will condition the responses available to them.

By the New Deal, however, elites had largely abandoned this commitment to the rule of law, protection of private property rights and private ordering as the foundation for economic prosperity and stability. Today, American elites are, if anything, more hostile to the values of the rule of law and constitutional government than are ordinary democratic citizens, at least during periods of Democratic governance. Since the Progressive era, intellectual sophisticates have denigrated the rule of law and formal constitutional procedures, advocating for executive-centred government that ignores the restraints of Congress and the Constitution (Zywicki 2003). The long-standing hostility to the rule of law was exacerbated by subsequent arguments by 'critical' legal scholars that the rule of law was not only undesirable but also impossible, owing to the ambiguities of language. In this sense, the excesses of 'pen and phone' lawmaking under President Obama represent simply an extreme strain of the mindset, exaggerated by the absence of any effort at principled explanation or even strong principled resistance.

To the extent that elite opinion is seen as a component of the maintenance of the rule of law in times of crisis, therefore, it appears that elite opinion is by and large hostile to the ideas of the rule of law and especially so when executive discretion is exercised by Democratic presidents, for which elites provide very little opposition.

3.4.3 Popular ideology

If elites cannot be counted on to support the rule of law in a time of crisis, what of a populist pro-constitutionalist ideological movement that can force their views upon the government – even in the face of hostility from elites?

Although the term 'ideology' has multiple and specific meanings in social science literature, for current purposes I will use the term less rigorously, to refer

54   *Todd Zywicki*

to a set of beliefs among the population at large that differs from and constrains the decision-making options available to elites. For current purposes, it is irrelevant whether elites are hostile or merely indifferent to the views of the public, but does not include situations in which the views of elites and the populous are aligned.

Perhaps the most clearly articulated analysis of the role of ideology in shaping the political response to economic crises is provided by Robert Higgs (1987 and Chapter 2, this volume). Higgs models 'ideology' as shaping the choice set available to the government in responding to crises and other emergency situations. And he contends that the change from the restraint of the nineteenth century to the activism of the twentieth century is best explained by evolving ideological views of the public and politicians. One implication of Higgs's analysis is clear – where the public and politicians are aligned in their dominant ideological viewpoints, or at least not opposed, that view will tend to prevail. Left unanswered, however, is the question: what happens if there is a majoritarian political ideology in the public at large that is contrary to the dominant views of elites?

In a conflict between elites and public opinion, elites would seem to have many advantages. First, elites generally hold the power to act first – to act proactively to implement their plans, subject to later ratification or disapproval from the public in subsequent elections. This provides elites with an agenda control and momentum that makes it more difficult to fully undo actions already taken. Moreover, as suggested above, once the government acts, those actions create a new set of political winners who can be counted on to take action to entrench the action, no matter how 'temporary' it was intended to be.[7] Second, elites hold control over the information-shaping portions of society: media, education and political institutions. Finally, in some cases elites hold the power to simply impose their values directly, such as when the Supreme Court chooses to create new rights under the Constitution, rewrites legislation to further the Court majority's ideological preferences, or refuses to enforce constitutional limits.

The rapid rise of the Tea Party movement as a political force in the United States, however, seemingly raises the potential for a populist, pro-constitutionalist movement to impose restraints on the government in times of crisis.[8] Galvanized into being by the bank bailouts during the financial crisis, the Tea Party movement rose rapidly into a powerful political force, peaking during the 2010 midterm election cycle when it claimed success in several states electing several longshot anti-establishment candidates who defeated either incumbents or establishment-supported candidates. These major electoral successes, as well as some positive media coverage, provided a tantalizing promise of a similar movement coming into being during a future crisis.

Despite these victories, however, the long-run success of the Tea Party in pushing back on politicians and well-organized interest groups that have coalesced around the rent-seeking state would seem to be modest at best. Indeed, perhaps the most striking example are the bank bailouts themselves, which brought the Tea Party into existence – despite widespread public opposition beginning with the Bear Stearns bailout in spring 2008 (Jacobe 2008), The federal government

The rule of law 55

provided over $700 billion of bailout money to stabilize banks later that year. The inability to prevail on even this core issue against political elites and powerful special interests may be indicative of the limited potential for populist movements to constrain those actors. Moreover, even the initial auto bailouts were opposed by a majority of Americans (Newport 2008) and opposition rose to 72 per cent when the Obama Administration proposed another round of bailout funds in the spring 2009 (Saad 2009). Still, the Administration went ahead with the bailouts because, despite this deep popular opposition, the bailouts were popular with an important special interest group with large presences in several politically important states.

Moreover, the Tea Party movement is anomalous in terms of its purported support for limited government and the rule of law. History suggests that, by and large, the public is more interventionist in times of crisis than elites. Most notably, the US Constitution was an elite project designed to tame the excesses of populist state legislatures. Similarly, many of the banking panics and recessions during the nineteenth century were met with concerted efforts by various groups – farmers, veterans, workers – for more government activism and intervention, which was resisted by elite politicians and especially judges.

In fact, despite its ability to garner headlines and win some modest electoral victories, even this tepid version of the Tea Party ideology seems to be out of step with the bulk of public opinion. For example, one poll taken at the end of 2014 found that only 21 per cent of respondents considered themselves to be 'supporters' of the Tea Party movement, while 67 per cent did not (Hart Research Associates and Public Opinion Strategies 2014). According to Gallup polls, while the popularity of the Tea Party movement peaked at the time of the 2010 midterm elections, still only 32 per cent of Americans considered themselves to be 'supporters' of the Tea Party, while 30 per cent opposed the Tea Party and the remainder who answered were neither supporters nor opponents (USA Today/Gallup 2010). Indeed, by the 2014 midterm elections, only 19 per cent of Americans considered themselves to be supporters of the Tea Party, while 50 per cent were 'neither' supporters nor opponents (CNN/ORC 2014). This data suggests that, even at the peak of President Barack Obama's unpopularity and even before the concerted effort of Republican Party and other elites to discredit the Tea Party, a broad-based grassroots ideological movement for fiscal restraint still was able to garner the support of, at most, one-third of the population. According to one poll conducted in April 2010 close to the peak of the Tea Party's popularity and influence, only 25 per cent of respondents said that the Tea Party reflected their beliefs while 36 per cent said that they did not (Montopoli 2012). In addition, by the 2014 midterm elections, the number of respondents claiming to be 'strong opponents' of the Tea Party (19 per cent) was substantially higher than those who still claimed to be 'strong supporters' of the Tea Party (11 per cent) (Newport 2014; Post-ABC News Poll 2013).[9] In addition, those who identified as supporters of the Tea Party were more likely to be white, male and married than the population at large – all groups that are shrinking in terms of electoral influence. However, Tea Party members are better-educated than average (Montopoli 2012).

56   Todd Zywicki

Nor is it clear that, were the Tea Party's views to become ascendant, it would actually address the looming entitlement state budget problems that are likely to precipitate the next fiscal crisis. Indeed, despite a rhetorical commitment to shrinking government, Tea Party members are also strong supporters of Social Security and Medicare. For example, during the 2011 budget showdown in Washington, one poll found that 76 per cent of Tea Party supporters opposed the inclusion of cuts to Social Security and Medicare in any proposed deficit reduction plan, while only 22 per cent supported it, barely indistinguishable from the population at large (Marist Poll National Registered Voters 2011). Moreover, Tea Party supporters tend to be older on average than Republicans in general, which suggests that their support for expensive programmes such as Social Security and Medicare are likely to strengthen over time, further exacerbating the nation's fiscal crisis (Newport 2014).

Perhaps most striking about the Tea Party movement is the lengths to which the political and intellectual establishment went to try to marginalize it and destroy its credibility. Reporters and politicians strained to falsely brand the Tea Party as ignorant, racist and extremist (Cooke 2013; Gainor 2014; Dickens 2011). One academic study of the Tea Party ascribed sympathy to the Tea Party as motivated by 'racism and the belief that subordinate groups should remain in their respective places' (Parker and Barreto 2014, 157) and that they 'are firmly opposed to the idea of group equality' (ibid., 165). The Republican Party establishment even coordinated a well-funded effort to defeat Tea Party primary challengers and to marginalize the Tea Party's influence (Zeleny 2013). As suggested by the declining popularity of the Tea Party in public polls, these efforts by media and political elites to discredit the movement have had great success.

Finally, movements such as the Tea Party also must deal with the fundamental dynamics of the logic of collective action, as described by Mancur Olson (1965). Broad-based movements seeking fiscal discipline and reform, such as the Tea Party, would seem to be a prototype example of a dispersed, heterogeneous group in the Olsonian sense. Although it is possible for some groups to coalesce temporarily around issues with broadly dispersed benefits, it is difficult to maintain enthusiasm and political organization over the long run, which tends to lead to a reinstatement of ordinary political dynamics (Boudreaux and Pritchard 2013). Moreover, conflicts between broad-based ideological preferences and specific self-interested political demands – such as Tea Party opposition to cutting Social Security and Medicare – will further weaken the influence of such groups. Given the high maintenance costs and internal conflicts of interest for members of such groups, over the long run political elites would seem to be able to wait patiently for these grassroots movements to burn themselves out and eventually to return to business as usual. Arguably, this describes the life-cycle of the Tea Party's influence.

3.4.4 Inevitability and the weakness of legal constraints

Law professors Eric Posner and Adrian Vermeule (2010) launch a more direct attack on the argument for the importance of adhering to the rule of law in times

The rule of law   57

of crisis, making the case that assertion of executive authority during times of crisis is both appropriate and inevitable in the modern world. Ironically, many of their arguments *for* unleashing executive discretion in times of crisis mirror the arguments made above *against* the same. Before analysing their argument, therefore, it is useful to understand it.

The core of Posner and Vermeule's argument is an effort to dismiss the position that they refer to as 'liberal legalism', which is essentially the position described above, namely an executive constrained by rules and processes established by the legislature and interpreted by the judiciary. Posner and Vermeule's assault on liberal legalism is comprehensive: it is unwise, unrealistic and unnecessary. Consider each in turn.

They argue that legalistic restraints on the executive are unwise because crises, whether national security or economic crises, necessitate government action to address the crisis and only the executive holds sufficient will and focus to respond quickly to stabilize matters. As Posner and Vermeule tellingly put the point describing the onset of the financial crisis in 2008, 'The Fed and Treasury did *not* simply apply general norms established by a policy-making Congress. The nature of the crisis, including the overwhelming uncertainty, *forced* these two agencies to take an ad hoc approach' (ibid., 38, emphasis added). Moreover, they argue that *only* the Executive could act, as Congress was too cumbersome and scattered and courts were irrelevant as 'Judicial review or other oversight would slow down the process when quick action was essential' (ibid., 39). In their telling, when faced with the purported threat of a collapse of the economy, Treasury Secretary Hank Paulson and Federal Reserve Chairman Ben Bernanke acted to restore confidence and predictability to markets when Congress and the courts could have only obstructed those actions.

Second, Posner and Vermeule argue that even if assertion of executive authority is unwise, it is nevertheless inevitable. As they put the matter, 'We live in a regime of executive-centered government, in an age after the separation of powers and the legally constrained executive is now a historical curiosity' (ibid., 4). In short, crises demand swift action and only the executive can respond with sufficient speed and force to meet the public demand for action.

> Legislatures and courts ... are continually behind the pace of events in the administrative state; they play an essentially reactive and marginal role, modifying and occasionally blocking executive policy initiatives, but rarely taking the lead. And in crises, the executive governs alone, at least so far as law is concerned.
>
> (Ibid.)

As a result, 'liberal legalism' (i.e. rule of law constraints on executive discretion) cannot work in the modern state and cannot constrain the executive in times of crisis.

Third, they argue that formal restraints on the executive are unnecessary, because informal restraints on the president are both more effective and more useful than legal rules. The executive is not constrained by laws but by 'politics

58   *Todd Zywicki*

and public opinion' (ibid.). Posner and Vermeule argue that proponents of legal liberalism fallaciously equate 'a constrained executive with an executive constrained by law' (ibid., 5). In turn, they argue that the loosening of legal constraints on the executive cause proponents of liberal legalism to develop 'tyrannophobia, or unjustified fear of dictatorship' (ibid.). This fear is unjustified, they argue, because it ignores the 'de facto constraints that have grown up and, to some degree, substituted for legal constraints on the executive. As the bonds of law have loosened, the bonds of politics have tightened their grip' (ibid.). They add, 'The executive, "unbound" from the standpoint of liberal legalism, is in some ways more constrained than ever before.' Indeed, not only is tyrannophobia unjustified, they argue that its presence in American politics may actually unintentionally promote the virus of tyranny that it is intended to restrain (ibid., 202–3).

Yet while Posner and Vermeule may be correct that the lawless expansion of executive authority may be inevitable in times of crisis, their normative justification is badly flawed. Most significant, their justifications for the extraordinary actions taken by the Treasury and Fed during the financial crisis rest on a string of dubious arguments. They claim, for example that 'overwhelming uncertainty' in the market 'forced' the government to take 'ad hoc' actions to restore confidence to the market – yet they provide no explanation for how 'ad hoc' interventions and bailouts were supposed to reduce uncertainty rather than exacerbating it. They rehash the myth that 'allow[ing]' Lehman Brothers to fail resulted in 'disastrous short-term consequences because many other firms had accounts with Lehman' (ibid., 38), when, in fact, there is no evidence that Lehman's failure did or would have resulted in the failure of any other banks because of their interconnectedness with Lehman (Wallison 2013). More important, they ignore the gross moral hazard that led to Lehman's collapse and resulted in the entirely avoidable failure of Lehman rather than its absorption by a healthier firm (Posner and Vermeule 2010). Finally, as economist John Taylor (Taylor 2009) has convincingly demonstrated, there is no evidence that Lehman's failure itself spooked markets – it was Hank Paulson's panicked response to Lehman's failure that spread contagion through the markets. As noted by Richard Kovacevich (2014, 543), CEO of Wells Fargo during the financial crisis, prior to TARP and a month after the Lehman bankruptcy, 'markets had declined but were still behaving reasonably well, except for those financial institutions that were having liquidity issues'. It was only when TARP was announced that 'isolated liquidity issues turned into a tsunami impacting all banks and all industries' (ibid.). In short, Paulson *created* the very panic that Posner and Vermeule claim that Paulson's panicked and erratic behaviour supposedly stemmed.

Posner and Vermeule are also on shaky ground in dismissing what they consider to be overwrought and unrealistic fears of tyrannophobia and their belief that formal institutions are irrelevant to controlling the abuse of discretionary powers in the president. While it is undoubtedly true that public opinion plays an important role in restraining excessive and abusive (i.e. politically motivated) actions by the president, it is unwise to dismiss the role of institutions in restraining such action. Moreover, there is good reason to believe that many of the

The rule of law 59

informal constraints that have restrained the President in the past have become sufficiently desiccated that they no longer bind and, in many situations, may actually empower.

First, while Posner and Vermeule argue persuasively that liberal legalistic rules do little to constrain executive action today, legal restraints are not entirely irrelevant. For example, in recent years the Supreme Court has, on several occasions, nullified examples of egregious executive overreach, often by 9–0 votes. Perhaps most notable, the Supreme Court invalidated President Obama's illegal recess appointments, despite support from Democratic leaders in Congress willing to surrender Congress's constitutional power to vote on nominees for partisan advantage (*NLRB v. Noel Canning* 2014). Courts have also invalidated several other examples of extreme executive action from property rights to religious freedom to criminal procedure (Somin 2013). In virtually all of these cases, the Democratic partisans in Congress and the mainstream media raised no objection to the President's actions.

More telling, as discussed above, the historical record suggests that judges during the nineteenth century were not as passive as current judges in deferring to the Executive in times of economic crisis. Judges frequently intervened to uphold property rights, the rule of law and constitutional constraints, going so far as to strike down on constitutional grounds legislation as far-reaching as the income tax. It is true that, over time, many of these decisions were reversed by constitutional amendment and changes in court composition (such as the infamous Supreme Court flip-flop on the constitutionality of legal tender laws [Zywicki 2005]). Still, it is evident that the Supreme Court can and has played a role in checking government overreach and lawlessness during times of economic crisis.

Formal restraints may also provide a context for reinforcing informal constraints, serving as a sort of focal point or coordinating device for preventing constitutional transgressions (Hadfield and Weingast 2013). Although it is rarely explicit, reviewing the historical record regarding the debates over government intervention to address economic downturns in the pre-New Deal era suggests that politicians believed that many proposed interactions were not only unwise, but also illegal and violated the Constitution (and in some cases, as noted, the Supreme Court interposed to enforce those limits). The tendency of modern presidents to focus largely on the politics and ignore the legality of their actions unless formally ordered by a court seems to be largely a modern tendency, not one that suggests any inherent limits in liberal legalism – although, as suggested above, the deterioration of legal constraints on the executive is consistent with changing elite attitudes over time.

In addition, Posner and Vermeule's appeals to politics and public opinion as constraints on the executive are flaccid and ill-defined. As noted above, one important function of the rule of law is to constrain politicians and special interests intent on capturing government power for their own purposes. Under Mancur Olson's well-understood theory of the dynamics of collective action in politics, government tends to the production of laws that provide concentrated benefits to well-organized interest groups at the expense of the dispersed public. There is

60   *Todd Zywicki*

certainly no reason to believe that this tendency is *less* pronounced in times of crisis – indeed, as discussed, the disproportionate distribution of TARP funds to politically connected banks demonstrates that interest-group politics are not suspended in times of crisis. More generally, the belief that constraints of politics and public opinion will constrain runaway executive discretion is simply unrealistic and even naive: the crony capitalist enterprise is bipartisan in nature, as the TARP legislation itself was proposed by a Republican president and passed into law by predominantly Democratic votes. The illegal diversion of TARP funds to bail out General Motors and Chrysler – a decision that was made by the Bush Administration immediately after Congress voted down an appropriations proposal to provide bailout funds to the car-makers – was met by nothing more than a feeble letter of protest by several United States Senators (Rattner 2010).[10] Meanwhile, public opinion polls taken at the time of the bank bailouts identified widespread public opposition to providing tax money to bail out banks, suggesting that public opinion provides little constraint on opportunistic politicians in times of crisis.

If dismissal of the importance of formal constraints on the executive is anachronistic, then their confidence in the constraining power of informal constraints is archaic. While considerations of public opinion and, especially, the watchdog function of an independent and free press may have constrained executive excess in the past, these forces appear much weaker today, at least with respect to Democratic presidents.

Posner and Vermeule point to several examples to support their claim that informal constraints, such as public opinion, render concerns about tyrannophobia ungrounded, such as the failure of Roosevelt's court-packing plan and the impeachment of Richard Nixon for abuse of power. Yet to the extent that these historical examples support their argument they also reveal the different circumstances that prevail today and cast doubt on the validity of these examples.

Consider, first, the public rejection of Roosevelt's effort to pack the court in response to the early judicial defeat of his New Deal programmes. This is, of course, a questionable example because, while the causes of the Supreme Court's 'switch in time that saved nine' are open to dispute, in the end the Supreme Court relented on its opposition to Roosevelt's programme, essentially mooting Roosevelt's need to pack the court. Still, to the extent that this historical example supports Posner and Vermeule's thesis, it is not clear that similar circumstances prevail today among the public or elites to resist such an action.

In large part, scepticism about the constraining power of informal structures follows from the weakened consensus among American elites regarding the importance of following constitutional practices in lawmaking. While presidential attacks on the Supreme Court have recurred over time in the United States, few recent presidents have so directly attacked the independence of the Supreme Court as much as President Obama. Obama's pre-emptive attacks on the Supreme Court prior to its ruling on *Sibelius v. NFIB* (regarding the constitutional challenge to the Affordable Care Act) or his direct criticism of the Court's ruling protecting political speech under the First Amendment in the *Citizen United* case were different in both

The rule of law   61

motivation and tone from comments by most sitting presidents who disagreed with the Supreme Court's rulings. Not only has the ostensibly independent media not questioned these attacks, in many instances also they have endorsed and emboldened them.

Analogies to the impeachment of Richard Nixon may provide an even clearer illustration of the degraded state of the media and elites in policing overreach by Democratic presidents. For example, when President Clinton committed perjury before a grand jury, the media and elite opinion were aghast that an impeachment proceeding would result. And although a Republican majority in the House of Representatives voted out Articles of Impeachment, Democrats in the Senate voted on a near party line vote not to convict him and remove him from office, despite the obvious fact that perjury in testimony before a grand jury quite plainly constitutes a 'high crime or misdemeanor' under the Constitution and that the President of the United States is the nation's chief law enforcement official. Indeed, not only were the media and elite opinion silent with respect to the President's crimes, also they attacked the Republican leaders who brought the case.

Posner and Vermeule's argument also fails to address a larger question: even if the short-term benefits of violating the rule of law exceed the costs, is that true in the long term? While acknowledging many of the critiques made above, namely that short-term deviations from the rule of law typically are ratified and often even enlarged after the crisis abates, they never address the question of whether, on balance, these short-term deviations are justifiable. Moreover, because they essentially ignore arguments about moral hazard (that the potential for executive discretion compels executive discretion) and minimize the risks that discretion will be used for favoured special interests rather than the public, they do not seem to even consider the potential that the long-term costs of abandoning the rule of law exceed the benefits.

They do, however, inadvertently support the thesis advanced above – that in a world where elite support for the rule of law is weak and potential for political opportunism is high, the expansive assertion of executive authority is more or less inevitable. The recognition of the forces pushing in favour of executive authority in times of crisis, combined with the weakened formal and informal restraints on the government of recent years, suggests that, for those concerned about the preservation of the rule of law, solutions must lie elsewhere.

3.5 The rule of law and the next crisis

The foregoing discussion presents a sombre diagnosis about the prospects for the survival of the rule of law during the next major constitutional crisis. Unlike prior crises, the genesis of the next crisis is likely to be a fiscal crisis caused by the implosion of the entitlements and rent-seeking states under the twin weights of exploding obligations for middle-class entitlements combined with continued slowing economic growth caused by the burden of regulatory overreach and the distortions of crony capitalism.

62   *Todd Zywicki*

Although precise estimates vary, estimates of America's unfunded entitlements liabilities run into the tens of trillions of dollars. The United States cannot and will not repay these debts. Chronic deficits have become a standard way of life in the United States, with the only question being their size, not their existence. It is well known that the impending retirement of the baby boom generation will put further strain on entitlement programmes. Ironically, while most hand-wringing about government activity is focused on the distortions introduced by rent-seeking by well-organized interest groups, the genesis of the American fiscal crisis is easily recognized by a reader of 'Federalist No. 10' – the problem of majority faction. Today, the most potent faction in the United States is not Wall Street banks or green energy welfare recipients, it is the mass of middle-class voters who drive government policy, including major entitlements, and for which politicians of both parties engage in a bidding war for support. As Pogo famously said, 'We have met the enemy, and it is us.'

The prospect for reform of middle-class entitlements before a fiscal crisis occurs is weak. Politicians are unwilling to risk proposed reductions in entitlements for fear of attack by other politicians. Indeed, astoundingly, at the time this is being written (spring 2015) leading Democratic Party politicians such as Elizabeth Warren are actually advocating for an *increase* in Social Security benefits. Illustrating the point, state and local governments have been largely unsuccessful in reining in the excessive obligations of public employee pension programmes, even as the obligations owed to current and future retirees exacts an increasingly large toll on local budgets and current services.

At the same time that middle-class interest-group politics has been loading increasingly unsustainable public expense burdens, economic dynamism has been suffocating under the accumulating weight of regulation and the crony capitalist political and economic structure (Zywicki 2015b). Much as Mancur Olson (1982) predicted, interest groups have increasingly sunk their tentacles into the spending and regulatory powers of the federal government, securing special-interest benefits, absorbing taxpayer subsidies and erecting barriers to entry for new rivals (or using government to bring down more efficient rivals). The accumulation of this regulatory weight of institutionalized rent-seeking and the crony capitalist symbiotic relationships between big government, big business and big labour, have conspired to stifle economic growth and dynamism. Indeed, for the first time in recent history – including periods of recession – last year the number of American businesses that failed exceeded the number of new businesses created (Hathaway and Litan 2014).

With respect to some aspects of constitutional government during times of crisis, history does provide lessons. For example, it is evident that the United States government cannot create a credible commitment not to bail out financial institutions in the midst of a financial crisis, especially in light of the received conventional wisdom that Lehman Brothers failed because of the government's reluctance to bail it out. It is significant that, underneath all of the bailouts in 2008, in the end Henry Paulson decided to bail out banks because it was 'expected' by the markets – in short, expectations of a government bailout became a self-fulfilling prophecy that generated bailouts (Zywicki 2013b).

The rule of law 63

Given the inability of the government to credibly commit to not bailing out big banks during a financial crisis, in the world of the second-best it may be that the best possible approach is to forcibly break up big banks and to restrict them from growing to the degree of size or complexity that bailouts in times of crisis become inevitable (Zywicki 2013a; Tarulo 2012).[11] Pursuing that policy would require an assessment of the costs of artificially limiting the size of banks in terms of any lost efficiencies of size or scope and weighing those costs against the benefits of avoiding the externalities imposed on taxpayers by bank bailouts.[12] A financial system grounded in the rule of law that created binding restraints on the power of the government to bail out large banks would be the ideal solution, as formally neutral rules would allow banks to compete on equal terms and to find their own efficient sizes, but given the inability to enforce formal rule of law constraints, avoidance of the situation may be the best available option, rather than the naive belief that Dodd-Frank will actually work to eliminate bailouts.

Are there similar lessons that can be applied for fiscal policy in the world of the second-best? James Buchanan argued for his entire career for a balanced budget amendment to the Constitution that would constrain the ability of the government to run chronic deficits. At the end of his career he supplemented this with a call for a 'monetary constitution' to isolate monetary authorities from the pressure of political authorities to monetize the debt and to otherwise compensate for bad fiscal policy (Buchanan 2010).

Recent history suggests that constitutional rules that prohibited budget deficits or currency inflation would be little more than parchment barriers in the face of any crisis, which is when they were most needed. For example, the United States Constitution already likely prohibits the issuance of paper money with 'legal tender' status that must be accepted by private parties in payment of private debts (Zywicki 2005). Yet the United States government issued 'greenbacks' to fund the Civil War and further declared them to hold the status of legal tender. Following the conclusion of the Civil War, in 1870 the validity of the legal tender law was challenged, which the Supreme Court originally sustained by a 4–3 vote. Following the appointment of two new Justices, however, the Supreme Court reversed itself in 1871, upholding the legal tender laws.

The case involving the legal tender laws, therefore, followed the standard rules for the deterioration of constitutional constraints – a crisis (in this case the Civil War) which the government met by an extra-legal exigency. Following the abatement of the crisis, however, it was thought too disruptive to restore the Constitution to its original rules and, as a result, the exercise of exigent power was eventually ratified by the Supreme Court and Congress rather than reversed. It seems likely that a balanced budget amendment to the Constitution similarly would be rendered a dead letter in a time of crisis. Thus, one suspects that constitutional constraints on the ability to accumulate or monetize the debt would likely prove unenforceable in times of crisis.

Similarly, the 14th Amendment, Section 4, provides that the 'validity of the public debt of the United States ... shall not be questioned'. Yet it hardly takes a great deal of imagination to recognize that this provision would provide little

64   *Todd Zywicki*

constraint on a federal government determined to repudiate its debts. For example, the government could argue that, as its debt burden increases, parties should have declining expectations that their debts will be paid at face value, and that the validity of their debt was limited to what they could reasonably expect in payment on the debt. Thus, it seems doubtful that a court would be likely to try to enforce this constitutional provision against the federal government.

This argument, in fact, mirrors the argument that was made to reject the claims of the secured creditors in the Chrysler case that they were entitled to be paid in full before the payment of the unsecured creditors in Chrysler. And, indeed, it may be that the auto bankruptcy cases provide the most likely template for what would happen in the event of a fiscal crisis in the United States. The Bankruptcy Code provides a well-established set of rules to deal with a firm's financial distress, specifying the procedures, creditor priorities and how to sell assets and distribute proceeds in bankruptcy. Yet in the auto bankruptcies, the political intervention of the government ran roughshod over the established rules, violating virtually every established rule of bankruptcy. The Chrysler case ignored standard rules of priorities and bidding procedures, engaging in a *sub rosa* plan of reorganization outside of the rules of the Bankruptcy Code, all designed to transfer taxpayer monies to a politically powerful interest group, the United Auto Workers. Moreover, when aggrieved secured creditors of Chrysler challenged the kangaroo-court processes, the Obama Administration browbeat the Supreme Court into not reviewing the case, arguing that Chrysler was like a 'melting ice cube' and that if the plan was not approved the company would collapse imminently. The Supreme Court obliged, refusing to stay the sale of the company to Fiat or to review the case. Eventually, however, the Supreme Court did take the case on *certiorari*, only to dismiss it as moot – the only effect of which was to vacate the lower court opinion approving the sale. The dynamics of the Chrysler case have many of the features of the typical constitutional crisis – a powerful interest group, a group of self-interested politicians, a breach of the rule of law and courts that, in the end, are unwilling to stand up and enforce the rule of law. If the federal government chooses to repudiate its debts, one suspects that the story will be similar. The government will not likely simply repudiate or write down its debts wholesale, but will instead pick and choose, honouring some debts and not others, depending on the political influence of competing interest groups.

Can anything be done to try to hope that the next constitutional crisis turns out more like 1787 than 2008? If so, then I am not aware of it. Without a commitment of societal elites to the Constitution and the rule of law, it seems that politicians can act largely unconstrained by the rule of law. Indeed, as Posner and Vermeule's book nicely illustrates, elite opinion has concluded that adherence to the rule of law, especially in times of crisis, is, at best, not even feasible and, at worst, an antiquated formalism. Engaged civic education could strengthen public understanding and support for the rule of law – yet because elites shape the content of civic education, 'better' civic education seems like an unlikely source as well.

Notes

1 While the national security crisis associated with the 9/11 terrorist attacks would be worthy of study as well, I will focus on the response to the financial crisis. First, because I know more about it. And, second, it seems likely that a future constitutional crisis in the United States will be economic in nature, whether caused by a financial panic or a fiscal crisis, such as 1787 and the Great Depression.

2 Debtor in possession financing refers to the provision of operating capital to a corporation so that it can operate in bankruptcy. Because post-bankruptcy debtor in possession financing is usually paid first out of the debtor's operating revenues and assets, it typically presents very low risk of non-payment, especially with debtors with substantial assets and revenues such as General Motors and Chrysler. Thus, their inability to easily obtain debtor in possession financing reasonably can be attributed to the liquidity problems in credit markets at the time.

3 Finding difference in funding costs of 18 basis points and arguing that it may not be attributable to an implicit TBTF subsidy.

4 It should be noted that the failure to find a significant TBTF subsidy today does not eliminate the possibility of its existence if the risk of bank failure is seen as sufficiently distant in the future. More relevant would be to determine whether such a subsidy is identified during a period of financial stress.

5 Protestations to the contrary, empirical studies suggest that makers of brand-named pharmaceuticals benefited from the ACA (along with hospitals), whereas generic drug makers and health insurers suffered. This suggests that while the pharmaceutical industry's behaviour is best understood as rent-seeking, the support of health insurers might be explainable as rent-extraction by Washington.

6 Rothbard's analysis of the panic of 1819 portrays President Monroe as a relatively passive and perhaps even out of touch observer of contemporary economic developments, seemingly delegating most of these economic policy decisions to his advisors. Rothbard does not make clear whether Monroe's restraint was a matter of philosophy or indifference. This passivity itself may reflect Monroe's prevailing opinion that there was little Washington could do to try to confront the recession.

7 The entrenchment of the perception that too-big-to-fail banks will be bailed out in the future, for example, illustrates the point.

8 The grassroots anti-tax revolts in the 1970s, such as Proposition 13 in California, potentially is another example of populist constraints on government becoming effective.

9 Results of a survey that 10 per cent of registered voters strongly supported the Tea Party while 32 per cent strongly opposed it.

10 According to Steven Rattner's book on the auto bailouts, when General Motors originally proposed to Treasury Secretary Henry Paulson that he divert TARP funds to the car-makers, Paulson told him that he was not authorized to do so and that GM would need a special appropriation from Congress. Yet when Congress voted down the appropriation Paulson provided TARP funds – he did not, however, provide any explanation for why, all of a sudden, he believed his actions to be legal (Zywicki 2011).

11 An alternative would be to try to regulate banks through antitrust law in order to limit merger activity. In fact, the Dodd-Frank financial reform legislation specifically permits the Federal Reserve to consider 'added risk to the stability of the US banking or financial system' in deciding whether to approve a merger. *See* Daniel Tarullo, http://www.federalre serve.gov/newsevents/speech/tarullo20121010a.htm. On the other hand, this approach does not address situations where banks grow internally to systemically risky size and interconnectedness (if such a thing exists), nor does it deal with current mega-banks, which are already deemed to be systemically risky.

12 Most studies suggest that while there are increasing marginal returns to size, eventually, the marginal returns level off and become zero at some point below the size of modern mega-banks, suggesting that banks could be reduced in size without suffering major losses in efficiencies.

66   *Todd Zywicki*

References

Ababneh, Musab, and Alex Tang. 'Market Reaction to Health Care Law: An Event Study'. *International Journal of Accounting and Financial Reporting* 3, no. 1 (2013): 108–27.

Acharya, Viral V., Deniz Anginer and A. Joseph Warburton. 'The End of Market Discipline? Investor Expectations of Implicit Government Guarantees'. *Social Science Research Network*, 2014. http://papers.ssrn.com/sol3/papers.cfm?abstract_id=1961656

Balasubramanian, Bhanu, and Ken Cyree. 'The End of Too-Big-to-Fail? Evidence from Senior Bank Bond Yield Spreads Around the Dodd-Frank Act'. *Social Science Research Network*. 2012. Accessed 26 February 2015. http://papers.ssrn.com/sol3/papers.cfm?abstract_id=2089750

Barro, Robert J., and David B. Gordon. 'A Positive Theory of Monetary Policy in a Natural Rate Model'. *Journal of Political Economy* 91, no. 4 (1983): 589–610.

Bernstein, David. *Rehabilitating Lochner: Defending Individual Rights against Progressive Reform*. Chicago: University of Chicago Press, 2011.

'Big Pharma's ObamaCare Reward: For Helping Pass the Law, the Drug Companies Get Price Controls'. *Wall Street Journal*, 5 February 2015. http://www.wsj.com/articles/big-pharmas-obamacare-reward-1423180690

Black, Lamont K., and Lieu N. Hazelwood. 'The Effect of TARP on Bank Risk-taking'. *Journal of Financial Stability* 9, no. 4 (2013): 790–803. http://www.sciencedirect.com/science/journal/15723089/9

Blau, Benjamin M., Tyler J. Brough and Diana W. Thomas. 'Corporate Lobbying, Political Connections, and the Bailout of Banks'. *Journal of Banking and Finance* 37, no. 5 (2013): 3007–17.

Boudreaux, Donald A. and A.C. Pritchard. 'Rewriting the Constitution: An Economic Analysis of the Constitutional Amendment Process'. *Fordham Law Review* 62, no. 1 (October 2013): 111–62.

Buchanan, James M. 'The Constitutionalization of Money'. *Cato Journal* 30, no. 2 (Spring/Summer 2010): 251–8. http://object.cato.org/sites/cato.org/files/serials/files/cato-journal/2010/5/cj30n2-1.pdf

Burton, Michael, Richard Gunther and John Higley. 'Introduction: Elite Transformations and Democratic Regimes'. In John Higley and Richard Gunther, eds, *Elite and Democratic Consolidation in Latin America and Southern Europe*. Cambridge, UK: Cambridge University Press, 1992, pp. 1–37.

Carney, Timothy P. 'Goldman and JPMorgan Sit Safely Behind the Walls of Dodd-Frank'. *Washington Examiner*, 12 February 2015. http://www.washingtonexaminer.com/goldman-and-jpmorgan-sit-safely-behind-the-walls-of-dodd-frank/article/2560179

CNN/ORC. 2014. http://www.pollingreport.com/politics.htm

Cooke, Charles C.W. 'The Maligned Tea Party: The Left's Characterizations Just Aren't True'. *National Review*, 21 October 2013. http://www.nationalreview.com/article/361725/maligned-tea-party-charles-c-w-cooke

Couch, Jim F., Mark D. Foster, Keith Malone and David L. Black. 'An Analysis of the Financial Services Bailout Vote'. *Cato Journal* 31, no. 1 (2011): 119–28. http://object.cato.org/sites/cato.org/ files/serials/files/cato-journal/2011/1/cj31n1-8.pdf

Dickens, Geoffrey. 'A Tale of Two Protests: Media Cheer Wall Street Occupiers but Jeered Tea Partiers'. *Media Reality Check*, 13 October 2011. http://www.mrc.org/media-reality-check/tale-two-protests-media-cheer-wall-street-occupiers-jeered-tea-partiers

Dodd-Frank Wall Street Reform and Consumer Protection Act of 2010. Public Law 111-203, (2010), H.R. 4173.

The rule of law 67

Dorsch, Michael. 'Bailout for Sale? The Vote to save Wall Street'. *Public Choice* 155, no. 3–4 (2011): 211–28.

Duchin, Ran, and Denis Sosyura. 'TARP Investments: Financials and Politics?' Ross School of Business Working Paper No. 1127 (January 2010): 1–72. http://deepblue.lib.umich.edu/bitstream/handle/2027.42/63451/1127_r10_duchin.pdf?sequence=6. Accessed 30 January 2015.

Duchin, Ran, and Denis Sosyura. 'The Politics of Government Investment'. *Journal of Financial Economics* 106, no. 1 (October 2012): 24–48. http://papers.ssrn.com/sol3/papers.cfm?abstract_id=1426219. Accessed 30 January 2015.

Duchin, Ran, and Denis Sosyura. 'Safer Ratios, Riskier Portfolios: Banks' Response to Government Aid'. *Journal of Financial Economics* 113, no. 1 (February 2014): 1–28. http://papers.ssrn.com/sol3/papers.cfm?-abstract_id=1925710. Accessed 30 January 2015.

Evans, David S., Howard Chang and Steven Joyce. 'The Impact of the US Debit Card Interchange Regulation Caps on Consumer Welfare: An Event Study Analysis'. University of Chicago Coase-Sandor Institute for Law and Economics Research Paper No. 658 (2013). http://www.law.uchicago.edu/files/file/658-dse-hj-sj-impact-fixed.pdf

Gainor, Dan. '5 Years After: 7 Worst Media Attacks on Tea Party'. *NewsBusters*, 27 February 2014. http://newsbusters.org/blogs/mike-ciandella/2014/02/27/5-years-after-7-worst-media-attacks-tea-party

Grant, James. *The Forgotten Depression: 1921: The Crash That Cured Itself.* New York: Simon and Schuster, 2014.

Greve, Michael S. *The Upside-Down Constitution.* Cambridge, MA: Harvard University Press, 2012.

Hadfield, Gillian K., and Barry R. Weingast. 'Constitutions as Coordinating Devices'. USC CLEO Research Paper No. C11-20, 2013. http://papers.ssrn.com/sol3/papers.cfm?abstract_id=1963451

Hart Research Associates (D) and Public Opinion Strategies (R). 'Do You Consider Yourself a Supporter of the Tea Party Movement?' *NBC News/Wall Street Journal Poll*, 14–17 November 2014. http://www.pollingreport.com/politics.htm

Hathaway, Ian, and Robert E. Litan. 'Declining Business Dynamism in the United States: A Look at States and Metros. *Brookings Institution.* May 2014. http://www.brookings.edu/~/media/research/files/papers/2014/05/declining%20business%20dynamism%20litan/declining_business_dynamism_hathaway_litan.pdf

Higgs, Robert. *Crisis and Leviathan: Critical Episodes in the Growth of American Government.* New York: Oxford University Press, 1987.

Hummel, Jeffrey Rogers. 'Martin Van Buren: The Greatest American President'. *Independent Review* 4, no. 2 (Autumn 1999): 255–81.

Igan, Deniz, Prachi Mishra and Thierry Tressel. 'A Fistful of Dollars: Lobbying and the Financial Crisis'. NBER Macroeconomics Annual 26, no. 1 (2011): 195–230. http://www.nber.org/papers/w17076

International Monetary Fund. *Global Financial Stability Report, March: Big Banks Benefit from Government Subsidies.* USA: International Monetary Fund, 2014. http://www.imf.org/external/pubs/ft/survey/so/2014/POL033114A.htm

Jacobe, Dennis. 'Six in 10 Oppose Wall Street Bailouts: But Majority of Americans Support the Government Helping People Stay in Their Homes'. *Gallup*, 3 April 2008. http://www.gallup.com/poll/106114/six-oppose-wall-street-bailouts.aspx

Kelly, Brian Y., Hanno N. Lustig and Stijn Van Nieuwerburgh. 'Too Systemic to Fail: What Option Markets Imply About Sector-Wide Government Guarantees'. Chicago

68   *Todd Zywicki*

Booth Research Paper No. 11–12, 2012. http://papers.ssrn.com/sol3/papers. cfm?abstract_id=1762312

Koppl, Roger. *From Crisis to Confidence: Macroeconomics After the Crash*. London: Institute of Economic Affairs, 2015.

Kovacevic, Richard. 'The Financial Crisis: Why the Conventional Wisdom Has It All Wrong'. *Cato Journal* 34, no. 3 (Autumn 2014): 541–56.

Lester, John, and Aditi Kumar. 'Do Bond Spreads Show Evidence of Too Big To Fail Effects?' *Oliver Wyman Financial Services*, 2014. http://www.oliverwyman.com/insights/ publications/2014/apr/do-bond-spreads-show-evidence-of-tbtf-effects.html#.VO9r_fnF-sw

Lux, Marshall, and Robert Greene. 'The State and Fate of Community Banking'. M-RCBG Associate Working Paper No. 37, 2015. http://www.valuewalk.com/ wp-content/uploads/2015/02/Final_State_and_Fate_Lux_Greene.pdf

Marist Poll National Registered Voters. 'Please Tell Me Whether You Think Each of the Following Should or Should Not Be Included in the Super Committee's Deficit Reduction Proposal: Major Cuts in Social Security and Medicare?' *Marist Poll*, 8–10 November 2011. https://maristpoll.marist.edu/wp-content/misc/usapolls/US111108/ Congress_Flat%20Tax_Mill%20Tax/Deficit%20Reduction%20Agreement_Cuts%20 to%20Social%20Security%20and%20Medicare.htm

McChesney, Fred S. *Money for Nothing: Politicians, Rent Extraction, and Political Extortion*. Cambridge, MA: Harvard University Press, 1997.

Montopoli, Brian. 'Tea Party Supporters: Who They Are and What They Believe'. *CBS News*, 14 December 2012. http://www.cbsnews.com/news/tea-party-supporters-who-they-are-and-what-they-believe/

Newport, Frank. 'Americans Still Not Buying In to Auto Bailout: No Ringing Endorsement of Federal Assistance'. *Gallup*, 9 December 2008. http://www.gallup.com/poll/112993/ americans-still-buying-auto-bailout.aspx

Newport, Frank. 'Tea Party Support Holds at 24%: Ideology is the Major Factor in Tea Party Support Within the GOP'. *Gallup*, 1 October 2014. http://www.gallup.com/ poll/177788/tea-party-support-holds.aspx

NLRB v. Noel Canning. 134 S. Ct. 2550 (2014).

'ObamaCare's Secret History: How a Pfizer CEO and Big Pharma Colluded with the White House at the Public's Expense'. *Wall Street Journal*, 13 June 2012. http://www. wsj.com/articles/SB10001424052702303830204577446470015843822

Olson, Mancur. *The Logic of Collective Action: Public Theories and Groups*. Cambridge, MA: Harvard University Press, 1965.

Olson, Mancur. *The Rise and Decline of Nations: Economic Growth, Stagflation, and Social Rigidities*. New Haven: Yale University Press, 1982.

Parker, Christopher S., and Matt A. Barreto. *Change They Can't Believe In: The Tea Party and Reactionary Politics in America*. Princeton, NJ: Princeton University Press, 2014.

Pashigian, B. Peter. 'A Theory of Prevention and Legal Defense with an Application to the Legal Costs of Companies'. *Journal of Law and Economics* 25, no. 2 (October 1982): 247–70.

Pierce, Hester, Ian Robinson and Thomas Stratmann. 'How are Small Banks Fairing under Dodd-Frank?' George Mason University Mercatus Center Working Paper No. 14-05, 2014. http://mercatus.org/publication/how-are-small-banks-faring-under-dodd-frank

Posner, Eric A., and Adrian Vermeule. *Executive Unbound: After the Madisonian Republic*. New York: Oxford University Press, 2010.

Post-ABC News Poll. 'What's Your View of the Tea Party Political Movement: Would You Say You Support It Strongly, Support It Somewhat, Oppose It Somewhat or

The rule of law   69

Oppose It Strongly?' *Washington Post*, 13 November 2013. https://www.washingtonpost. com/politics/polling/whats-party-tea-political/2014/01/27/8b1b18a2-8647-11e3-aff8-191f8d178325_page.html

Rattner, Steven. *Overhaul: And Insider's Account of the Obama Administration's Emergency Rescue of the Auto Industry*. New York: Haughton Mifflin Harcourt, 2010.

Rothbard, Murray N. *The Panic of 1819: Reactions and Policies*. New York: Columbia University Press, 1962.

Rouan, Rick. 'Dimon says Dodd-Frank Puts "Bigger Moat" Around JPMorgan Chase'. *Columbus Business First*, 5 February 2013. http://www.bizjournals.com/columbus/ blog/2013/02/dimon-says-dodd-frank-puts-bigger.html. Accessed 30 January 2015.

Saad, Lydia. 'Americans Reject Sequel to Auto Bailout: More Than 7 in 10 Say Congress Should Not Approve Loans'. *Gallup*, 26 February 2009. http://www.gallup.com/ poll/116107/americans-reject-sequel-auto-bailout.aspx

Schleicher, David. 'The Seventeenth Amendment and Federalism in an Age of National Political Parties'. George Mason University Law and Economics Research Paper No. 13–33, 2013. http://papers.ssrn.com/sol3/papers.cfm?abstract_id=2269077

Siegan, Bernard. *Economic Liberties and the Constitution*. New Brunswick, NJ: Transaction, 2006.

Skeel, David A. *The New Financial Deal: Understanding the Dodd-Frank Act and Its (Unintended) Consequences*. Hoboken, NJ: John Wiley & Sons, 2011.

Somin, Ilya. 'Supreme Court Shutouts Reveal Reckless Decisions'. *USA Today*, 23 July 2013. http://www.usatoday.com/story/opinion/2013/07/22/supreme-court-losses-column/2576625/

Tarulo, Daniel K. 'Financial Stability Regulation'. At the Distinguished Jurist Lecture. Philadelphia, Pennsylvania. 10 October 2012.

Taylor, John B. *Getting Off Track: How Government Actions and Interventions Caused, Prolonged, and Worsened the Financial Crisis'*. Stanford, CA: Hoover Institution Press, 2009.

USA Today/Gallup. 'Do You Consider Yourself to be a Supporter of the Tea Party Movement, An Opponent of the Tea Party Movement, or Neither?' *USA Today/Gallup Poll*, 4–7 November 2010. http://www.pollingreport.com/politics.htm

Wallison, Peter J. *Bad History, Worse Policy: How a False Narrative About the Financial Crisis Led to the Dodd-Frank Act*. Washington, DC: American Enterprise Institute Press, 2013.

Zeleny, Jeff. 'Top Donors to Republicans Seek More Say in Senate Races'. *The New York Times*, 2 February 2013. http://www.nytimes.com/2013/02/03/us/politics/top-gop-donors-seek-greater-say-in-senate-races.html?_r=0

Zywicki, Todd J. 'Beyond the Shell and Husk of History: The History of the Seventeenth Amendment and Its Implications for Current Reform Proposals'. *Cleveland State University Law Review* 45, no. 2 (1997): 165–235.

Zywicki, Todd J. 'The Rule of Law, Freedom, and Prosperity'. *Supreme Court Economic Review* 10 (2003): 1–26.

Zywicki, Todd J. 'The Coinage Clause'. In David Forte and Matthew Spalding, eds, *Heritage Guide to the Constitution*. Washington DC: Regnery, 2005, pp. 145–7.

Zywicki, Todd J. 'The Auto Bailout and the Rule of Law'. *National Affairs* 7 (Spring 2011): 66–80.

Zywicki, Todd J. 'Making Financial Regulation *Antifragile'*. *Library of Law and Liberty*. 15 December 2013a. http://www.libertylawsite.org/book-review/making-financial-regulation-antifragile

Zywicki, Todd J. 'The Next Financial Crisis: What Will the Market "Expect"?' *Library of Law and Liberty*. 19 May 2013b. http://www.libertylawsite.org/book-review/the-next-financial-crisis-what-will-the-markets-expect

Zywicki, Todd J. 'The Corporatist Legacy of the Auto Bailouts'. *Library of Law and Liberty*. 13 January 2014. http://www.libertylawsite.org/2014/01/13/the-corporatist-legacy-of-the-auto-bailouts/

Zywicki, Todd J. 'Bruno Leoni's Legacy and Continued Relevance'. *Journal of Private Enterprise* 30, no. 1 (Spring 2015a): 130–41.

Zywicki, Todd J. 'Rent Seeking, Crony Capitalism, and the Crony Constitution'. Presented at the Ends of Capitalism Conference, New York. 26 February 2015b.

Zywicki, Todd J., Geoffrey A. Manne and Julian Morris. 'Price Controls on Payment Card Interchange Fees: The US Experience'. George Mason Law and Economics Research Paper No. 14-18, 2014. http://papers.ssrn.com/sol3/papers.cfm?abstract_id=2446080

Part II
Fiscal crisis

4 Fiscal crisis as a quality of progressivist democracy

Richard E. Wagner

4.1 Introduction

The American federal government has run budget deficits almost continuously since 1960; not since the 1920s has there been any significant effort to reduce the federal debt. Today that debt stands at around \$18 trillion, or about \$60,000 per person in a nation of 300 million. That growth of deficits and debt, moreover, shows no sign of stopping, let alone reversing. The same situation prevails on a smaller scale throughout our state and local governments. The total volume of state and local indebtedness now stands at around \$4 trillion, and continues to grow despite the existence of balanced budget requirements in 49 states. At the federal level, moreover, legislation was enacted in 1978 to prohibit budget deficits after 1981. This legislation, named Byrd-Grassley after its sponsors, was never repealed, but neither were deficits eliminated, as David Primo (2007, 109) explains. For the better part of a century, Democratic governments have shown a strong tendency to operate with budget deficits and accumulate public debt, as Buchanan and Wagner (1977) explore and Wagner (2012) amplifies and elaborates.

Traditional measures of public debt show only the proverbial tip of the iceberg. Just as the larger part of an iceberg lies below the surface, so too does the larger part of the looming fiscal crisis. This unseen component of public debt is described as unfunded liability. The major sources of unfunded liability in the United States reside with the Social Security and Medicare programmes. State and local governments also create unfunded liabilities, often through pension programmes, which have been implicated in recent years in a number of municipal bankruptcies (Moberg and Wagner 2014). Unfunded liabilities, unlike ordinary public debt, are not made explicit at the time they are created. Hence their magnitude must be estimated. While there is variation in estimated magnitudes that depends on the estimator and the technique used, a magnitude in the vicinity of \$100 trillion seems to be a reasonable estimate. This unfunded liability thus amounts to more than \$300,000 when placed on a per capita basis, and which Kotlikoff (2005) and Kotlikoff and Burns (2012) describe as looming generational storms.

It seems clear that the present path of budget deficits and public debts can't continue. What can't continue won't continue. Hence, an alternative fiscal trajectory is looming. Just what that trajectory might be will be determined through

74 *Richard E. Wagner*

political and social controversy and conflict. Public perceptions about the sources of the crisis will surely have significant bearing on that future fiscal trajectory. In this respect, two types of trajectory can be identified. One trajectory is relatively conservative in that it would reinforce the Progressivist political economy of the past century by presenting a convincing narrative to the effect that the present crisis illustrates what can happen when a well-working Progressivist system is buffeted by strong external shocks. In this case, nothing is required to overcome the crisis other than to keep the faith with the political authorities who are working hard to get beyond the crisis. The crisis does not point to any kind of systemic failure, but rather illustrates the damage that a long string of bad luck can do to a well-working system.

The alternative trajectory entails a relatively bold narrative grounded in growing recognition that the crisis is a systemic reflection of a century-long morphing of the original American constitution of liberty into a Progressivist constitution of democratic oligarchy. Through this morphing, the original presumption that people were largely responsible for their own governance has largely given way to the presumption that the many are governed by an elite few. This alternative trajectory would embrace something like Richard Epstein's (2014) articulation of the classical liberal foundations of the American Constitution.[1] The present crisis is, in any case, an intelligible feature of the democratic competition for power, and this trajectory can be changed only by rearranging the constitutional framework through which that competition proceeds.

The ability of democratic governments to generate fiscal crises has long been recognized by scholars prior to the advent of the Progressivist era. For instance, William Niskanen (1978, 159) quotes Alexander Tytler, a Scottish historian from the eighteenth century who summarized thusly the views across two millennia of scholarship about the tenuous character of a well-working democracy:

> A democracy can't exist as a permanent form of government. It can only exist until the majority discovers it can vote itself largess out of the public treasury. After that, the majority always votes for the candidate promising the most benefits with the result that democracy collapses because of the loose fiscal policy ensuing, always to be followed by a dictatorship, then a monarchy.

While there seems to be some uncertainty as to whether Tytler actually put those words to paper or if, instead, they were part of some oral tradition, there is no doubt that Tytler's words resonate well with two millennia of political thought on democracy, as amplified by modern scholarship on public choice, which Richard Wagner (2006) sets forth in his analysis of retrogressive regime drift.

In explaining how the present crisis is a facet of the democratic competition for power that generated the present system of oligarchic democracy, I start with the theory of public debt. The theory of public debt is a source of huge public confusion because of the strong proclivity people have to treat public debt as similar to personal or corporate debt. There are points of similarity, to be sure, because

Fiscal crisis 75

indebtedness always spans time in that obligations incurred today won't be discharged until tomorrow or the day after tomorrow. For personal or corporate debt, however, it is clear who is indebted to whom. It is not so clear with respect to public debt, so straight-thinking on this matter is essential for gaining a solid understanding of fiscal crises and democratic public finance. After exploring the theory of public debt, the rest of the chapter examines how a constitutional system of limited or liberal democracy can morph into a system of essentially unlimited or oligarchic democracy. That morphing arises through the constitution and reconstitution of democratic power. After exploring how democratic competition can reconstitute the pattern of power, the rest of the chapter explores some possible paths for the restoration of a constitutional system of liberal democracy where the reach of politics is limited, in contrast to its presently unlimited reach.

4.2 Public debt and contractual mythology

Public debt is often treated as similar in form to personal debt. This has the effect of covering public debt with the mythology of contract. Nearly everyone has experience with personal debt. Such debts are genuine forms of contract. A person or a business wants to buy an asset today, but doesn't want to sell another asset to acquire the funds. So the person borrows the money by promising to repay the lender with interest, according to the terms to which the borrower and lender agree. All debtor–creditor relationships entail a bridging of time that maintains an open relationship between the debtor and creditor until that contract has been discharged at some later date. There is a fundamental distinction between spot and credit transactions. Spot transactions are concluded at the instant of transaction. Credit transactions are not, and are concluded only when the debt is repaid. When transactions extend into the future, as credit transactions do, opportunities arise for what are effectively fraudulent transactions with respect to public debt, in that a borrower might not repay the debt.

The open-ended character of credit markets provides opportunities for post-contractual opportunism that don't result with spot transactions. In the face of these opportunities, participants in credit markets have developed numerous practices and conventions to protect such market transactions against post-contractual opportunism. Credit reports help to provide assurance about a borrower's reliability. Provisions for collateral offer added security to lenders. Borrower's concerns with their reputations add further security. Through these and numerous other features of credit markets, the unavoidable riskiness that accompanies open-ended contractual relationships is mitigated and the size of the market expands.

Most references to public debt treat such debt as analogous to personal debt. The earlier reference to present federal indebtedness as being about $60,000 on a per capita basis draws an explicit analogy between public debt and personal debt. It is easy enough to understand the ready acceptability of this analogy, for it expresses what seems to be intuitively obvious. As an individual you incur debts that you are obligated to repay. It seems intuitively obvious that it is the same

76   *Richard E. Wagner*

with governments. What is intuitively obvious, however, is not always true. That the sun rises in the east and sets in the west is readily apparent, and was widely believed until Copernicus. It could still be widely believed today for all I know, as I know of no surveys that have posed this question to a broad population. Still, we have an accepted scientific theory that countermands what appears to be intuitively obvious. Public debt presents us with the same problem of what appears to be intuitively obvious. Each of us has personal experience of what it means to be indebted. It is easy to recognize that someone can accumulate debts sufficiently large that servicing that debt might become difficult or even impossible. We also recognize that our indebtedness is a product of previous choices we have made. Normal morality thus tells us that we should make good on our debts because they are the current manifestations of past promises we have made.

It is accurate to say that the debt of the American federal government now exceeds $18 trillion, with about one-third of that debt held by foreigners. It is not accurate, however, to identify the federal government as the entity that is indebted. To do this is to participate in a shell game where the game's host diverts the attention of the spectators. To understand this shell-game quality, it is necessary to ask just who owes what to whom when it comes to public debt (see Wagner 1996). We can ask such questions for personal or commercial debt, but the answers are obvious: borrowers owe repayment plus interest to lenders, and this is all there is to the matter. Public debt creates an entirely different situation.

To illustrate this distinction between public and personal debt, suppose a town of 10,000 decides, through a town council, to borrow $10 million, when the alternative is to raise that money through taxation. Further suppose that doing this is agreeable to all residents of the town and not just to the members of the town council and some of their supporters. James Buchanan (1958) explains that the analysis of public debt is the same regardless of whether the creditors live inside or outside the borrowing unit. The former situation is described as internal debt, while the latter situation is described as external debt. The analytical properties of debt creation are the same in either case, so I shall focus on internal debt because it is simpler to illustrate. At a superficial level, it looks as though the town becomes indebted because it raises $10 million by selling bonds to a subset of town residents. But how can that town be liable for that debt? The deep as distinct from superficial answer is that the town can't be liable because the town itself has no wealth from which it can amortize the debt. The ability of the town to service the debt depends on its ability to extract taxes from residents.

Liability for the debt resides with taxpayers. The town itself is simply an intermediary in a transaction between two sets of residents within the town. One set of residents buys the bonds. In doing this, they are paying current taxes for the other residents. The other set of residents pays taxes in later years to service the debt and retire the bonds. The people who buy the bonds are replacing what would have been tax payments by other town residents with the expectation that those bonds would be redeemed according to the terms of the debt issue. The remaining residents acquired an obligation to make future tax payments in exchange for the ability to escape having to make higher tax payments now. It is worth noting that

Fiscal crisis 77

this obligation is never assigned explicitly to these residents at the time the debt is created, though such an obligation could easily have been assigned. Instead, the apportionment of that obligation among residents is left to be worked out in future years as the debt is serviced. The town itself is a form of financial intermediary that stands between the people who buy the bonds and the people who will pay higher taxes in future years to amortize the bonds. Suppose we now ask why the town council would have issued bonds rather than increasing taxes? The answer to this question matters hugely with respect to the political economy of public debt.

The essence of democratic public debt resides in recognition that it creates patterns of liability and obligation among the citizenry that extend through time, only with those obligations and liabilities never being made explicit. Contrary to Buchanan's (1958) argument, present as well in Kotlikoff (2005) and Kotlikoff and Burns (2012), that public debt shifts the burden of current spending from present to future generations, public debt is actually a means by which some citizens shift burdens onto other citizens, as Wagner (2014b) explains. Yes, public debt still spans time by passing encumbrances forward, but those encumbrances are concentrated on subsets of the population and not distributed uniformly across the population. Public debt is but one among numerous instruments of fiscal domination by which some people exercise dominion over others. This quality of public debt requires recognition that there are two distinct situations under which political entities can create debt, one relatively innocuous and also rare and one more serious and also common. I shall address the innocuous case first under the heading of consensual democracy, before turning to the more serious case under the heading of factional democracy.

4.3 Public debt within a system of consensual democracy

Conventional ideology treats democracy as necessarily being a system where people govern themselves. Within this ideology of self-governance, there can be no principled limit to the reach of government because governments do only what people want it to do, as Bertrand de Jouvenel (1993) explains lucidly in his examination of the tendency of democratic power to become unlimited, in contrast to monarchical power. This common ideological formulation is vague and vacuous, as it must be. There is no way that a collective entity can act as an entity. All collective action originates in desires of particular people who take leadership positions in gaining acceptance for those desired actions. Once this simple point is placed in the analytical foreground, it is easy enough to recognize that there are two broad categories of democratic action. One category reflects a general consensus within the relevant polity. In the early years of the American republic, this notion was reflected in the general welfare clause of the Constitution which limited federal appropriations to items of general welfare throughout the republic. In his masterful treatment of *Congress as Santa Claus*, Charles Warren (1932) described the morphing of the general welfare clause from a limit on the power of Congressional appropriation to subsequent recognition that the general

78 *Richard E. Wagner*

welfare meant whatever a dominant Congressional coalition declared it to mean. The growing interest in the expansion of governmental programmes that was then underway led to reinterpretation of the general welfare clause to accommodate that expansion. Along with this accommodation comes the morphing of what largely had been a system of consensual democracy into more of a system of factional democracy, wherein government increasingly becomes an instrument through which some people are able to profit at the expense of others, while laying down an ideological smokescreen to obscure some of the cruder facets of the arrangement.

Public debt plays out differently within a system of consensual democracy than it does within a system of factional democracy. Suppose an earthquake destroys a town-owned stadium. To keep within the motif of consensual democracy, suppose there is overwhelming if not universal support to rebuild the stadium. This situation might come about because all town residents make repeated use of the stadium in many ways throughout the year. In this situation it would not be surprising to find universal support for building a new stadium. The only publicly relevant issue is how to pay for rebuilding the stadium. In this regard there are two options. One option is to adopt an extraordinary tax, which would entail a one-time doubling of the tax rate to raise the $10 million to reconstruct the stadium. The alternative option is to sell bonds to a willing subset of town residents, with those bonds being amortized over a ten-year period. To further solidify this point about consensual governance, we can even imagine that liabilities for those future amortization payments are assigned at the time the bonds are sold. Each resident of the town would thus receive an explicit liability for their shares of future amortization payments.

Should the tax option be selected by the town, some people will discharge their tax liability by drawing down their cash balances or selling other assets. Others will turn to the credit market to borrow the money to discharge their liabilities. The stadium will be built, the town will issue no debt, and some number of town residents will borrow on the credit market to finance their share of the extraordinary tax liability. Should the town pursue the debt option instead, nothing of genuine significance is changed except that private financial intermediaries are replaced by the town as a financial intermediary. It is reasonable to wonder about the town's qualities as an intermediary relative to those of private credit institutions. The general rule when private operation is replaced by public operation is some combination of less efficient operation in conjunction with bias in the execution and enforcement of contractual provisions.

With the tax alternative combined with recourse to private debt for those who choose not to fund the extraordinary tax from their current accounts, the contracted debts are personal liabilities. Those debts reside with the debtor regardless of future changes in economic circumstances, whether the debtor moves away from the town, or dies, with the debt becoming a charge against the debtor's estate. When public debt replaces what would have been an extraordinary tax increase, the situation changes in several respects, each of which operates in the direction of increasing support for public spending when it is financed by borrowing – even

Fiscal crisis 79

when that spending is desired by everyone in general. For one thing, what was an individual's explicit debt obligation is now rendered implicit and contingent on a number of different circumstances; Buchanan (1967) explains the contingent character of the liability that public debt entails. One of those circumstances is future changes in taxation. Another is changes individuals make to their actions relative to the town's tax base. At this point the situation is morphing into one suitable for a system of factional democracy.

4.4 Public debt within a system of factional democracy

While some town residents might value the stadium highly, many others might place little or no value on reconstructing the stadium. We might also presume that those who support reconstructing the stadium do so only because they will not bear the full cost of that reconstruction. In this respect, James Bennett (2012) provides a lucid explanation of how billionaire owners and millionaire players are able to dominate ordinary taxpayers in securing subsidized construction of stadiums and arenas. This is factional democracy at work. In this type of case, those who support reconstruction would not support the reconstruction if they had to pay for it themselves. Tax financing shifts much of the burden onto ordinary taxpayers. Suppose a majority of the council members likewise supports stadium reconstruction and faces the problem of deflecting opposition to that reconstruction. Where the imposition of an extraordinary tax to finance the reconstruction will surely galvanize the opposition, the resort to debt will surely stimulate less opposition, especially when liabilities for future amortization payments are not assigned at the time the debt is approved. In this case the town debt divides taxpayers into two sets: (1) supporters of the stadium and (2) opponents. Those town residents who bought the bonds gain from that transaction through the terms on which the debt is serviced. Among the remaining town residents, some gain and some lose. Those who support the added spending gain, while the others lose. These people have become forced debtors.

A deep fallacy is involved in treating public debt as an obligation that one entity owes to another. This fallacy is perpetuated in accounts that speak of aggregate public debt or place that aggregate debt on a per capita basis. There is nothing wrong with such figures, for they are real and not fictional. There are federal bonds in existence that aggregate to a face value of some $18 trillion. All the same, it is false to think of public debts as something equivalent to what one person owes to another. In the days when monarchs borrowed from wealthy people within their realms, the monarch's debts were personal debts owed to other people. The situation is very different for democratic regimes.

It is not sensible to describe public debt as something that 'we owe to ourselves'. As an exercise in aggregate accounting, this aphorism is an identity that is established by double-entry accounting. The situation is no different, for that matter, in speaking about household debts. Those debts arise through contracts between borrowers and lenders; the aggregate amount of household debt in the United States is currently around $12 trillion. One could always

80   *Richard E. Wagner*

aggregate all such debt throughout the nation, and declare that this aggregate debt is something we owe to ourselves. As a statement about aggregate accounting, this assertion is necessarily true. That truth, however, is a fiction that is created by constructing an artificial entity that is not an action-taking and responsibility-bearing entity. Indeed, it is the absence of any genuine locus of responsibility that is the source of democratic fiscal crises.

A monarch is an action-taking and responsibility-bearing entity. So is a business corporation. Even if that corporation is constituted through a plurality of investors, the corporation must attract investors in an environment where those investors are free to choose where to invest. Democratic political bodies, however, are not like corporations or monarchs. To be sure, it is possible to imagine how democratic political bodies could be transformed into corporate bodies with willing owners, as illustrated, for instance, by MacCallum (1970), Foldvary (1994) and Wagner (2011). When those bodies operate with transferable ownership shares, market values would be established for those entities. Short of such bold institutional reconfiguration, however, public debt will remain categorically distinct from personal debt because the locus of responsibility for personal debt that private property creates evaporates with public debt. Democratic debt is one of those proverbial tips of the iceberg that conceal the below-surface context in which that debt is created.

4.5 Two forms of democratic budget tragedy: commons and factional

There are two distinct formulations of the fiscal crises that plague democratic governments. One formulation treats democratic budgeting as a form of tragedy of the commons. Economists have long recognized that there is a tendency for excessive resource exploitation in common property settings. Frank Knight (1924) recognized this tendency with respect to highway congestion. Scott Gordon (1954) used the excessive exploitation of fishers to illustrate the same point. Elinor Ostrom (1990) presents several case studies where people have been able to transcend the common tragedies they faced. In these instances, the ability to transcend the commons tragedy entailed the establishment of some form of ownership rights within the commons, as illustrated by assigning quotas on how much water someone might remove from an irrigation system.

Democratic budgeting creates a type of fiscal commons (Brubaker 1997; Wagner 1992, 2007). Within the image of the commons, taxation denotes the assignment of liabilities among taxpayers to stock the fiscal commons while appropriation denotes the removal of items from the fiscal commons. The outcome of budgeting on the fiscal commons entails the same excessive exploitation that holds for other commons settings. Suppose 100 people dine in a restaurant that operates according to the conventions of private property. The aggregate bill incurred by those diners might be $5,000, or $50 per diner on average. Within a setting of democratic budgeting, these people will comprise a dining club where the aggregate bill will be settled through taxation. With private property, someone

Fiscal crisis 81

who chooses a $30 item over a $50 item will save $20. This won't happen with common property because that $20 saving will be distributed among all the diners and will amount to 20 cents per diner. Under these circumstances, we can appreciate that the less expensive option is less likely to be chosen under common property budgeting. We can also appreciate the strong tendencies that exist for spending to increase. After all, someone who adds $20 to be bill will add only 20 cents to his or her share of the tax. The cost of taking an action is lower to any action-taker under common property budgeting, as Buchanan (1969) shows in explaining how cost varies with different settings for making choices. With common property budgeting, the aggregate bill might end up being $7,000 or $70 per diner. In this tragedy of the commons setting, everyone loses pretty much equally within the commons.

The tragedy of the commons is general or universal. Everyone loses through the excessive exploitation that occurs on the fiscal commons. It follows from the logic of the situation that everyone potentially can gain by eliminating that excessive exploitation. This situation is illustrated nicely by William Niskanen's (1971) widely recognized theory of bureaucracy, which argued that there were universal tendencies for governmental bureaus to spend more on their activities than private firms would spend because bureau officials could not directly remove profits from their bureaus. What they could do, though, was operate in more costly fashion to the extent such greater costliness supplied them with desired advantages.

Factional democracy points to a distinctly different form of democratic tragedy. This form of tragedy is better characterized not by excessive provision of collective activities but by qualitative changes in the character of collective activities and the governance of human activities. This is not a model of mutual exploitation on the commons but a model where some parts of the population gain at the expense of the remainder of society. This is a world of domination and subordination. This is the world where billionaire owners and millionaire players are heavily subsidized by ordinary taxpayers (Bennett 2012). Within the American system of federal income taxation, for instance, about half the population of voting age is free of tax liability. To the extent state activities are financed through the federal income tax, we would normally expect to find little opposition to increased spending. The income tax is not, of course, the sole source of federal revenue. Still, income tax burdens are highly concentrated on a small subset of the population, which means that the cost of government is low if not zero.

This situation can be described by a model of coalitional politics where winning subsets of the population gain by imposing burdens on the remainder of the population. The standard model of the fiscal commons is susceptible to correction through recognition that everyone is being overburdened by excessive exploitation of the commons. The coalitional politics of factional democracy is not susceptible to such a simple remedy. In this case the democratic processes mask a process where there are subsets of the population that are able to dominate other subsets, often using ideological tools to do so as Pareto (1935) explained.[2] Pareto recognized that only some actions people took entailed consequences they experienced directly and could appraise. These actions Pareto described as logical, to

82 *Richard E. Wagner*

denote a direct link between the action taken and the consequence experienced. Often, however, there is no direct link between action and consequence. These actions involve what are denoted as credence goods, in contrast to experience goods. The quality of a credence good offered by a vendor is accepted, or not, on faith and not through experience. Two prime categories of credence goods involve religion and politics.

Pareto explained that political competition largely involved candidates in making claims about credence goods, where competitive success resides in creating images that allow voters to feel good about their actions. Ideological competition in the realm of credence goods takes the form of allowing voters to embrace rationalizations that they wish to embrace in any case. For instance, someone who might support a subsidized stadium might embrace the claim that the stadium provides public-good benefits for the town while shying away from recognizing the private benefit of being a contractor in the reconstruction. Political competition in the presence of credence goods is principally about finding the right buttons to push when no independent testing through experience of claims is possible. To end this form of crisis requires bold moves of some type, as in lowering the progressivity of a tax system so as to bring the cost of government home to more people. This form of crisis arises through expansion in the number of tax eaters relative to tax suppliers, with reform requiring some form of rebellion by the tax suppliers – along the lines that Stephen Walters (2014) describes as taking place in the 1970s in California and Massachusetts, setting in motion a period of what he describes as boom towns.

4.6 Unfunded liabilities: more of the same

An unfunded liability is just public debt to which a different name is attached. With ordinary public debt a government sells bonds to buyers. The revenues required to retire those bonds will be imposed on taxpayers in future years, save to the extent that those future revenues are extracted from the buyers of bonds through default or inflation. However that revenue is acquired, it is easy to assign a value to the amount of public debt, for it is given by the amount governments promise to pay bondholders in future years, regardless of how future governments actually deal with those promises.

The situation is really no different for an unfunded liability, save only that no explicit liability is acknowledged at the time the liability is incurred. For an unfunded liability, the future liability is left implicit rather than being made explicit. The open-ended quality of the liability means that the actual extent of the liability won't be known until some future point in time. Yet a liability is there all the same, with that future liability being a product of preceding political commitments. For the federal government, the bulk of unfunded liabilities accrue through the Social Security and Medicare programmes. Those programmes contain provisions to make payments in future years, with liabilities to provide those payments likewise to be imposed in those future years. For both unfunded liabilities and public debts, a present commitment is made to make payments in

Fiscal crisis   83

future years, with those payments to be extracted from taxpayers in those future years. The only difference is purely nominal: that with public debt the magnitude of those future payments is established at the time the debt is created, though just on whom those future payments will be extracted will be determined in the future. By contrast, with unfunded liabilities the magnitude of those future payments won't be determined until the future arrives.

Ordinary public debt entails a contingent liability, in that any person's tax payments to service public debt is contingent upon the tax system in play when that future arrives, as well as on the taxpayers' personal situations relative to the future tax structure. In contrast, unfunded liability entails a double contingency. One element of contingency is identical with what exists for ordinary public debt, in that a taxpayer's liability for future payments will depend on his or her economic position at the time of tax extraction relative to the tax structure in place at the time those taxes are extracted. But unfunded liability has a second layer of contingency, in that the amount of liability is also to be determined in the future, whereas with public debt it is stipulated at the time the debt is created. Hence, we know that the explicit debt of the American federal government is around $18 trillion because this is the face value of the bonds that holders of public debt have bought over the years. We don't know, today, what the exact amount of the public debt associated with Social Security and Medicare is, or that for the various state and local health and pension programmes that are also sources of unfunded liability. These amounts will be determined only in the future as people make their retirement choices and incur covered medical expenses. Unfunded liabilities are, thus, projections of a double contingency. They entail projections of future revenues and expenditures, usually over a 75-year period, with existing legislation assumed to remain unchanged over that period. When looked at from an accounting standpoint, unfunded liabilities seem to indicate a discrepancy that will have to be resolved in the coming years. That discrepancy can be resolved either through increasing taxes in future years or through reducing payments of benefits, or through some combination of both.

This accounting-based point of view treats growing public indebtedness as a temporary reflection of unusual circumstances that will be corrected as the years pass. What is unsustainable will not continue indefinitely, of course, so we may be sure that there will be some future change in the trajectory of unfunded liabilities. But is it reasonable to think that this unsustainable trajectory was simply a product of unforeseen and unforeseeable circumstances and forces? The alternative line of explanation is that the present trajectory reflects the playing out of intelligible political and economic forces at work. For instance, Social Security and Medicare are operated as defined-benefit programmes, which means that future payments cannot be known until future conditions are known. There is, however, no necessity that these programmes be operated in this manner. Social Security originally was modelled after private insurance programmes, but was transformed into a defined-benefit programme when politicians saw the accumulating surplus as something that could be spent, as Carolyn Weaver (1982) explains, and which gave a big boost to the present scheme of unfunded liabilities.

84   *Richard E. Wagner*

Unfunded liabilities do not reflect errors due to natural complexities. It is easy enough to recognize that complexities in budgeting will generate errors. It is not easy to estimate revenues and expenditures a year or more in advance. In some years estimated revenues will exceed what was actually collected, while in other years they will fall short of what was collected. Complexity means that budgeting will be inaccurate. Sometimes revenues will exceed expenditures. Other times the expenditures will exceed the revenues. Over a period of years, however, the imbalances will roughly even out. There should be no systematic tendency towards budget deficits, at least not to the extent that the complexity of budgeting means that there will always exist gaps between *ex ante* projections of budgetary magnitudes and the *ex post* realization of those magnitudes.

The persistence of budget deficits and the accumulation of public debt can only be attributed to the operation of systematic qualities of political competition as this competition gets reflected in democratic budgetary processes. Unfunded liabilities reflect a form systemic lying, in that the democratic process countenances the making of contradictory political promises to different people. On one side are the promises made to taxpayers regarding the future cost of programmes. To be sure, these promises are only implicit, but should be understood in contractual terms. That contractual frame of reference means that present taxes are sufficient to fund future payments, so that taxpayers, in evaluating present programmes, have some reasonable basis for doing so. On the other side are promises made to beneficiaries about what they can expect from those programmes. The two sets of promises don't balance, and the deficit is an unfunded liability. This liability will probably worsen in the coming years, and is not sustainable in any case. What is not sustainable will necessarily end sometime, but how will it end?

Two divergent paths can be discerned. The popular path will entail strengthening the forces of democratic oligarchy that have created the present situation. This path will entail a parade of tax increases and reductions in benefit, along with increased regulation to cover over remaining deficiencies. The other, uncommon path will entail a reconstitution of the American civil order and of the place of governments within that order. The Progressivist century will be recognized as having been a playing out of fiscal tragedy that the ancient Greeks understood as the down-side of democracy. Pursuit of this alternative path offers the prospect of transcending the democratic budget tragedy. To achieve that transcendence requires renewed recognition of how democratic governance must be restrained by the prior claims of private property and the social relationships that arise from this recognition.

4.7 Time, democracy and political capital accounts

Public debts and unfunded liabilities point to significant problems that democratic governments have in dealing with programmes and situations that extend through some duration of time. Each of us faces situations where the actions we take today will have consequences that will extend over some future interval of time. Many of these situations entail incurring debt today that we must repay at some

Fiscal crisis   85

future time. That future payment might be inconvenient, but typically we repay the debt anyway, and that repayment is supported by several interrelated institutional reasons that are largely absent for public debts. One major institutional reason resides in private property as the basic social arrangement for governing relationships among individuals. The presence of private property means that individuals operate under conditions of residual claimancy, wherein individuals own the difference in value between good and bad choices. If the choice to borrow works out well in the end, they gain from having done so. Should that decision work our poorly, they will bear the loss. Either way, private property creates institutional conditions under which people are responsible for the value consequences of their actions.

This position of ownership means that borrowers will exercise care in taking on loans by virtue of the resulting obligation to repay the loans. To be sure, people can differ in how they appraise such future obligations. A debt contract that one potential borrower might accept might be rejected by another potential borrower. Economists typically describe this difference among people as time preference. In the children's story of the *Three Little Pigs*, the pig who built the house of straw would be described as having high time preference while the pig who built the house of bricks would be described as having low time preference. Also significant for private debt is the position of the lender. Loans are the private property of lenders, and a loan is a rental of an asset. With all such rental contracts, the owner of the asset faces the problem of getting the asset back according to the terms of the contract. Among other things, this situation means that lenders will exercise care in extending loans, at least so long as the institutional rules of private ordering are in place. Under such rules, a lender who extends loans on which the borrower defaults will lose the value of that loan to the extent collateral wasn't attached to the loan.

To be sure, contemporary credit markets don't operate exclusively under private ordering because political regulation impinges on the operation of credit markets in many ways. Within wholly private ordering of credit transactions, whether a debt is extended and the terms on which it is extended is a matter that is determined exclusively between the lender and the borrower. A lender is not obligated to lend to a particular borrower nor does a borrower have some entitlement to a loan. The contractual principle of gains from trade pervades privately ordered credit markets. Modern credit markets, however, are not exclusively privately ordered because political regulation has high presence within modern credit markets. Those regulations do such things as regulate the portfolios of lenders, which in turn include such things as placing constraints on how a loan portfolio must be distributed among various classes and categories of borrowers. The intrusion of public ordering means that actual credit markets will involve lenders in making loans they would not make based on prudent commercial calculation, but instead make such loans as part of the cost of doing business within the contemporary regulatory environment. That environment requires firms to make a mixture of what would be described as good and bad loans under private ordering, though much of the anticipated loss from bad loans is further covered through political guarantees, largely financed by taxpayers.

86   *Richard E. Wagner*

The situation changes dramatically with public debt, in several ways. All corporate bodies have the property that the creation of liabilities rests with the entity and not with the officers who created the liability. For commercial corporations, however, there are various institutional arrangements relating to private property that provide strong inducements for corporate officials to manage their enterprises in a value-maximizing manner. With a small exception, there is no ownership value associated with politically managed enterprises. This exception arises with local governments that operate under institutional conditions that largely disappeared during the twentieth century. Those conditions entailed local governments that were financed by taxes on real estate and in which most residents owned real estate. Within this institutional setting, a form of tied sale was created between the ownership of real estate and the ownership of the town. Should a town be mismanaged, the demand for residency in the town would fall relative to demands elsewhere. This situation would show up as a decline in the value of real estate and, at the same time, also provide information about the efficiency of town management. Under such institutional conditions, there is much similarity between towns and commercial corporations with respect to their tendencies towards managerial efficiency.

Over the past century or so, however, the institutional arrangements regarding municipal operation have moved away from this efficiency-enhancing framework. Localities are no longer financed wholly or even predominately by taxes on real estate. A good deal of local financing now comes from state and federal governments. Voting, moreover, is no longer the exclusive province of property owners. Tenants face a different situation with respect to supporting public debt than do property owners. For an owner of property, there is no significant advantage to borrowing over taxing because Ricardian equivalence is a feature of ordinary credit markets (Barro 1974). For tenants, however, borrowing is less costly than taxation, provided only that tenant can reasonably expect the leave the locality within a few years.

This institutional constraint on limiting future promises because of its impact on valuations through the capital market weakens even more as fiscal activity moves to state and federal governments. A city might use pension promises as a short-term measure to gain political support, but doing that places encumbrances on the city's tax base that will create problems in future years, as Moberg and Wagner (2014) explore for municipal bankruptcy. At the federal level of government, there can be no territorially based competition among governments, save for emigration across national borders. There can be competition between Lubbock and Detroit because people can choose between the locations. For the federal government, however, leaving aside migration there is no locational competition because the federal tax base is approximately invariant to the locational choices people make between Lubbock and Detroit. At the federal level of government, political officials can afford to play Santa Claus, to borrow from Charles Warren's (1932) masterful recounting of the denigration of the General Welfare clause of the American constitution from around 1800 to around 1930. In other words, the scale at which democratic governments operate matters greatly for the

Fiscal crisis 87

performance properties of those governments, with the forces of oligarchy intensifying as the scale of government expands.

4.8 Expanding governmental scale and intensifying democratic oligarchy

Within the framework of the economic theory of markets organized under conditions of open competition, the sizes of enterprises are pretty much irrelevant. Economies of scale may play out differently across different types of enterprises. Those enterprises that manufacture simple products that are in high demand will typically be larger than those that manufacture complex products for which manufacturing requires paying particular attention to idiosyncratic differences and desires among customers. Construction firms that specialize in high-rise office buildings operate on a larger scale than firms that build houses or apartments. Economists have long recognized that the most efficient scale or range of production can differ significantly among types of production. Hence, a market economy organized through open competition will feature enterprises of widely differing scale. But these differences of scale typically give no advantage to larger firms relative to smaller ones. Economists have long recognized that free competition tends towards a situation where the expected return on different lines of activity tends towards equality across those lines. This tendency is just a tendency because its operation is also continually buffeted by the creation of new enterprises and new lines of production. Hence, the static state where returns on capital would be equalized is never reached. All the same, however, this property of open competition explains why the scale of enterprises is generally irrelevant with respect to the rate of return that can be earned by investing in different-sized enterprises.

The situation is strikingly different when it comes to the size of governments, more so at national than at local levels. For instance, economies of scale would limit the sizes of schools in a system of open competition more so than they would when governments provide schooling. Market-based schools, or market-based providers of any service, must attract customers in open competition with other providers. A provider whose output declines in quality or increases in costliness will lose customers to more efficient producers within a system of open competition. Governmental entities, however, don't face competition, save for a few, limited margins of competition. A public school faces limited competition from private schools and from home schooling – exceedingly limited, however, in that people who use private schools or who turn to home schooling must still pay taxes to support public schools. In this simple fact resides stark recognition of the competitive infirmities of public provision. To illustrate the extent of that infirmity, suppose groceries were provided through public commissaries which would be financed through taxation and with people picking up their designated bag of groceries once a week. With private schooling or home schooling, the equivalent situation is one where people don't pick up their designated bags and instead shop at a private store despite having paid through taxation for the public store's bag of groceries.

88 *Richard E. Wagner*

In the theory of networks, an important distinction is that between networks that are scalable and networks that are free of scale (Barabási 2002). A network is a mapping that contains a number of entities along with various links that connect those entities. A new entity enters the network and establishes connections with some of the entities already in that network. One possible pattern of connection is random, which means that the pattern of new connections resembles the pattern of previous connections. Whatever pattern of connection might exist for a network of 1,000 entities would be duplicated for a network of 10,000 entities. In contrast, scale-free networks undergo changes in their patterns of connection as they expand. In particular, scale-free networks often experience dominance by a few nodes as scale expands. A random network might feature a normal distribution of enterprises in terms of the number of their connections. There would be about as many enterprises with a below-average number of connections are there are enterprises with an above-average number of connections. In contrast, scale-free networks feature highly skewed distributions of connection, with a few enterprises having several times the average number of connections while many enterprises have a number of connections that is well below average.

To illustrate how scale might matter with respect to governments, compare Switzerland today with the United States, both in 1789 and today. Switzerland has around 7 million people distributed among 26 cantons, or an average of about 270,000 persons per canton. In 1790, the United States contained around 4 million people distributed among 13 states, or about 300,000 persons per state. Contemporary Switzerland and Colonial America had similar scales of government when appraised in terms of the number of citizens per canton or state. Today, the United States has in excess of 300 million people distributed among 50 states, or about 6 million persons per state. To restore governance on the scale of contemporary Switzerland or colonial America would require the United States now to have over 1,000 states. The scale of governance in the United States today is vastly larger than it was in 1790 or is in Switzerland today. But is this larger scale truly of any significance?

Compare, for instance, the scales of governance as between a town of 9,000 and a city of 90,000. In each case, suppose the unit is governed by a council of nine members elected by district. For the town, each official represents 1,000 people, whereas for the city each official represents 10,000 people. It is reasonable to think that for the town each official can know something about and have personal contact with each person. Much of that knowledge and contact, moreover, will take place informally, as illustrated by chance meetings in grocery stores, theatres, churches and parking lots. A network diagram of those connections would have pretty much a random character, created mostly by chance meetings.

By contrast, a network diagram for the city would have power law features, meaning that only a subset of the citizenry had contact with the representative. One person can't truly know something about 10,000 people and have random contact with them in consequence of the daily pursuit of life. The pattern of contact will acquire a representational structure, by which I mean contact will flow through organized patterns of representation. Representatives will be linked

Fiscal crisis 89

with representatives of particular interest groups that claim to speak for large numbers of citizens who themselves have no contact with the representative. In this manner, representative democracy takes on oligarchic character as its scale increases, which Bertrand de Jouvenel (1961) illustrates crisply for the operation of representative assemblies. A gulf inexorably arises between governing officials and those who are governed, with the width of that gulf varying directly with the scale of governance. For instance, 435 representatives combined with a population in excess of 300 million gives something like 700,000 per district.

Democracy is a generic term as it is commonly used. It means only that a subset of political officials is selected through an election. Democracy is a purely formal term that covers a wide variety of particular types of democracy. The relation between liberty and democracy, however, is surely one of those things that depend on particular details more than generic form. As oligarchic tendencies grow within democracies, the scope expands for political officials to act independently of the interests and concerns of constituents. Indeed, it can't be any other way because the scale of governance prevents any pattern of interaction and communication that reflects subject-to-subject relationships, and instead takes on properties of subject-to-object relationships which Martin Buber (1958) explores.

4.9 Liberty and democracy: towards constitutional reconciliation

What is the relationship between liberty and democracy? There is a strong ideological current running throughout contemporary society that asserts that democracy and liberty are necessarily and inescapably complementary. According to this current, a democratic form of government is the appropriate way that a self-governing people manage their public affairs. This image is taught in schools starting from early years, and is repeated throughout the various social media. So strongly does this current run throughout our society that little scepticism is voiced when politicians and other public figures express their hope that the reach of democracy will soon extend throughout the world. According to this ideology, democracy is the political value *par excellence* for a people who aspire to excellence in the practice of self-governance.

Yet democracy and liberty cannot be complementary political values, at least not without a significant effort at constitutional reconciliation. At base, democracy embraces the principle that majorities dominate minorities. In contrast, liberty is a principle of non-domination whereby interaction among people is governed by principles of private property and not by majority rule. Only to the extent that people have agreed to abide by majority in particular instances is democracy consistent with liberty.

Liberty was the founding value of the American republic, as was recognized in the Declaration of Independence's assertion that governments derive their just powers from the consent of the governed. The principle of liberty holds that people use their prior rights of property to establish governments to preserve and protect those rights. In sharp contrast, the Progressivist strand of democratic

90   *Richard E. Wagner*

ideology holds that the determination of property rights is the province of government. What is called private property is nothing but a grant from government as a type of usufruct, which governments can bestow or remove as they choose. In this respect, two contemporary philosophers, Liam Murphy and Thomas Nagel (2002), claim that private property is a myth. It is, perhaps, easy enough to understand the popularity of this Progressivist sentiment. Vilfredo Pareto (1935) recognized that people will tend to embrace ideological articulations that enable them to feel good about themselves. America is governed by a democratic form of government, and most Americans like to think of themselves as constituting a free people. An ideology that links democracy in the service of liberty is surely an easy product to sell, particularly when the historical experience of the past century has been dominated by various forms of totalitarian bestiality. And yet there is always a potential conflict between liberty and democracy.

Constitutions do not enforce themselves any more than laws rule over men. Law can't rule; only people can do that, as Rajagopalan and Wagner (2013) explain. Constitutions are what someone with authority to dominate the issue in question says it will be. In any conflict between guns and parchment, guns will win (Wagner 1993). What keeps that conflict in check and a liberal order from eroding is some conjunction of strong belief combined with arrangements of governance that require concurrence among different possessors of guns, as it were, with each possessor able to maintain his own position, leading effective governance to require concurrence among the different possessors of guns.

In this respect, Federalism is a form of government that possibly has some potential to resist the scale-free qualities of democratic polities, as Vincent Ostrom (1997) explains. The original American constitution mostly had this kind of federalist feature. The federal government was limited to a few explicitly enumerated powers. Everything else was reserved for the states or for individual citizens. The establishment of cities and towns and their jurisdictions, moreover, was the province of states and not the federal government. It is much less costly to move from one state to another than it is to change nations of residence. It is less costly still to change localities within a state. In addition, capital market principles operate with localities to the extent those activities are financed by taxes on real estate.

Furthermore, one of the two chambers of the Federal Congress was appointed by the states. This meant that the Federal Senate sat as a kind of chamber of the states, with individual senators subject to recall by the states they represented. The federal government, moreover, could not tax individual earnings, and federal revenues were pretty much limited to revenues from tariffs, which meant in turn that most federal spending was limited to military affairs. Furthermore, the federal government had no central bank that could accommodate an expansion in federal activity by buying federal debt as a particular way of printing money. The monetary authority of the federal government was limited to the certification of weights and measures, as illustrated by a dollar being defined as a unit of measure represented by one-20th of an ounce of gold of a particular fineness. In other words, monetary policy at this time was directed at offering protection against counterfeiting. In sharp contrast, monetary policy became a form of legalized counterfeiting after establishment of the Federal Reserve, with the value of a dollar having declined some 100-fold since the Federal Reserve was established.

This federalist arrangement stayed in place pretty well until early in the twentieth century, when the Constitution was amended to create direct election of senators and the federal government granted the power to tax incomes. Also, the Federal Reserve was established. These three shifts in constitutional authority were all significant moves in the direction of democratic oligarchy, and we have been living under these oligarchic arrangements for a century now. To be sure, democratic oligarchy is not a term currently in use, but it is an accurate description of contemporary democratic processes, all the same. The constitutional promise is one which holds governments accountable to the same standards of conduct as private entities in society. The Fifth Amendment to the American Constitution exemplifies this standard nicely, as Richard Epstein (1985) explains in his examination of the Fifth Amendment limitation to the takings power under the Constitution. That Amendment allows governments to take property through eminent domain, though that taking is subject to two conditions: (1) it must be for a genuine public purpose, as distinct from a purpose that advances the interests of some at the expense of others and (2) it must be accompanied by just compensation, with just meaning that the owner of the taken property is left as well off as he or she would have been by selling that property. Where the original constitutional arrangement created what could reasonably be called a system that entailed more competition than collusion among governments, that system has been largely replaced by a system of collusive federalism over the past century or so, as Michael Greve (2012) examines in his explanation of how the American Constitution has been turned upside-down.

4.10 A closing peroration

The American republic was founded on a rejection of the European feudal heritage wherein a few within a society were born to govern, with the remainder of society born into their various stations of servility. Where the feudal regimes were governed by relationships grounded in status, the American republic was to be governed by relationships grounded in private property and freedom of contract. Governments were established to preserve and protect this new order where people largely governed themselves through a variety of civic associations that they created. The robust commercial republic that emerged through this constitution of liberty clearly warranted the designation of American exceptionalism. That exceptionalism has been under assault for around a century now as the consensual principle on which the American regime was founded has come increasingly to give way to the factional principle, whereby government becomes an instrument that confers advantage on some people by imposing costs on other people, which the original American Constitution sought to resist.

The key feature of Progressivist governance is that some self-anointed few govern the many. In his chapter on democratic despotism in *Democracy in America*,

92 *Richard E. Wagner*

Alexis de Tocqueville explained that democratic despotism would feature people wearing velvet gloves and not mailed fists. It would take the form of shepherds guiding sheep. An open question concerns how much of the population truly wants to live as sheep rather than living their lives on their own terms. Hillary Clinton (1996) was surely right when she claimed that it took a village to raise a child. Her conception of that village, however, was of a Health and Human Services bureaucracy and not as a republic of free and responsible people whose creative abilities to manage their affairs dwarfs the talents and capacities of any political bureaucracy.

Steven Walters (2014) explains how tax limitations in California and Massachusetts changed dramatically the framework of political incentives operating in those states in the late 1970s. Before tax limits were imposed, politicians continually sought to reward supporters by increasing public spending. Some of this spending was financed by taxation, with the rest financed by borrowing, which is just deferred taxation. These political incentives, however, operated contrary to the conditions for economic flourishing which requires: (1) protecting private property by allowing its owners to reap the returns from their property and (2) maintaining public property in good order. Tax limits forced politicians in California and Massachusetts to do this more than they had been doing, creating boom towns in the process.

What holds for the state and local governments that Walters examined holds even more strongly for the federal government. It is not difficult to set forth the contours of what would be required to re-establish a constitution of liberty. At base, it would be to put the Constitution right-side up, recurring to Michael Greve's image of an upside-down constitution. It's doubtful that income tax could be repealed, but its progressive rate structure could certainly be lowered, which would bring more people within the purview of the income tax. With government becoming more costly to more people, the demand for governmental activity at the federal level would decline. Within the context of this chapter, a significant step towards turning the Constitution right-side up would be to eliminate unfunded liabilities by requiring governments to use defined contribution plans and to operate under genuine insurance principles. A related significant step would be to require governments to assign personal liabilities for the amortization of public debt at the time that debt is created. In such manners as these, the conduct of governments would become more compatible with the central operating principles of the private property that governments are instituted to preserve and protect in a regime where no privileged status positions exist.

Notes

1 Richard Wagner (2014a) provides a flying buttress to Epstein's book from the perspective of public choice theory.
2 The length of Pareto's analysis exceeds 2,000 pages. Raymond Aron (1967: 99–176) presents a cogent distillation of Pareto's thought. So does Andrew Bongiorno (1930).

Fiscal crisis 93

References

Aron, Raymond. *Main Currents in Sociological Thought, Vol. II*. New York: Basic Books, 1967.

Barabási, Albert L. *Linked: The New Science of Networks*. Cambridge, MA: Perseus, 2002.

Barro, Robert J. 'Are Government Bonds Net Wealth?'. *Journal of Political Economy* 82 no. 6, (1974): 1095–118.

Bennett, James T. *They Play, You Pay: Why Taxpayers Build Ballparks, Stadiums, and Arenas for Billionaire Owners and Millionaire Players*. New York: Copernicus, 2012.

Bongiorno, Andrew. 'A Study of Pareto's Treatise on General Sociology'. *American Journal of Sociology* 36, no. 3 (1930): 349–70.

Brubaker, Earl R. 'The Tragedy of the Public Budgetary Commons'. *Independent Review* 1, no. 3 (1997): 353–70.

Buber, Martin. *I and Thou*. New York: Scribner's, 1958.

Buchanan, James M. *Public Principles of Public Debt*. Homewood, IL: Richard D. Irwin, 1958.

Buchanan, James M. *Public Finance in Democratic Process*. Chapel Hill: University of North Carolina Press, 1967.

Buchanan, James M. *Cost and Choice*. Chicago: Markham, 1969.

Buchanan, James M., and Richard E. Wagner. *Democracy in Deficit: The Political Legacy of Lord Keynes*. New York: Academic Press, 1977.

Clinton, Hillary R. *It Takes a Village, and Other Lessons Children Teach Us*. New York: Simon & Schuster, 1996.

De Jouvenel, Bertrand. 'The Chairman's Problem'. *American Political Science Review* 55, no. 2 (1961): 368–72.

De Jouvenel, Bertrand. *On Power*. Indianapolis: Liberty Fund, 1993 [1953].

De Tocqueville, A. *Democracy in America*. Chicago: University of Chicago Press, 1835 [2002].

Epstein, Richard A. *Takings: Private Property and the Power of Eminent Domain*. Cambridge, MA: Harvard University Press, 1985.

Epstein, Richard A. *The Classical Liberal Constitution*. Cambridge, MA: Harvard University Press, 2014.

Foldvary, Fred. *Public Goods and Private Communities*. Hants, UK: Edward Elgar, 1994.

Gordon, H. Scott. 'The Economic Theory of a Common Property Resource: The Fishery'. *Journal of Political Economy* 62, no. 2 (1954): 124–42.

Greve, Michael S. *The Upside-Down Constitution*. Cambridge, MA: Harvard University Press, 2012.

Knight, Frank H. 'Some Fallacies in the Interpretation of Social Cost'. *Quarterly Journal of Economics* 38, no. 4 (1924): 582–606.

Kotlikoff, Lawrence J. *The Coming Generational Storm*. Cambridge, MA: MIT Press, 2005.

Kotlikoff, Lawrence J., and Scott Burns. *The Clash of Generations*. Cambridge, MA: MIT Press, 2012.

MacCallum, Spencer H. *The Art of Community*. Menlo Park, CA: Institute for Humane Studies, 1970.

McChesney, Fred S. *Money for Nothing: Politicians, Rent Extraction, and Political Extortion*. Cambridge, MA: Harvard University Press, 1997.

Moberg, Lotta, and Richard E. Wagner. 'Default without Capital Account: The Economics of Municipal Bankruptcy'. *Public Finance and Management* 14, no.1 (2014): 30–47.

Murphy, Liam, and Thomas Nagel. *The Myth of Ownership*. Oxford: Oxford University Press, 2002.

94 *Richard E. Wagner*

Niskanen, William A. *Bureaucracy and Representative Government*. Chicago: Aldine, 1971.

Niskanen, William A. 'The Prospect for Liberal Democracy'. In James M. Buchanan and Richard E. Wagner, eds, *Fiscal Responsibility in Constitutional Democracy*. Leiden, NL: Martinus Nijhoff, 1978, pp. 157–74.

Ostrom, Elinor. *Governing the Commons*. Cambridge, UK: Cambridge University Press, 1990.

Ostrom, Vincent. *The Intellectual Crisis in American Public Administration*. Tuscaloosa: University of Alabama Press, 1973.

Ostrom, Vincent. *The Political Theory of a Compound Republic*, 2nd edn. Lincoln: University of Nebraska Press, 1987.

Ostrom, Vincent. 'Faustian Bargains'. *Constitutional Political Economy* 7, no. 4 (1996): 303–8.

Ostrom, Vincent. *The Meaning of Democracy and the Vulnerability of Societies: A Response to Tocqueville's Challenge*. Ann Arbor: University of Michigan Press, 1997.

Pareto, Vilfredo. *The Mind and Society: A Treatise on General Sociology*. New York: Harcourt Brace, 1935.

Primo, David M. *Rules and Restraint: Government Spending and the Design of Institutions*. Chicago: University of Chicago Press, 2007.

Rajagopalan, Shruti, and Richard E. Wagner. 'Constitutional Craftsmanship and the Rule of Law'. *Constitutional Political Economy* 24, no. 4 (2013): 295–309.

Wagner, Richard E. 1992. 'Grazing the Budgetary Commons: The Rational Politics of Budgetary Irresponsibility'. *Journal of Law and Politics* 9: 105–19.

Wagner, Richard E. *Parchment, Guns, and Constitutional Order*. Cheltenham, UK: Edward Elgar, 1993.

Wagner, Richard E. 'Who Owes What to Whom? Public Debt, Ricardian Equivalence, and Governmental Form'. *Review of Austrian Economics* 9, no. 2 (1996): 143–57.

Wagner, Richard E. 'Retrogressive Regime Drift within a Theory of Emergent Order'. *Review of Austrian Economics* 19, no. 2 (2006): 113–23.

Wagner, Richard E. *Fiscal Sociology and the Theory of Public Finance*. Cheltenham, UK: Edward Elgar, 2007.

Wagner, Richard E. 'Municipal Corporations, Economic Calculation, and Political Pricing: Exploring a Theoretical Antinomy'. *Public Choice* 149 (2011): 151–65.

Wagner, Richard E. *Deficits, Debt, and Democracy*. Cheltenham, UK: Edward Elgar, 2012.

Wagner, Richard E. 'Richard Epstein's The Classical Liberal Constitution: A Public Choice Refraction'. *New York University Journal and Law and Liberty* 8 (2014a): 961–90.

Wagner, Richard E. 'James Buchanan's Public Debt Theory: A Rational Reconstruction'. *Constitutional Political Economy* 25, no. 3 (2014b): 253–64.

Walters, Stephen J.K. *Boom Towns: Restoring the Urban American Dream*. Stanford, CA: Stanford University Press, 2014.

Warren, Charles O. *Congress as Santa Claus: National Donations and the General Welfare Clause of the Constitution*. Charlottesville, VA: Michie, 1932.

Weaver, Carolyn L. *The Crisis in Social Security: Economic and Political Origins*. Durham, NC: Duke University Press, 1982.

Webber, Carolyn L., and Aaron Wildavsky. *A History of Taxation and Public Expenditure in the Western World*. New York: Simon and Schuster, 1986.

White, Joseph, and Aaron Wildavsky. *The Deficit and the Public Interest: The Search for Responsible Budgeting in the 1980s*. Berkeley: University of California Press, 1989.

5 The consequences of a United States default or repudiation

Jeffrey Rogers Hummel

5.1 Introduction

Many now realize that the US government is rushing headlong towards a major fiscal crisis. Promised future outlays, mainly for Social Security, Medicare (including Obamacare) and Medicaid, far exceed projected future revenue. Although the size of this unfunded government liability is very sensitive to both demographic changes and economic fluctuations, all estimates are sizable. Jagadeesh Gokhale (2014) of the Cato Institute, using techniques that he and Kent A. Smetters of the Wharton School (2006) developed, calculates the fiscal gap's present value as of 2012 at $54.4 trillion in 2012 dollars. This estimate relies on the Congressional Budget Office's (CBO's) baseline scenario in which the national government's existing tax and spending laws remain unchanged. The CBO also has an alternative scenario in which Congress does *not* actually implement assorted future tax increases and benefit cuts that are currently scheduled to kick in. This alternative scenario increases Gokhale's estimate to $91.4 trillion. Laurence J. Kotlikoff, a Boston University economist who helped develop generational accounting to provide a more comprehensive measure of the shortfall, puts its present value at the bone-crushing level of $205 to $210 trillion (Kotlikoff 2013; Kotlikoff and Michel 2015).

Beginning in 1992, the government's official budget documents briefly included estimates of the fiscal gap based on generational accounting. But under presidents Bill Clinton and George W. Bush these reports were suppressed. Yet even the CBO's most recent long-term outlook (2014) has federal expenditures in its alternative fiscal scenario – *not counting interest on the accumulating national debt* – rising by 2089 to more than 30 per cent of gross domestic product (GDP), whereas revenues will still be below 20 per cent of GDP, a gap of over 10 per cent of GDP. As for the national debt, the CBO throws up its hands and halts its estimates for the alternative scenario after 2050, when the debt already exceeds 250 per cent of GDP, with interest alone commanding more than half of federal revenue.

All these projections admittedly assume no drastic entitlement or tax changes in the future. But whatever the size of this gap, it should not be construed as a problem that is confined merely to the future. There is a real sense in which this number already impinges on the present. For it represents, in present value terms, the total amount by which promised government benefits must be cut, or future

96 *Jeffrey Rogers Hummel*

taxes must be hiked, or some combination of the two. There is absolutely no other alternative. Those who put their faith in some set of politically feasible reforms to close this gap therefore have an honest way to present and compare such proposals. They could take an estimate of the shortfall or even a range of estimates, and clearly state how much of this looming gap each proposal is going to cover with increased tax revenue, how much by reducing benefits and how much is ignored with hand waving. To my knowledge, few of the proposed reforms actually report this because most, if not all, of them involve a lot of smoke and mirrors. One can also make the shortfall appear more manageable by assuming utterly fantastic rates of economic growth without historical precedent, but that moves us far away from serious economic analysis into the realm of science fiction.

Extreme advocates of the American welfare state often try to deny the seriousness of the fiscal gap by focusing on Social Security *alone* (for instance, Madrick 2015) or by claiming that President Obama's Affordable Care Act of 2010 has reduced Medicare costs. And there is a smidgen of truth in both claims. Social Security by itself probably could be made sustainable with a judicious combination of tax increases and sizable benefit reductions, although many who deny the problem actually oppose benefit reductions and instead contend that benefits could and should be increased. But Social Security is only one part of several transfer programmes responsible for the shortfall, and they have perverse, reinforcing interactions. Obamacare has shifted some costs to the private sector and raised some taxes, and there are claims that, in the long run, it will reduce health care expenditures overall. Yet Obamacare has pushed out the estimated bankruptcy of the Hospital Insurance (Medicare Part A) trust fund by merely six years and made a trivial difference in the CBO's long-run estimates of the shortfall.

Only the naively optimistic believe that politicians will fully resolve this looming fiscal crisis with some drastic combination of tax hikes and programme cuts. Many who recognize the magnitude of the fiscal gap, however, predict that it will lead to an inflationary crisis. But, as I have argued elsewhere, it is far more likely that the United States will be driven to an outright default on Treasury securities, openly reneging on the interest due on its formal debt and probably repudiating part if not all of the principal (Hummel 2007, 2009, 2010; Henderson and Hummel 2014; Lemieux 2013). So after explaining below why I think this is the likely outcome, I will explore the consequences of a default by the US government on Treasury securities and then, inevitably, on its implicit entitlement obligations. Once a tipping point is reached, such a default will probably unwind swiftly, leaving American politicians with no other options. Whether the default will result in a restructuring that only reduces the US government's fiscal burden or in something approaching a more complete repudiation is impossible to foretell. Either way, the short-run consequences for financial markets and the economy will be painful. But the long-run consequences, both economic and political, will be largely beneficial, and the more complete the repudiation, the greater the benefits.

5.2 Why default or repudiation is the most likely outcome

The Federal Reserve can theoretically try to eliminate the shortfall between government outlays and receipts by printing money. To understand why this is extremely unlikely, we must look at US fiscal history. Economists refer to the revenue that government or its central bank generates through monetary expansion as *seigniorage*. Apart from two hyperinflations (during the Revolution and under the Confederacy during the Civil War), seigniorage in America peaked during the Civil War under the Union, when the creation of greenback paper money covered about 15 per cent of the war's cost. By World War II, seigniorage was financing only a little over 6 per cent of government outlays, which amounted to about 3 per cent of GDP (Friedman and Schwartz 1963, 571). By the Great Inflation of the 1970s, seigniorage was below 2 per cent of federal expenditures or less than 0.5 per cent of GDP (Hummel 2007). This was partly the result of sophisticated financial systems, with fractional reserve banking, in which most of the money that people actually hold is created privately, by banks and other financial institutions, rather than by government. Consider how little of your own cash balances are in the form of government-issued Federal Reserve notes and Treasury coin, rather than in the form of bank deposits and privately created money market funds. Such privately created money, even when its quantity expands, provides no income to government. More recently, increased globalization has permitted international competition to discipline central banks. Consequently, seigniorage has become a trivial source of revenue, not just in the United States, but also throughout the developed world. Only in poor countries, such as Zimbabwe, with their primitive financial sectors, does inflation remain lucrative for governments.

The financial crisis of 2007–8, moreover, reinforced the trend towards lower seigniorage. Buried within the 3 October 2008 bailout bill, which set up the Troubled Asset Relief Program (TARP), was a provision permitting the Fed to pay interest on bank reserves, something other major central banks were doing already. Within days, the Fed implemented this new power, essentially converting bank reserves into more government debt. Fiat money traditionally pays no interest and, therefore, allows the government to purchase real resources without incurring any future tax liability. Federal Reserve notes will, of course, continue to earn no interest. But now, any seigniorage that government gains from creating bank reserves will be greatly reduced, depending entirely on the gap between market interest rates on the remaining government debt and the interest rate on reserves. The smaller this gap, the less will be the seigniorage. Indeed, this new constraint on seigniorage becomes tighter as people replace the use of currency with bank debit cards and other forms of electronic fund transfers. In light of all these factors, even inflation well into the double digits can do little to alleviate the US government's potential bankruptcy.

Admittedly seigniorage is not the sole government benefit from inflation. Another way the government gains arises through transfers to debtors from creditors. If inflation is totally unanticipated or unexpectedly high, interest rates will not have yet have risen enough to compensate for the decline in money's purchasing

98   *Jeffrey Rogers Hummel*

power. Net debtors gain and net creditors lose. And government is the economy's biggest debtor. Unanticipated inflation therefore reduces the real value of government debt. During the Great Inflation of the 1970s, private investors holding long-term US Treasury securities actually earned negative real returns despite receiving positive nominal interest. As a consequence, from 1946–82, while the nominal debt that the US government owed to the general public rose from $242 billion to $925 billion, that debt in 1946 dollars had actually fallen to $201 billion.

The unexpected inflation of the 1970s, thus, actually generated about twice as much income for the US government through reducing the national debt's real value as did direct seigniorage. That still is not a lot, and investors are much savvier these days. Globalization, with the corresponding relaxation of exchange controls in all major countries, allows investors easily to flee to foreign currencies, with the result that changes in central bank policy are almost immediately priced by exchange rates and interest rates. Add to this the ability to purchase government securities that are now indexed to inflation, and it becomes highly unlikely that anyone will be caught off guard by anything less than sudden, catastrophic hyperinflation (defined as more than 50 per cent per month) – and maybe not then. Even if they are caught off guard, that will do little to eliminate the main source of the fiscal shortfall. Very high rates of inflation cannot possibly drive down the real costs of programmes such as Social Security and Medicare so long as these programmes are indexed to inflation.

Nonetheless, let us run some numbers to estimate how much inflation might be needed to close the looming 'fiscal imbalances' (as they are euphemistically styled) through seigniorage alone. Accepting the CBO's 2014 lower-bound baseline projection, in 25 years, counting interest on the national debt, a mere 12.3 per cent of GDP will be needed to close the US government's fiscal gap. Given that 10 per cent inflation during the 1970s generated revenue amounting to 0.5 per cent of US GDP, a straight-line extrapolation suggests that covering the growing fiscal shortfall would require more than a tripling of the price level, year after year after year. Within three years the dollar would be worth only about 6.7 per cent of its original value. Such continual triple-digit inflation would be unprecedented, the highest the US has ever experienced outside its two hyperinflations. Moreover, seigniorage itself faces its own Laffer curve (known as the Bailey curve, after the economist Martin Bailey). To avoid the depreciation on their real cash balances, people spend their money faster as inflation rises, which further accelerates the inflation. As prices spiral upward, the central bank must continually increase the money supply at an ever faster rate, in order to generate the same amount of real seigniorage, in a self-reinforcing cycle that can eventually explode into hyperinflation. Once we also acknowledge that the CBO's projections are probably too optimistic, we can see why our estimate that annual inflation of 256 per cent will finance increasing Social Security, Medicare and Medicaid payments is almost certainly too low.

What about increasing the proceeds from explicit taxes? Examine Figure 5.1, which graphs both federal outlays and receipts as a per cent of GDP from 1940 to 2012 (Carter *et al.* 2006, vol. 5, Series Ea584-678; US Office of Management

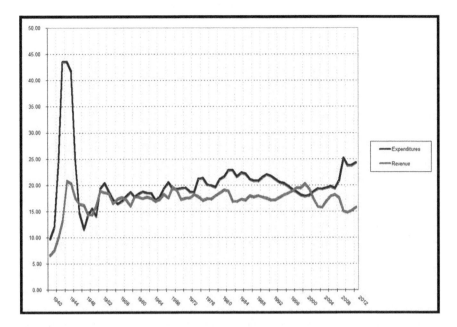

Figure 5.1 Federal outlays and receipts as a per cent of GDP, 1940–2012.

Sources: Carter *et al.* 2006, vol. 5, Series Ea584-678; US Office of Management and Budget 2015

Note: In order to keep the series consistent with respect to GDP, I have not brought the graph forward beyond 2012. In 2013 the Bureau of Economic Analysis instituted a comprehensive revision of all its GDP estimates, past and present. The revisions have raised all past estimates of GDP slightly and only the revised series is available from 2013 on. Replacing the old series throughout this graph with the revised series, which I consider inferior to the old series, would lower both lines slightly, but not affect their relative relationships

and Budget 2015). Two things stand out. First is the striking behaviour of federal tax revenue since the Korean War. Displaying less volatility than expenditures, it has bumped up against 20 per cent of GDP for well over half a century. That is quite an astonishing statistic when you think about all the changes in the tax code over the intervening years. Tax rates go up, tax rates go down and the total bite out of the economy remains relatively constant. It suggests that 20 per cent is some kind of structural-political limit for federal taxes in the United States. It also means that variations in the government's deficit resulted mainly from changes in spending rather than from changes in taxes. The second fact that stands out in the graph is that federal tax revenue at the height of World War II never quite reached 22 per cent of GDP. That represents the all-time high in US history for federal taxes as percentage of GDP, should future tax increases conceivably break through the postwar ceiling of 20 per cent. Comparing these percentages with the CBO's expenditure estimates mentioned above makes it clear that closing the

100 *Jeffrey Rogers Hummel*

fiscal gap with taxation would require that Americans put up with, on a regular peacetime basis, a higher federal tax burden than they briefly endured during the widely perceived national emergency of World War II.

The government, along with its liabilities, does have assets and an extreme expedient would be to sell some of them. But the Treasury Department's financial report for fiscal year 2015 (2016) estimates the value these assets at only $3.23 trillion, less than a quarter of the formal national debt, and most of them are financial rather than real assets. The largest component, $1.02 trillion, is student loans. True, the government does underestimate its gold holdings of $11.1 billion at the historical price of $42 per ounce. If somehow the entire amount could be sold for the exceptionally high price of nearly $2,000 per ounce, that would still only raise a bit over $0.5 trillion, a one-time drop in the bucket.

Although the government's financial report values its real assets – property, plant and equipment – at a mere $893.9 billion, this omits what it refers to as 'stewardship land and heritage assets', such as the enormous expanses of land and ocean containing the national parks and forests, mineral rights and offshore drilling rights. The Institute for Energy Research (2013) claims that all these resources are, unsurprisingly, underutilized. While better management would undoubtedly increase receipts from these physical assets, the Institute places the total value of the government's oil, natural gas and coal resources at the astonishing total of over $150 trillion. This estimate relies on several debatable assumptions: including a constant price of $100 per barrel of oil over the distant future, plus opening to development the vast 90 per cent of these areas currently held off the market for legal or regulatory reasons. Even if the estimate is accurate, it is virtually inconceivable that the government would or could sell a large enough segment of these assets at their full value within a short span of time.

We all know that there is a limit to how long an individual or institution can pile on debt if future income is rigidly fixed. Federal tax revenues are probably capped around 20 per cent of GDP; reliance on seigniorage is not a viable option; and public-choice dynamics tell us that politicians have almost no incentive to rein in Social Security, Medicare and Medicaid. These constraints make a fiscal crisis inevitable.

5.3 The cascade into default

US Treasury securities have long been considered risk-free. The financial structure of the US government currently has two apparent firewalls. The first, between Treasury debt and unfunded liabilities, is provided by the separate trust funds of Social Security, Medicare and other, smaller federal insurance programmes that rely on specific taxes designated exclusively to maintain them. These give investors in Treasury securities the illusion that the shaky fiscal status of social insurance has no direct effect on the government's formal debt. But, according to the latest *intermediate* projections of the Trustees (Boards of Trustees of the Federal Hospital Insurance and Federal Supplementary Medical Insurance Trust Funds 2014), the Hospital Insurance (HI-Medicare Part A) trust fund will be out of

The consequences of a US default or repudiation 101

money in 2030, whereas the Social Security (OASDI) trust funds will be empty by 2033. The Trustees' *pessimistic* projections have Hospital Insurance out of money by 2021 and Social Security by 2028. The Trustees do not provide any estimates of how much sooner the Social Security trust funds might empty out if they transfer money into the Medicare trust fund when that fund runs dry.

Yet what is clear is that at some point, whenever all the trust funds are finally and fully depleted, payroll taxes will be insufficient to finance these programmes and general revenues will have to take up the shortfall. Although other parts of Medicare and all of Medicaid already dip into general revenues, when HI and OASDI need to do so, the first firewall is gone. Investor anticipation of this event is a potential tipping point, as it strips away the illusion that the unfunded liabilities of Social Security and Medicare are somehow independent of the Treasury's ability to service its more formal debt. If investors react by requiring a risk premium on Treasury securities, the cost of rolling over the national debt will immediately rise. As of December 2014, one-third of the Treasury securities held by private investors, or approximately $3 trillion, had a maturity of one year or less (US Treasury Department 2015c). This would set off a self-reinforcing cycle, in which the rising risk premium would exacerbate the federal government's financial straits, further raising the risk premium. Events would then move very fast, much like the sudden collapse of the Soviet Union in 1990–1. As the emergence of the Greek debt crisis in 2009–10 illustrates, the market can shift abruptly from a high-confidence regime, with little or no risk premium on government debt, to a low-confidence regime, with a major risk premium on government debt (Kling 2012).

The second financial firewall is between US currency and government debt. The Federal Reserve *could* unleash the Zimbabwe option and repudiate the national debt indirectly through hyperinflation, rather than have the Treasury default directly. But my expectation is that, faced with the alternatives of seeing both the dollar and the debt collapsing towards worthlessness or defaulting on the debt while saving the dollar, the US government will choose the latter. Treasury securities are second-order claims to central-bank-issued dollars. Although both may be ultimately backed by the power of taxation, that in no way prevents government from discriminating between the priority of the claims. After the American Revolution, the United States repudiated its paper money but it only postponed interest payments on its formal debt for a few years before eventually honouring it in full with gold and silver coins (Ferguson 1961; Riley 1978; Anderson 1983; Perkins 1994). True, fiat money, as opposed to a gold standard, makes it harder to separate the fate of a government's money from that of its debt. But Russia in 1998 is just one recent example of a government choosing partial debt repudiation over a major depreciation of its fiat currency (Chiodo and Owyang 2002).

Other events, of course, might serve as tipping points, igniting such a self-reinforcing loss of investor confidence. On the one hand, Carmen M. Reinhart and Kenneth S. Rogoff (2009, 2010), in their comprehensive studies of past financial crises, have suggested that government debt equal to 100 per cent of GDP has passed a dangerous threshold. The CBO, in its alternative fiscal scenario, projects

102 *Jeffrey Rogers Hummel*

that the US will breach this threshold by 2029. On the other hand, Paul Krugman (2010a, 2010b) disputes the significance of the 100 per cent threshold. The US national debt reached over 100 per cent of GDP during World War II, and the United Kingdom was able to successfully manage and reduce a World War II-government debt that had climbed all the way to 250 per cent of GDP.

Perhaps a more meaningful, related, but even less predictable indicator is the total interest on government debt as per cent of total revenue. Instead of comparing the fiscal gap, a stock, with GDP, a flow, it compares a flow with a flow. This ratio varies not only with the debt's size but also with changes in both government revenue and interest rates. Although net interest payments approached 20 per cent of federal revenue in the early 1990s, they are currently safely well below 10 per cent of revenue. During the early years of George Washington's presidency, interest on the Revolutionary War debt swallowed more than half of federal revenue; after the Civil War interest payments topped one-third of revenue; and in 1933 as the US abandoned the gold standard the ratio exceeded 30 per cent (Carter 2006). But these earlier peaks are mitigated somewhat by the much smaller size of the central government relative to the economy in the distant past. And as mentioned above, the CBO's most recent alternative scenario has government interest payments reaching 50 per cent of total revenue by 2050.

Particularly sobering was a brief report six years ago from Doug Elmendorf (2009), director of the CBO. The report's alternative fiscal scenario estimated that, if federal revenues remained in the neighbourhood of 20 per cent of GDP for the next 75 years, while federal expenditures net of interest rose to 35 per cent of GDP (only 5 per cent higher than the current CBO estimate), adding interest payments from the accumulating national debt would drive total federal expenditures up to 75 per cent of GDP by 2083. That would entail interest amounting to a fantastic 40 per cent of GDP, *nearly twice assumed total revenue*. Obviously, government finances will have reached an explosive tipping point long before that level is ever reached and, indeed, well before interest payments even equal total revenue.

Some have suggested that a US government default or repudiation is impossible because it would violate Section 4 of the Constitution's 14th Amendment. The first sentence reads: 'The validity of the public debt of the United States, authorized by law, including debts incurred for payment of pensions and bounties for services in suppressing insurrection or rebellion, shall not be questioned.' While technically making unconstitutional any judicial or congressional *ex post* tampering with the national debt, this provision did nothing to inhibit the partial default on government promises when the US went off the gold standard domestically during the Great Depression or when it went off the gold standard internationally under President Nixon. It is therefore hard to imagine that it would stand in the way during a full-fledged fiscal crisis.

5.4 Short-run consequences

As of February 2015, the gross outstanding Treasury debt was $18,155,854 million, or more than 100 per cent of GDP (US Treasury Department 2015b). But

The consequences of a US default or repudiation   103

Table 5.1 How big is the national debt? (September 2014, in $ billions)

Gross Treasury debt*	17,824
Held by government agencies	−5,039
Outstanding debt	12,785
Held by Federal Reserve	−2,452
Held by private investors (including commercial banks)	10,333
Held abroad	−6,066
Held domestically	4,267
(US GDP as of 2014–Q4: $17,704 billion)	

Source: US Treasury Department 2015c.
Note: *Omits $24 billion of debt issued by government-owned agencies and $6,265 billion of liabilities issued by government-sponsored enterprises.

government agencies, mainly the Social Security and Medicare trust funds, held $5,081,818 million of that total. So, the more conventionally cited figure is the $13,074,036 million held by the public (including the Federal Reserve System), equalling 73 per cent of GDP. (See Table 5.1 for comparable numbers as of September 2014.) Even economists debate which is the more relevant of the two numbers, with Reinhart and Rogoff emphasizing the larger number and Krugman the smaller of the two. If one is concerned only about current formal obligations, then Krugman is correct, given that the trust funds simply represent past surplus revenues from some government programmes 'loaned' to cover past expenses of other government programmes. However, this total *does* omit a trivial $24 billion of debt issued by government-owned agencies and a far more ominous $6,265 billion of liabilities for such government-sponsored enterprises as Fannie Mae and Freddie Mac. It does not include approximately $15 trillion of contingent liabilities that arise from loan guarantees and deposit insurance that could leave the government suddenly on the hook for a part of that amount, albeit not all or even most of it, in the event of some crisis (Walter and Weinberg 2002; Hamilton 2014).

Yet if one is concerned about the looming fiscal gap, then one needs to add not just the trust funds but also the remainder of the fiscal shortfall, yielding, as already pointed out, a total variously estimated between $54 and $210 trillion. Fortunately, for analysing the short- and long-run consequences of a Treasury default, how to count the trust funds diminishes in importance. By the time a fiscal crisis occurs, the trust funds will already have been run down if not entirely depleted, whereas the amount held by the public will have increased. We can therefore concentrate on exactly who in the 'public' holds the debt, under the probable although uncertain assumption that the relative proportions between different holders will not alter too much as the debt grows (see Tables 5.2 and 5.3; the numbers in these tables have been updated from Hummel 2012). These proportions offer some idea of how losses from the national debt's total repudiation, to take the extreme case, would be distributed.

The Federal Reserve (which is misleadingly considered part of the public in official reports) holds about $2.5 trillion in Treasury securities, or almost 20 per cent of the publicly held debt. That percentage is only slightly higher than it was

104   *Jeffrey Rogers Hummel*

before the financial crisis. Although the quantitative easing that occurred during the crisis brought about an enormous increase in the Fed's balance sheet, much of that increase involved the Fed purchasing, for the first time, large quantities of mortgage-backed securities rather than Treasury securities. The amount of Treasury debt owned by the Fed could grow substantially if the Fed monetizes more of it in the future, even should the Fed offset such purchases by unloading its nearly $2 trillion worth of mortgage-backed securities and assorted miscellaneous assets. But the Fed is now paying interest on bank reserves at a rate that exceeds the return on short-term Treasuries. So, in essence, banks are loaning their reserves to the Fed, which then uses the money to buy securities. Thus the Fed's portion of the national debt can be thought to partly represent indirect support of the government debt by private commercial banks and other financial institutions.

Treasuries still currently constitute about half of the Fed's total assets. Although a total repudiation of Treasury debt would thus make the Fed technically bankrupt, that represents simply an accounting fiction. Most of the interest that the Fed earns on its financial assets is now remitted to the Treasury. The only significant impact of bankrupting the Fed is that the Treasury would lose the fairly minor annual flow of these remittances. The Fed's ability to issue fiat money would in no way be compromised, so long as Federal Reserve notes remain payable for taxes, and such money creation could easily cover the Fed's relatively small operating expenses. Coins today are put into circulation not by the Fed but by the Treasury, without the Treasury acquiring any genuine offsetting assets, and government accountants have

Table 5.2 Holdings by sector of the outstanding national debt (2014–Q4, percentages of $12,995 billion total)

	%
Households and non-profit organizations	5.44
Non-financial corporate business	0.31
Non-financial non-corporate business	0.40
State and local governments	4.63
Rest of the world	47.47
Federal Reserve	18.90
Commercial banks and other depositories	3.90
Insurance companies	2.17
Private pension funds	2.57
State and local government employee retirement funds	2.08
Federal government retirement funds*	1.51
Money market mutual funds	3.18
Mutual funds	5.60
Closed-end and exchange-traded funds	0.58
Government-sponsored enterprises	0.50
Issuers of asset-backed securities	0.18
Security brokers/dealers and holding companies	0.57

Source: Board of Governors, Federal Reserve System 2015.

Note: *This percentage is somewhat misleading because federal government retirement funds also hold about $1.4 trillion of non-marketable Treasury securities counted within the government's trust funds.

The consequences of a US default or repudiation   105

had no trouble dealing with these purely fiat 'liabilities'. More disturbing is the prospect that the Fed might then put new money into circulation by expanding its purchases of assorted private securities, making it an even bigger player in the allocation of savings than it has already become as a result of the financial crisis. A few have expressed concern that even a small fall in the value of Fed assets that wipes out the Fed's capital account will create political problems for the independence of the Fed (Stella 1997; Greenlaw *et al.* 2013). But this is a concern only because lack of independence might result in a more expansionary monetary policy. For reasons already discussed, we are considering the more likely case where a repudiation of Treasury debt results from an effort to avoid significant currency depreciation.

What about the remaining portion of US Treasury debt not held by the trust funds or the Fed? Over half (60 per cent) of it is owned abroad, and two-thirds of that belongs to foreign governments and their central banks (Bertaut and Tryon 2007; Hamilton and Wu 2012; Rietz 2011). The remainder is owned domestically. China and Japan are the largest foreign investors in US Treasuries, with their holdings (including both government and private) equalling $1.239 trillion each as of January 2015, or together 40 per cent of foreign holdings (US Treasury Department 2015a). Any repudiation of foreign holdings of Treasury securities would obviously not hurt Americans directly, at least initially, and most of that loss would be borne by foreign governments. I consider the potential long-run consequences, both political and economic, of this hit to foreign creditors in the subsequent section of this chapter.

But initially, to assess repudiation's impact on domestic owners of Treasury securities, we need to examine the question from two angles. First, we must look at the proportion of national debt held in various sectors of the economy. And then we must examine for each sector the size of their holdings relative to the size of their total portfolio of financial assets. According to the Fed's flow of funds accounts for the fourth quarter of 2014 (Board of Governors, Federal Reserve System 2015), mutual and closed-end funds (including money market funds and exchange-traded funds) are the financial institutions holding the largest share domestically (9.36 per cent of the total $13 trillion publicly held debt, with the total now including both the Fed's portion and that held abroad). Commercial banks and other depositories directly own only 3.90 per cent, with private pension funds close behind (2.57 per cent) and insurance companies with only 2.17 per cent. State and local governments directly hold 4.63 per cent, while their retirement funds hold another 2.08 per cent. That leaves a remaining 8.92 per cent, or less than a fifth of the *domestically* held portion of the national debt, in the hands of other investors. Investment banks, government-sponsored enterprises, non-financial corporations and non-corporate private businesses own negligible amounts, less than a per cent each. The holdings of hedge funds and trust funds are not reported separately and are lumped into the 5.44 per cent belonging to households and non-profits.

Initial direct losses to the US private sector, if a total repudiation took place today, would total little more than $4 trillion, significantly less than any estimate of the US government's enormous fiscal gap, even less than the $10 trillion fall in the value of the US stock market between 2007 and 2008 and about equal to the fall in the value of US real estate between 2007 and 2009 (Board of

106 *Jeffrey Rogers Hummel*

Table 5.3 Foreign holdings of Treasury securities (January 2015, in $ billions)

China, Mainland	1,239.1
Japan	1,238.6
Belgium	354.6
Caribbean banking centres*	338.5
Oil exporters**	290.8
Brazil	256.5
United Kingdom	207.4
Switzerland	205.5
Luxembourg	176.0
Hong Kong	172.0
Taiwan	170.6
Ireland	137.1
Singapore	109.7
India	91.2
Mexico	85.8
Turkey	82.4
Russia	82.2
France	75.5
Norway	73.6
Canada	70.0
Germany	69.6
South Korea	65.6
Philippines	40.8
Sweden	38.3
Netherlands	36.9
Colombia	36.1
Thailand	33.3
Australia	33.0
Italy	32.5
Kazakhstan	31.3
Poland	29.6
Spain	27.1
Chile	25.2
Israel	24.6
Denmark	17.0
Vietnam	14.0
Peru	10.3
All other	<u>1,956.9</u>
Grand total	6,217.9
Foreign governments	4124.3
Of which Treasury bills	340.1

Source: Treasury Department, http://www.treasury.gov/resource-center/data-chart-center/tic/Documents/mfh.txt

Notes: *Caribbean banking centres include Bahamas, Bermuda, Cayman Islands, Netherlands Antilles and Panama.
**Oil exporters include Ecuador, Venezuela, Indonesia, Bahrain, Iran, Iraq, Kuwait, Oman, Qatar, Saudi Arabia, the United Arab Emirates, Algeria, Gabon, Libya and Nigeria.

The consequences of a US default or repudiation 107

Governors, Federal Reserve System 2011, 94, 106). Outside the household sector, with its unknown amount of hedge and trust-fund holdings, the largest total dollar losses would fall on mutual and closed-end funds, as well as state and local governments with their retirement funds.

Looking at the overall portfolios *within* these domestic sectors as of the fourth quarter of 2014 (Board of Governors, Federal Reserve System 2015) in Table 5.4, state and local governments have the most serious exposure, with 20.3 per cent of their *financial* assets invested in Treasuries, while 5.0 per cent of their retirement funds are likewise tied up. Among private institutions, unsurprisingly, the heaviest hit would be money market funds, whose holdings of Treasuries constitute 15.4 per cent of their total assets. Other mutual and closed-end funds hold only 5.7 per cent of their portfolios in Treasuries. For private pension funds, the percentage is 3.9. Commercial banks and other depositories are still the economy's most important financial intermediaries, holding nearly $17 trillion in total financial assets. Treasury securities are only 3.0 per cent of that total (although government agency and GSE-guaranteed securities constitute a whopping 11.7 per cent). The *direct* exposure of the household and non-profit sector is only 1.0 per cent, but this is both an overestimate and underestimate; an overestimate because it is a percentage of the household sector's financial assets only, not counting any of its real assets, but more important, an overestimate because, of course, the financial sector *indirectly* has claims backed by Treasuries through its investments in mutual funds, pension funds, commercial banks and other financial intermediaries.

Table 5.4 Treasury securities as a per cent of each sector's total financial assets (2014–Q4)

	%
Households and non-profit organizations	1.04
Non-financial corporate business	0.24
Non-financial non-corporate business	1.30
State and local governments	20.26
Rest of the world	——
Federal Reserve	54.03
Commercial banks and other depositories	2.99
Insurance companies	3.60
Private pension funds	3.91
State and local government employee retirement funds	4.95
Federal government retirement funds*	4.39
Money market mutual funds	15.35
Mutual funds	5.78
Closed-end and exchange-traded funds	1.93
Government-sponsored enterprises	1.02
Issuers of asset-backed securities	1.69
Security brokers/dealers and holding companies	0.98

Source: Board of Governors, Federal Reserve System 2015.

Note: *This percentage is somewhat misleading, because federal government retirement funds also hold about 39 per cent of their assets as non-marketable Treasury securities counted within the government's trust funds.

108   *Jeffrey Rogers Hummel*

To be sure, such a crude reckoning ignores a vast array of potential secondary effects on the US economy. The short-run economic consequences could be very severe for some firms and households. Treasuries are currently highly liquid assets that serve as collateral for other loans in a complex and interconnected financial structure in which savings often passes through two, three, or more layers of inter-mediating institutions. Default will therefore reverberate throughout credit markets, possibly imposing losses on financial intermediaries with little direct exposure to government debt. As during the financial crisis of 2007–8, many firms will proba-bly face a temporary liquidity squeeze, unable to roll over their short-term debts as they suffer cash flow problems. Unlike the financial crisis, the impact will probably afflict Main Street as well as Wall Street. The stock market undoubtedly will take a hit, along with the bond markets. Bankruptcies and insolvencies will result and the economy will slide into a recession of unknown depth.

Yet the fact to keep in mind is that the economy's real assets – factories, buildings and other capital goods; shopping malls and inventories, homes; technological know-how; and human capital – will still be in place and largely undamaged. Indeed, most of these bankruptcies and insolvencies will represent merely changes in ownership. The real side of the US economy is what produces the bulk of goods and services, and it will not go away. More troubling is that these short-run financial problems might trigger unfortunate political interventions that impede the econo-my's adjustment. It is easy to conjure up apocalyptic scenarios of the sort that stam-peded Congress into adopting the infamous TARP and that are now terrifying European governments. But, as we will see, the realism of such scenarios is open to question.

Withal, such dollar losses will not close the government's fiscal gap. The gap consists mainly of other, promised government payments and transfers that may or may not occur in the future. Although repudiation could free up all the revenue otherwise allocated to servicing the national debt, this would still cover less than half of these implicit promises at best and, all likelihood, not even close to that. Moreover, any full accounting of how such an event would affect the US economy has first to consider that, prior to the crisis's final culmination, individuals and institutions will almost certainly start to dump Treasuries, fleeing to other assets. How the crisis ultimately plays out depends crucially on what they flee to. Indeed, cancelling government debt is itself a transfer. Treasury securities are assets with their own offsetting liabilities. And that brings us to the desirable long-run consequences.

5.5 Long-run consequences

One important long-run *political* benefit of a Treasury default would be that it would make it more difficult for the US government to borrow money. In other words, a default is a balanced-budget amendment with teeth, as David D. Friedman once characterized my argument. Sadly, that characterization is not strictly correct. Many defaulting governments have proved able to go back into the loan markets soon thereafter, although often at higher interest rates. This is especially true in the

The consequences of a US default or repudiation   109

modern world, in which other governments and international agencies bail out governments facing default in order to protect the foreign investments of politically well-connected creditors. Just how much trouble the US government will have borrowing after a default depends crucially on the severity of the default, with a total repudiation being the most crippling. But even if this effect fails to be as strong as would be ideal, a default still would encourage both greater fiscal responsibility and lower total expenditures on the part of the US government.

A Treasury default would also bring long-run *economic* benefits. But to fully appreciate these, we must carefully distinguish between two concepts that are often confused: *intergenerational transfers* and *intertemporal transfers*. Although many believe that the national debt and the government's unfunded liability impose a burden on future generations, this is a misleading way to think about it. You cannot magically transport real resources from the future into the present in an intertemporal transfer. Social insurance programmes that are run on a pay-as-you-go basis involve intergenerational transfers in the *present*, from today's young taxpayers or purchasers of Treasury securities to today's elderly Social Security and Medicare beneficiaries. To the extent that these programmes create an explicit or implicit government debt, they are merely imposing transfers that will all take place in the *future*, between future taxpayers and either the future owners of Treasury securities or future beneficiaries of social insurance.

The only way that such deficit financing can affect total real wealth in the future is through its impact on economic growth, mainly by discouraging saving and capital accumulation. The extent to which social insurance impinges on growth is controversial among economists, but the harshest critics have never claimed that these programmes will cause long-run economic growth to turn negative or to cease altogether. At their worst, these programmes might mean that future generations, instead of being, let's say, twice as wealthy as the current generation in 50 years (if real GDP per capita grows at 1.5 per cent annually), will only be about 65 per cent wealthier (with 1.0 per cent growth). In other words, the fiscal gap, including the part created by the formal Treasury debt, is not so much a *burden* on future generations from which the current generation benefits as it as a *problem* for future generations, setting in motion future transfers among members of those generations.

Thus, to determine the economic impact of repudiation, we must examine how it alters transfers that would otherwise take place at some future point. All loan transactions have two parties, the lender (or creditor) who forgoes the current use of money in exchange for a financial asset, and the borrower (or debtor) who gains the current use of money in exchange for a financial liability. Debt, whether private or public, therefore has both an asset and liability side, in which the debtor is supposed to transfer money to the creditor at some future date. If we disentangle distribution and net wealth (or net welfare) effects, a sudden and unanticipated but successful repudiation of a private debt has only a distribution effect, so long as no one expects it to be repeated or extended later to other debts. The debtor gains by the exact same dollar amount that the creditor loses, with no initial net wealth effect.

110   *Jeffrey Rogers Hummel*

So where is the offsetting liability that government debt creates? Although superficially it appears that government itself owes the liability, this impression misses the underlying economic reality. The liability ultimately rests on taxpayers because their taxes will be almost the entire source of revenue to pay interest and any principal on the government debt. Nearly every financial asset created by government borrowing, therefore, creates a corresponding tax liability. Even if the debt is perpetually funded forever and never repaid, the discounted present value of this stream of future taxes roughly equals the total value of the debt.

In short, the inevitable default on Treasury securities will reduce taxes required in the future, and the more complete the repudiation, the greater the tax reprieve. The real gainers from the looming fiscal crisis will not be the US government but its taxpayers. How this affects the value of taxable assets, including human capital, depends on how perfectly people anticipate future tax liabilities. The degree to which they do so is a technical issue much debated by macroeconomists. The claim that people completely and correctly anticipate these future levies is known as Ricardian Equivalence. If Ricardian Equivalence holds even approximately, then the decline in the value of Treasuries should be mostly offset by an eventual rise in the total value of privately issued assets such as shares of stock, taxable real assets and expected future wage income.

If Ricardian Equivalence does not hold, and people do not perfectly anticipate their future tax liabilities, then they erroneously believe that Treasury securities represent net wealth. Suffering from what is sometimes called 'bond illusion' or 'fiscal illusion', they think they are wealthier than they actually are. Whether this illusion has desirable or undesirable economic consequences is one of the many questions involved in economic controversies about business cycles, fiscal policy and economic growth. But, regardless of the answers to these questions, repudiation of the national debt will bring people's perception of their net wealth into greater consistency with reality. They will still enjoy a reduction in future taxes, despite never realizing that they would have had to pay them.

Even absent Ricardian Equivalence, repudiation of Treasury securities held abroad will represent a long-run net gain for Americans. Constituting a transfer to a wealthy US from the rest of the world, this distribution effect may appear unfair. But it has the advantage of ending the coerced support paid to foreign governments, particularly that of China, by US taxpayers. Indeed, the frequent and much-touted bailouts of insolvent governments to help them avoid or palliate sovereign defaults usually end up benefiting creditors, who have willingly taken on the risk of loaning money to governments, but at the expense of the taxpayers in the allegedly 'bailed out' country. Such will probably be the consequence of the ongoing fiscal crisis in Greece; it is what took place during the 1994 Mexico crisis; and it repeats a pattern that dates back at least as far as the notorious US military interventions into Latin America early in the twentieth century (Langley 1989) and the less blatant European interventions into the Balkans that started even earlier (Feis 1930; Krasner 1995–6).

Plus, bear in mind that foreigners also hold privately issued US securities, about $22 trillion worth as of the end of 2014, nearly three times foreign holdings of US government securities (Bureau of Economic Analysis 2015). To the extent

The consequences of a US default or repudiation   111

that the prices of these privately issued securities correctly reflect any future taxes earmarked to finance the US government's debt, these foreign investments in the long run will tend to rise in value after a US default. Foreign losses will be partly offset by such gains. Of course, these gains will accrue primarily to private citizens abroad, who hold the bulk of privately issued US securities, while the losses will fall primarily on foreign governments and their central banks.

Foreign governments will not be happy with this outcome, which will certainly strain US relations with them. But outside repudiating US holdings of their own sovereign debt (which in many cases may happen anyway because they face their own fiscal crises), there is little in the way of economic retaliation they can carry out that will not hurt their own economies at least as much as it hurts the American economy. The Federal Reserve owns only about $20 *billion* of foreign securities. We do not know how much of the $2.8 trillion of foreign debt in the hands of American citizens is government issued, but I suspect the proportion is not very large, even counting indirect holdings through foreign mutual funds and other intermediaries. China and Japan, being the largest holders of US Treasuries, are going to be the most severely affected by a Treasury default. As for any military repercussions from other countries after US default, the threat is ridiculously far-fetched. Although China's military spending is the second highest in the world, US military spending almost equals the military spending of all other countries combined.

Turning to the domestically held Treasury debt, its repudiation will bring no perceived change in national net wealth, if Americans perfectly anticipate their future tax liabilities. Moreover, the existence of these offsetting tax liabilities serves to mitigate any domestic distribution effects. Since nearly everyone pays taxes or owns assets whose value is reduced by taxation, it is impossible to predict even whether a particular owner of government securities will, over their entire investment portfolio, gain or lose. Those who have invested in some government securities plus an assortment of other assets, will find over the long run that, as their government securities are wiped out, their other assets (including human capital) increase in value. Even if people do not perfectly anticipate future tax liabilities, they clearly anticipate a part of them, so there should be some compensating rise in the value of private assets.

No matter how incompletely the gains show up in rising asset values, people *de facto* will tend to gain or lose on the basis of whether, over the entire range of their economic activities, they are net tax consumers or net taxpayers. Of course, the correspondence between net tax consumers and losers from repudiation, on the one hand, and net taxpayers and gainers from repudiation, on the other, will not be exact. Government debt is not the only means by which the state dispenses tax-generated largess. The correspondence, however, will be close enough to ensure that a non-trivial number of the government's creditors will be helped more than they are harmed in the long run.

Another consequence I have so far not discussed, however, is that those harmed *most* by repudiation will *not* be those who hold Treasury securities. The more unfortunate victims will be those anticipating benefits from Social Security, Medicare and Medicaid. Recall that a full Treasury repudiation would close no

112   *Jeffrey Rogers Hummel*

more than half the fiscal gap, and probably much less, so it would almost certainly entail a concomitant collapse of those programmes. Anyone relying upon these government promises suffers from his or her own, particularly egregious form of fiscal illusion. Here we need to be careful about what estimates of the fiscal shortfall to employ. Not all of it, particularly the part resulting from Medicaid, involves taxes specifically earmarked for implicit promises to particular individuals. Moreover, Social Security and Medicare both create two different types of gaps: (1) the 'open-group' obligation (or actuarial deficit), which includes future taxes and benefits of *all* future participants in the programme, and (2) the 'closed-group' obligation (or unfunded liability), which includes future taxes and benefits of only those current participants who have paid something in or received benefits. The latter obligation, which represents the present value of shutting down the programme immediately while honouring all existing promises – that is, converting it from a pay-as-you-go to a fully funded basis – is usually larger.

The closed-group unfunded liability is also a better proxy for the uncompensated losses inflicted by the elimination of these anticipated benefits. Both the Social Security Trustees and the Medicare Trustees annually estimate the present value of net expenditures over tax receipts for both the open and closed groups. As reported in the Treasury's *Financial Report of the United States Government: Fiscal Year 2015*, the 75-year closed-group shortfall for both Social Security and Medicare (Parts A, B and D) from $56.7 trillion for 2014, up from $53.0 trillion in 2013 (US Treasury Department 2016). The open-group shortfall for 2014 is only $41.9 trillion, or just about $15 trillion lower than for the closed-group. Whatever the correct number, these would represent devastating losses for the recipients. Yet the best way to alleviate future suffering is to repeatedly and emphatically warn the American people that these programmes will go under. For economists and politicians to take any other course is the height of callous irresponsibility. The more accurately people anticipate this inevitable outcome, the better prepared they will be to avoid or mitigate its suffering.

Indeed, I would go so far as to argue that, from the standpoint of justice and equity, the beneficiaries of Social Security and at least Part-A of Medicare (Hospital Insurance) deserve priority over those who hold Treasury securities. They were all forced into these programmes through past tax payments, while those who bought Treasuries voluntarily assumed the risk of making loans to a rapacious, profligate and ultimately insolvent state. Owners of the formal government debt should therefore not receive a single dime until those who were coerced into Social Security and Medicare are fully compensated for past tax expropriations. Alas, as mentioned above, a total repudiation will only partly reduce rather than come close to eliminating the fiscal gap created by these programmes. Ideally, any compensation to past taxpayers should be supplemented by making personally liable up to their entire fortunes every congressman and senator who voted for these unsustainable programmes and every president who signed them into law. Unfortunately, that will never happen in the real world.

None of the long-run effects, by definition, will occur instantaneously. Yet, as the inevitability of a US default becomes increasingly apparent, more and more

The consequences of a US default or repudiation 113

people will try to unload their government securities. Thus, some offsetting rise in the value of other assets should commence before default occurs. Exactly where individuals and institutions attempt to invest after selling Treasury securities will affect both the short run and the long run. Fleeing to assets dominated in foreign currencies is one theoretical possibility, especially for foreign holders of Treasuries. This will contribute somewhat to a depreciation of the dollar on foreign exchange markets. But precisely which, if any, foreign currencies will be considered safe havens when the US defaults is an open question.

Thus, the three primary alternatives for most Americans will be to move into either (1) real assets, including commodities such as gold, as well as real estate, consumer durables and physical capital goods; (2) dollar-denominated financial securities *other than* Treasuries or those that represent claims to Treasuries; or (3) dollars themselves, meaning Federal Reserve base money. If the shift of savings is primarily into (1), this could fuel inflation; a shift into (2) would mostly affect relative prices; but if the Fed successfully decouples its fiat money from Treasuries, as I expect, then we could instead see a major shift into (3), which, if severe enough, could be deflationary.

Deflation raises the spectre of prolonged recession and sluggish recovery, similar to what the US has gone through since 2008. But the duration and severity of the resulting depression would depend on what other government policies are imposed in response. Perhaps the most chilling prospect is that the US government could conceivably repudiate its debt and simultaneously raise taxes, thus confiscating the taxpayer gains from repudiation. Yet how politicians would get away with doing so when they are unable to raise taxes high enough to prevent default in the first place is highly questionable. What is more likely is that the government might try a debt restructuring that discriminates among those holding Treasury securities. Like Russia in 1998, the US might default on the domestic debt but honour its foreign debt. Or it could do the reverse. Discriminating among domestic debt holders would be far more complex, given how fungible and liquid Treasury securities are. But, as I emphasized before, even a total repudiation, by itself, does not close the fiscal gap. The ultimate success of such halfway measures is therefore doubtful.

In the final analysis, the future is unknowable and we can only speculate about what interventions would follow a Treasury default. Nonetheless, the national debt, by its nature, obligates the government to make future payments. That obligation can ultimately be honoured only through future taxation or through a monetary expansion that constitutes either indirect taxation, indirect default, or both. Repudiation, by definition, eliminates that obligation and alleviates future intergenerational transfers. It is always and everywhere a form of taxpayer relief, making it the most desirable among feasible alternatives.

5.6 Historical case study

Historical case studies can be a rich source of anecdotal evidence. For the sake of brevity, I will explore only one striking case, from the early history of the United States. Unlike more recent defaults, where international bailouts have

114   *Jeffrey Rogers Hummel*

short-circuited and foreclosed most of the desirable consequences, this case dramatically contradicts the common presupposition that sovereign defaults are necessarily dire. Indeed, it substantiates my argument that default can usher in such desirable results as decreasing government intervention, thereby encouraging prosperity. The case involves not the default of the national government but of several state governments in the 1840s.

After the War of 1812, New York State began construction of a canal connecting the Hudson River with the Great Lakes. The Erie Canal, completed in 1825, was one of those rare and curious instances where a socialist enterprise actually made a good profit, and it encouraged other states to emulate New York. An orgy of canal building resulted. Usually, state governments owned and operated these new canals. In those few instances where the canals were privately owned, the states contributed the largest share of the financing. By 1840, the canal boom had blessed the United States with 3,326 miles of mostly economically unjustified canals at an expense to the states of $125 million, a large sum in those days. Virtually all the new canals were a waste of resources and did not deliver the hoped-for monetary returns. Instead, the heavy state investments, when added to budget growth stimulated by the War of 1812, led to massive borrowing (Ransom 1964; Taylor 1951; Thies 2002).

Then, in May 1837, a major financial panic engulfed the country's 800 banks, forcing all but six to cease redeeming their banknotes and deposits for gold or silver coins. The panic brought on a sharp depression that was quickly over (McGrane 1924; Rezneck 1935). Amazingly, after recovery, the outstanding indebtedness of states nearly doubled, with a third of that invested in state-chartered banks in the Midwest and South (Wallis *et al.* 2004). By the end of 1839, a second bank suspension spread to half the country's banks. Over the next four years, nearly a quarter of state banks failed, the country's total money stock (M2) declined by one-third and prices plummeted 42 per cent (Hummel 1999; Temin 1969).

Needless to say, the state governments faced financial stringency and, during the deflation of 1839–1943, many became desperate. By 1844, $60 million worth of state improvement bonds were in default. Four states – Louisiana, Arkansas, Michigan and Mississippi – as well as the territory of Florida eventually repudiated debts outright, while four others – Maryland, Illinois, Pennsylvania and Indiana – defaulted temporarily. New York and Ohio escaped similar straits only by taking such extraordinary measures as abruptly halting infrastructure expenditures, temporarily jacking up property taxes (in Ohio's case by administrative decree rather than legislative approval), continuing to roll over their state debts at exorbitant interest rates and using their political control over their state-chartered banks to induce continued lending. They were also in slightly less serious straits to begin with because New York had the one profitable canal, whereas Ohio had never anticipated that its canals would generate significant revenue (Scott 1893; Ratchford 1941; Wallis 2002).

The Whig Party, under the leadership of Senator Henry Clay of Kentucky, saw the 1837 depression and the subsequent state defaults as a heaven-sent opportunity for a national bailout. They proposed in Congress that the national government

The consequences of a US default or repudiation   115

assume the state debts. Clay's party also advocated a national bankruptcy law that would allow individual debtors voluntarily to escape their obligations. But the Democrats, under the inspired leadership of Martin Van Buren, who had been elected president in 1836, not only blocked these initiatives but pushed government involvement in the opposite direction. Although total national expenditures suddenly spiked to $37.2 million in 1837, overall they declined through Van Buren's four years, from $30.9 million in 1836 to $24.3 million in 1840. That represents a 21 per cent fall in nominal terms, no more than half as much if you adjust for price changes, but somewhere in between if you also adjust for population growth or the economy's size (US Department of Commerce 1975).

Many of these federal spending cuts came in the realm of internal improvements, especially for rivers and harbours. As for revenue, tariff rates were already falling as a result of programmed reductions worked out during a previous compromise. The national government's only other source of revenue at the time was the sale of public land. So the President threw his weight behind two measures that would bring the allocation of public land into closer alignment with the homestead principle: pre-emption, giving settlers who cultivated the land first option to buy, and graduation, reducing the price on unsold land. Graduation failed to pass, but Congress renewed earlier pre-emption acts twice during Van Buren's term. At the end of the four years, with significant cuts in both national spending and revenue, the depression-generated national debt was holding near a modest $5 million, far less than one year's outlays.

Meanwhile, rather than having disastrous long-run effects, the combination of state defaults and repudiations generated a widening circle of benefits. To begin with, it prompted state governments to make major fiscal reforms. As the distinguished economic historian John Joseph Wallis (2001, 1) reports:

> Beginning with New York in 1846, almost two-thirds of the states wrote new constitutions in the next ten years. The constitutions restricted state investment in private corporations; limited or banned incorporation by special legislative act; created general incorporation laws for all types of business; altered the way state and local governments issued debt; put absolute limits on the amount of debt governments could issue; and fundamentally changed the structure of the property tax.

Economist Thomas J. Sargent asks in his Nobel Prize lecture (2011, 2012): how likely would have been such reforms if the state governments had indeed been bailed out by the national government?

States became wary of investing in internal improvements or in anything else. This ensured that, as railways came to dominate the next phase of the country's transportation revolution, the states left development and expansion of this network primarily to the market. State ownership of railways became negligible, as nearly all the previously state-owned lines were unloaded. Although the state and especially the local governments continued to subsidize railways through some direct investment and in less conspicuous ways, private sources ended up

116 *Jeffrey Rogers Hummel*

providing three-quarters of all the capital for American railways prior to 1860 (Fishlow 1965, 1972, 496). Indeed, the period after the fiscal crisis was when most of the states finally threw off their mercantilist heritage and, for the first time, moved towards a regime of *laissez faire*.

At the same time, foreign investors, particularly British, who had acquired about $100 million in state bonds, now became extremely cautious about loaning money to state governments. Wallis, along with co-authors Richard Sylla and Arthur Grinath (2004, 1) have aptly invoked parallels 'with LDC debt crises of the 1980s, the Mexican, Asian, Russian-LTCM, and Brazilian crises of the 1990s, and the Argentine crisis of the early 2000s'. Foreign caution even extended to the national government. When American agents investigated the possibility of borrowing money in Europe in 1842, they were told that US bonds could not be sold there because investors feared that the federal government would also default (English 1996; McGrane 1935). Moreover, the state constitutional restrictions on borrowing bequeathed a salutary fiscal legacy that, despite subsequent undermining, has lingered to the present day (Kiewiet and Szakaly 1996; Wallis 2005).

Nor did the economic distress of the deflation of 1839–43 extend far beyond the state governments and state-chartered banks. Many economists, including Milton Friedman, have been struck by the comparison between this episode and the Great Depression of 1929–33. Qualifying as the two most massive monetary contractions in American history, they were of identical magnitude and duration. But there the similarities end. During the Great Depression, as unemployment peaked at nearly 25 per cent of the labour force in 1933, US production of goods and services collapsed by 30 per cent. During the earlier nineteenth-century price decline, investment fell, but the economy's total output did not. Quite the opposite; it actually rose somewhere between 6 and 16 per cent, and real consumption rose even more. This episode was nearly a full-employment deflation. And, once it was over, the country continued to enjoy the sustained economic growth that had begun in the 1830s, with its rising real incomes and increasing prosperity (Temin 1969, 157; Friedman and Schwartz 1963, 299; Carter 2006, Table Ca219).

5.7 Conclusion

The US government will likely default on its explicit and implicit promises within the next two decades. Exactly how and when is less certain. But the fundamental and massive budgetary changes required to prevent a fiscal crisis are politically unimaginable. Whether the fiscal gap is $210 or $54 trillion, any proposed reform can only close it with some combination of benefit cuts and revenue increases whose total present comes close to equalling the shortfall. If politicians today abolished Medicare and Medicaid totally, then some judicious combination applied to the remaining gap might save Social Security on a pay-as-you-go basis. Or opening the borders to unrestricted immigration might funnel enough new taxpayers into the front end of these programmes to make the required reforms less drastic. Otherwise, only default can impose the necessary

The consequences of a US default or repudiation   117

fiscal discipline. Fortunately, the state government experience of the 1840s suggests that this may provide a better and more durable long-run solution.

Indeed, nearly all the social democracies are facing similar fiscal dilemmas, despite their higher taxes. Pay-as-you go social insurance is simply not sustainable over the long run. Even though the US initiated social insurance later than most other welfare states, it is approaching crisis at about the same time because Medicare, unlike the national health care characteristic of other welfare states, subsidizes rather than rations health care. In other words, the social-democratic welfare state will come to end, just as the socialist state came to an end. Socialism was doomed by the calculation problem identified by Ludwig von Mises (1951) and Friedrich Hayek (1935). Von Mises further argued that the mixed economy was unstable and that the dynamics of intervention would inevitably drive it towards socialism or *laissez faire*. But in this case, he was mistaken; a century of experience has taught us that the client-oriented, power-broker state is the gravity well towards which public-choice incentives drive both command and market economies.

What will ultimately kill the welfare state is that its centrepiece, government-provided social insurance, is simultaneously above reproach and beyond salvation. Fully funded systems could have survived, but politicians had little incentive to enact them and, once a pay-as-you-go system is in operation, the costs of converting it to a fully funded basis are too onerous to impose on a democratic electorate. Whether this inevitable collapse of social democracies will ultimately be a good or bad thing depends on what replaces them. But by recognizing and exposing this inevitability, the critics of the welfare state can help ensure that the replacement is a freer society.

References

Anderson, William G. *The Price of Liberty: The Public Debt of the American Revolution.* Chapel Hill: University of North Carolina Press, 1983.

Bertaut, Carol C., and Ralph W. Tryon. 'Monthly Estimates of US Cross-Border Securities Positions'. Federal Reserve Board International Finance Discussion Paper No. 1014. 2007. http://www.federalreserve.gov/pubs/ifdp/2007/910/default.htm

Board of Governors, Federal Reserve System. *Flow of Funds Accounts of the United States: Flows and Outstandings, Second Quarter 2011.* 2011. http://www.federalreserve.gov/releases/z1/Current/data.htm

Board of Governors, Federal Reserve System. *Financial Accounts of the United States: Flow of Funds, Balance Sheets, and Integrated Macroeconomic Accounts, Fourth Quarter 2014.* 12 March 2015. http://www.federalreserve.gov/releases/z1/Current

Board of Trustees of the Federal Old-Age and Survivors Insurance and Federal Disability Insurance Trust Funds. *Annual Report.* 2014. http://www.ssa.gov/oact/tr/2014/index.html

Boards of Trustees of the Federal Hospital Insurance and Federal Supplementary Medical Insurance Trust Funds. *Annual Report.* 2014. https://www.cms.gov/Research-Statistics-Data-and-Systems/Statistics-Trends-and-Reports/ReportsTrustFunds/Trustees-Reports-Items/2012-2014.html?DLPage=1&DLSort=0&DLSortDir=descending

118 Jeffrey Rogers Hummel

Bureau of Economic Analysis. US Department of Commerce. 'Balance of Payments (International Transactions)'. Interactive Website. 2015. http://www.bea.gov/iTable/iTable.cfm?ReqID=62&step=1#reqid=62&step=5&isuri=1&6210=5

Bureau of the Fiscal Service. US Department of the Treasury. *Financial Report of the United States Government–Fiscal Year 2014*. 2015. http://www.fiscal.treasury.gov/fsreports/rpt/finrep/fr/fr_index.htm

Carter, Susan B., Scott Sigmund Gartner, Michael R. Haines, Alan L. Olmstead, Richard Sutch and Gavin Wright, eds. *Historical Statistics of the United States: Earliest Times to the Present*. Millennial Edition. 5 vols. New York: Cambridge University Press, 2006.

Chiodo, Abbigail J., and Michael T. Owyang. 'A Case Study of a Currency Crisis: The Russian Default of 1998'. *Federal Reserve Bank of St Louis Review* 84 (November/December 2002): 7–18.

Congressional Budget Office. *The 2014 Long-Term Budget Outlook*. July. 2014. Supporting Data Spread Sheet at https://www.cbo.gov/publication/45308

Elmendorf, Doug. *Federal Budget Challenges*. Presentation at Harvard University introductory economics lecture, April 2009.

English, William B. 'Understanding the Costs of Sovereign Default: American State Debts in the 1840's'. *American Economic Review* 86 (March 1996): 259–75.

Feis, Herbert. *Europe: The World's Banker: An Account of European Foreign Investment and the Connection of World Finance with Diplomacy before World War I*. New Haven: Yale University Press, 1930.

Ferguson, E. James. *The Power of the Purse: A History of American Public Finance, 1776–1790*. Chapel Hill: University of North Carolina Press, 1961.

Fishlow, Albert. *American Railroads and the Transformation of the Ante-Bellum Economy*. Cambridge, MA: Harvard University Press, 1965.

Fishlow, Albert. 'Internal Transportation'. In Lance E. Davis, Richard A. Easterlin, William N. Parker, et al., eds, *American Economic Growth: An Economist's History of the United States*. New York: Harper & Row, 1972.

Friedman, Milton, and Anna Jacobson Schwartz. *A Monetary History of the United States, 1867–1960*. Princeton, NJ: Princeton University Press, 1963.

Gokhale, Jagadeesh. *The Government Debt Iceberg*. London: Institute of Economic Affairs, 2014.

Gokhale, Jagadeesh, and Kent A. Smetters. 'Fiscal and Generational Imbalances: An Update'. *Tax Policy and Economy* 20 (2006): 193–223.

Greenlaw, David, James D. Hamilton, Peter Hooper and Frederic S. Mishkin. 'Crunch Time: Fiscal Crises and the Role of Monetary Policy'. NBER Working Paper No. 19297, Cambridge, MA, 29 July 2013. http://www.nber.org/papers/w19297

Hamilton, James D. 'Off-Balance-Sheet Federal Liabilities'. *Cato Papers on Public Policy* 3 (2014).

Hamilton, James D., and Jing Cynthia Wu. 'The Effectiveness of Alternative Monetary Policy Tools in a Zero Lower Bound Environment'. *Journal of Money, Credit, and Banking* (Supplement, February 2012): 3–46.

Hayek, Friedrich A., ed. *Collectivist Economic Planning: Critical Studies on the Possibilities of Socialism*. London: G. Routledge & Sons, 1935.

Henderson, David R., and Jeffrey Rogers Hummel. 'The Inevitability of US Government Default'. *Independent Review* 18 (Spring 2014): 527–41.

Hummel, Jeffrey Rogers. 'Martin Van Buren: The Greatest American President'. *Independent Review* 4 (Autumn 1999): 255–81.

The consequences of a US default or repudiation 119

Hummel, Jeffrey Rogers. 'Death and Taxes, Including Inflation: The Public versus Economists'. *Econ Journal Watch* 4 (January 2007): 46–59.

Hummel, Jeffrey Rogers. 'Why Default on US Treasuries is Likely'. *Library of Economics and Liberty* (August 2009). http://www.econlib.org/library/Columns/y2009/Hummeltbills.html

Hummel, Jeffrey Rogers. 'Government's Diminishing Benefits from Inflation'. *The Freeman* 60 (November 2010): 25–9.

Hummel, Jeffrey Rogers. 'Some Possible Consequences of a US Government Default'. *Econ Journal Watch* 9 (January 2012): 24–40.

Institute for Energy Research. 'Federal Assets Above and Below Ground'. *Latest Analysis* (17 January 2013). http://instituteforenergyresearch.org/analysis/federal-assets-above-and-below-ground/

Kiewiet, D. Roderick, and Kristin Szakaly. 'Constitutional Limitations on Borrowing: An Analysis of State Bonded Indebtedness'. *Journal of Law, Economics, & Organization* 12 (April 1996): 62–97.

Kling, Arnold. 'How a Default May Play Out'. *Econ Journal Watch* 9 (January 2012): 51–9.

Kotlikoff, Laurence J. 'Assessing Fiscal Sustainability'. *Mercatus Research*. Arlington, VA: Mercatus Center, 2013.

Kotlikoff, Laurence J., and Adam N. Michel. 'Closing America's Fiscal Gap: Who Will Pay'. *Mercatus Working Paper*. Arlington, VA: Mercatus Center, June 2015.

Krasner, Stephen D. 'Compromising Westphalia'. *International Security* 20 (Winter 1995–6): 115–51.

Krugman, Paul. 'Debt and Transfiguration'. *New York Times Blog*, 12 March 2010a. http://krugman.blogs.nytimes.com/2010/03/12/debt-and-transfiguration/

Krugman, Paul. 'Bad Analysis at the Debt Commission'. *New York Times Blog*, 27 May 2010b. http://krugman.blogs.nytimes.com/2010/05/27/bad-analysis-at-the-deficit-commission/

Langley, Lester D. *The United States and the Caribbean in the Twentieth Century*. 4th edn. Athens, GA: University of Georgia Press, 1989.

Lemieux, Pierre. *The Public Debt: A Comprehensive Guide*. New York: Palgrave Macmillan, 2013.

Madrick, Jeff. 'The Rocky Road to Taking It Easy'. *New York Review of Books* 62, no. 4 (5 March 2015): 48–50.

McGrane, Reginald Charles. *The Panic of 1837: Some Financial Problems of the Jacksonian Era*. Chicago: University of Chicago Press, 1924.

McGrane, Reginald Charles. *Foreign Bondholders and American State Debts*. New York: Macmillan, 1935.

Perkins, Edwin J. *American Public Finance and Financial Services, 1700–1815*. Columbus: Ohio State University Press, 1994.

Ransom, Roger L. 'Canals and Development: A Discussion of the Issues'. *American Economic Review* 54 (May 1964): 365–76.

Ratchford, B.U. *American State Debts*. Durham, NC: Duke University Press, 1941.

Reinhart, Carmen M., and Kenneth S. Rogoff. *This Time Is Different: Eight Centuries of Financial Folly*. Princeton, NJ: Princeton University Press, 2009.

Reinhart, Carmen M., and Kenneth S. Rogoff. 'Growth in a Time of Debt'. *American Economic Review* 100, no. 2 (May 2010): 573–8.

Rezneck, Samuel. 'The Social History of an American Depression, 1837–1843'. *American Historical Review* 40, no. 4 (July 1935): 662–87.

Rietz, Justin D. 'Interest Rates During the 2009's: The Federal Reserve vs a Global Savings Glut'. Unpublished paper, May 2011.

120 *Jeffrey Rogers Hummel*

Riley, James C. 'Foreign Credit and Fiscal Stability: Dutch Investment in the United States, 1781–1794'. *Journal of American History* 65, no. 3 (December 1978): 654–78.

Sargent, Thomas J. 'Nobel Prize Lecture'. 8 December 2011. http://www.nobelprize.org/nobel_prizes/economics/laureates/2011/sargent-lecture.html?print=1

Sargent, Thomas J. 'United States Then, Europe Now'. 2012. https://files.nyu.edu/ts43/public/research/Sargent_Sweden_12.pdf

Scott, William A. *The Repudiation of State Debts: A Study in the Financial History of Mississippi, Florida, Alabama, North Carolina, South Carolina, Georgia, Louisiana, Arkansas, Tennessee, Minnesota, Michigan, and Virginia*. New York: Thomas Y. Crowell, 1893.

Social Security and Medicare Boards of Trustees. *Status of the Social Security and Medicare Programs: A Summary of the 2011 Annual Reports*. 2011. http://www.ssa.gov/OACT/TRSUM/index.html

Stella, Peter. 'Do Central Banks Need Capital?' *IMF Working Paper*, July 1997. http://papers.ssrn.com/sol3/papers.cfm?abstract_id=882586

Taylor, George Rogers. *The Transportation Revolution*. New York: Holt, Rinehart and Winston, 1951.

Temin, Peter. *The Jacksonian Economy*. New York: W.W. Norton, 1969.

Thies, Clifford F. 'The American Railroad Network during the Early 19th Century: Private versus Public Enterprise'. *Cato Journal* 22, no. 2 (Autumn 2002): 229–61.

US Department of Commerce. *Historical Statistics of the United States: Colonial Times to 1970*. 2 vols. Washington, DC: US Government Printing Office, 1975.

US Office of Management and Budget. 2015. *Budget of the United States Government: Historical Tables Fiscal Year 2016*. 2015. http://www.gpo.gov/fdsys/search/pagedetails.action?granuleId=&packageId=BUDGET-2016-TAB&fromBrowse=true

US Treasury Department. 'Major Foreign Holders of Treasuries' *Treasury International Capital System (TIC) – Home Page*. 16 March 2015a. http://www.treasury.gov/resource-center/data-chart-center/tic/Documents/mfh.txt

US Treasury Department. 'Monthly Statement of the Public Debt of the United States'. February 28, 2015b. http://www.treasurydirect.gov/govt/reports/pd/mspd/2015/2015_feb.htm

US Treasury Department. *Treasury Bulletin*. March 2015c. http://www.fiscal.treasury.gov/fsreports/rpt/treasBulletin/current.htm

US Treasury Department. *Financial Report of the United States Government: Fiscal Year 2015*. 26 February 2016. https://www.fiscal.treasury.gov/fsreports/rpt/finrep/fr/fr_index.htm

von Mises, Ludwig. *Socialism: An Economic and Sociological Analysis*. New Haven: Yale University Press, 1951.

Wallis, John Joseph. 'What Caused the Crisis of 1839?'. NBER Working Paper Series on Historical Factors in Long Run Growth, No. 133, 2001.

Wallis, John Joseph. 'The Depression of 1839 to 1843: States, Debts, and Banks'. Unpublished manuscript. 2002. http://scholar.google.com/scholar?q=The+Depression+of+1839+to+1843+wallis

Wallis, John Joseph. 'Constitutions, Corporations, and Corruption: American States and Constitutional Change, 1842 to 1852'. *Journal of Economic History* 65, no.1 (March 2005): 211–56.

Wallis, John Joseph, Richard E. Sylla and Arthur Grinath III. 'Sovereign Debt and Repudiation: The Emerging-Market Debt Crisis in the US States, 1839–1843'. NBER Working Paper 10753. 2004.

Walter, John R., and John A. Weinberg. 'How Large Is the Federal Financial Safety Net?' *Cato Journal* 21, no. 3 (Winter 2002): 369–93.

Part III
Regime crisis

6 The US military's role in national crises

Past, present and future

Paul Springer

6.1 Introduction

In many ways, the history of the United States is often taught in the form of crisis reaction anecdotes. Most textbooks focus more upon the dire emergencies of the nation's existence than the everyday lives of ordinary American citizens. Thus, a typical survey text will devote multiple chapters to the deadliest American wars, each of which lasted four years, and only a handful of pages to periods of domestic and international tranquility.[1] This is unsurprising, and reflects the tendency of American citizens to focus much of their attention upon the crisis of the moment, whether it is local or international in scope. Modern US media outlets devote a majority of their coverage to crises and responses, and if a crisis does not exist, a relatively minor issue can be trumpeted as a call to action, a means to rally the public and, at the same time, take in massive amounts of advertising dollars. This strategy pays enormous dividends for the major media providers, which in the twenty-first century must feed a rapacious public desire for constant information and updates. A failure to treat every incident as world-altering merely leads to a lower audience rating – the more sedate approaches to news delivery have haemorrhaged consumers to the sensationalists for more than a century.

Although the continual focus upon the crisis of the moment might rivet the target audience, and hence prove an effective means of generating revenue for the media, it is not a healthy approach to governance – in particular, to military activities. Modern military forces require a substantial period of time to formulate strategies and lurch into action – they are not a nimble instrument suitable to fickle employment so much as a ponderous bureaucracy capable of enormous undertakings and shocking levels of violent activity when necessary. Unfortunately, military forces in the Western democracies, and in particular the United States, have increasingly become the enforcement mechanism of choice for civilian leaders within the executive branch, causing them to perform functions for which they were never designed. This creates a dangerous situation in which the military, an organization specifically created to preserve the integrity of the nation and defend against its foes, might instead be morphing into a quasi-law enforcement organization that also provides emergency first-responder services. Such a shift places

124   *Paul Springer*

not only the constitutional liberties of the populace at risk, but also presents the very real threat that it will be incapable of effectively responding to truly existential threats, should they arise.

The oath of every American military officer clearly states that his or her allegiance is to the Constitution of the United States, and the republic it establishes, which must be defended against all enemies, foreign and domestic. The current oath came into being in 1959, although it does not markedly differ from versions of the oath that have been in existence for more than 200 years. The most notable change came in 1862, when officers stopped being asked to swear that they would obey all orders given them by the president. Of course, the oath does not cover every possible scenario that an officer might face, nor is it intended to do so. Rather, the personnel of the US military officer corps are expected to make reasoned, independent judgements about the nature of their service and, if given an unconstitutional order, to disobey. Very rarely have military commanders openly defied the authority of the president or other civilian leaders, and successfully bucking the chain of command has been rare in the extreme. Even when a military commander has had a legitimate reason to defy civilian authority, the consequences of doing so have typically been fatal to that officer's career.

In the twenty-first century, the US military will face increasing challenges associated with an increasingly dangerous world and reduced resources to combat the threats. The US Department of Defense's *Quadrennial Defense Review 2014* defined the military's key roles by stating that it 'prioritizes three strategic pillars: defending the homeland; building security globally by projecting US influence and deterring aggression; and remaining prepared to win decisively against any adversary should deterrence fail.' It also notes that the military must now accept 'the tough choices we are making in a period of fiscal austerity to maintain the world's finest fighting forces' (US Department of Defense 2014, i). In that regard, the *Review* reflects the statement of former Chairman of the Joint Chiefs Admiral Mike Mullen, who stated in 2011 'I've said many times that I believe the single, biggest threat to our national security is our debt, so I also believe we have every responsibility to help eliminate that threat' (Marshall 2011).

This chapter begins by establishing the historical roles of the military services in war and peace, and how the patterns of presidential behaviour have influenced the utility of the military for crisis response. It is important to note that wars do not inherently create a constitutional crisis, as the Constitution is relatively clear about the roles and responsibilities of the military and the president in wartime. This overview is not all-inclusive; rather, it attempts to demonstrate the wide variety of ways the president has chosen to employ the military to solve challenging problems, particularly in the domestic arena. A major theme that emerges in the domestic sphere is that the president will not tolerate direct challenges to federal authority, and uses the military to solve regional domestic problems as a very real reminder of the uncontested power of the federal government. Of late, the US government seems determined to remain in a crisis mode, perhaps due to the opportunities for action that a crisis often offers. However, the constant treatment of every challenge as a crisis creates a major stressor upon the civil–military relationship, and should be minimized whenever possible.

6.2 The military roles in war and peace

The military's role in wartime is relatively easy to discern. Simply stated, it is to fight and win the nation's wars, using any available tools within the parameters set by civilian authority and the laws of armed conflict (LOAC). The military does not choose which wars to fight, and has on occasion been ordered to engage in a conflict over the protests of senior uniformed commanders. Yet, according to Charles Stevenson,

> Civilian control is strong when the armed forces are engaged in major military operations. In war time, political leaders understand the stakes are high and they will be held accountable. The warriors accept their role and hope to be given clear and reasonable orders.
>
> (Stevenson 2006, 196)

A state of war carries with it very specific legal understandings – the allowable behaviour of belligerents has been codified over the centuries to create a substantial body of international law. One unresolved question, though, is whether the US military and the president have all of the constitutional privileges of wartime if a state of war has not been formally declared. There is an excellent reason for the Congressional prerogative to declare wars, and in large part to determine not just if they will be fought, but with what resources. James Madison summed up the importance of the Congressional role by stating:

> Those who are to *conduct a war* cannot in the nature of things, be proper or safe judges, whether *a war ought* to be *commenced, continued*, or *concluded.* They are barred from the latter functions by a great principle in free government, analogous to that which separates the sword from the purse, or the power of executing from the power of enacting laws.
>
> (Madison 1900–10, vol. 6, 148, emphasis original)

Madison, whose genius for managing the separation of governmental powers underpinned the entire Constitution, later held the presidency but refused to commit troops to war without Congressional permission and support in the face of British provocations.

If the presidency and Congress are in a state of competition regarding control over the military and the use of force, perhaps the nature of the conflict at hand is of paramount importance. In 1864, William Whiting noted that, although the Constitution cedes the responsibility for declaring war to Congress, such a declaration might be presumed to refer to war as an aggressor, including the deployment of troops beyond the nation's borders. Surely the founders did not intend for the president to sit idly by in the face of an invasion or insurrection,

126   *Paul Springer*

awaiting instructions from a Congress that might take months to return from a recess. Thus, a defensive war, marked by a rapidly developing emergency, would fall upon the president as commander-in-chief, who could respond as he saw fit to meet the crisis. A declaration of war, in comparison, might be reserved for times of more reasonable contemplation by the legislature (Whiting 1864, 38–40).

The military's traditional role in peacetime is far harder to pin down. Although the United States has never completely abolished its armed forces, prior to World War II the military tended to be a chronically underfunded, relatively tiny organization except during wars. A small professional officer corps, augmented by enlisted ranks whose numbers swelled during conflict periods, served to maintain the institutional memory and necessary expertise without bankrupting the nation. Even on the eve of American entry into World War I and II, the US Army was a ridiculously small force compared to both its peers and its impending opponents. The lone exception was the US Navy, which gradually grew to be one of the largest in the world by the end of World War I, and only increased its lead in that regard through World War II and beyond. Although the supposed primary role of the peacetime military is to maintain readiness for any potential conflict, in practice, the military has been used in a myriad of non-war activities while serving as the primary enforcement arm of the executive branch in all forms of domestic and international activities.

6.3 The presidency in wartime

Like the military, the president theoretically does not choose which wars to fight, so much as carry out the will of the people expressed through their representatives in Congress. In practice, the situation becomes a bit murkier. After all, the United States has not declared war for more than seven decades, even though it has fought in five major wars (Korea, Vietnam, Afghanistan and a pair of wars against Iraq) in the ensuing years, to say nothing of the dozens of smaller military engagements in the same time period. Thus, despite the lack of a formal declaration of war, it is clear that military force remains a major instrument of American power.[2] Some scholars consider all the undeclared wars of the postwar era as unconstitutional, largely on the grounds that Congress is either being cut out of its traditional role, or is abdicating responsibility for the decision about when and how the nation's military forces should be utilized (Griffin 2013, 11–17).

Other scholars argue that the modern world, where existential dangers threaten the nation as never before, absolutely requires a strong and decisive executive, even one who might be termed 'imperial' at times. To those authors, a slow decision-making process should not be considered a careful and deliberate approach, but rather an unnecessarily delayed and dangerous form of government (Posner and Vermeule 2010, 14–15). The modern world, it follows, presents challenges that call for a dynamic leader with the ability to quickly decide upon and enact policies for the defence of the nation and its interests. Such a decisive position, though, can create its own problems if there is no limit upon the presidential

The US military's role in national crises 127

power to respond to emergencies, particularly warfare. Perhaps Chris Edelson put the issue best:

> Emergency presidential power is not a new idea. However, the way in which it is used in the twenty-first century, especially in the context of the war on terror, presents new challenges. If, in the past, one way to limit presidential power was by publicly debating the justifications presidents gave for using emergency power, what happens when power is exercised in secret, with justifications initially provided only in classified memoranda? If one way to limit emergency power is to require that it be temporary, that it be used only for as long as a particular crisis demands, what happens when crisis is open ended, when Americans find themselves in a war against terrorism that has no clear end point?
>
> (Edelson 2013, 6)

Thus, if the existence of a state of war conveys extraordinary powers to the presidency, and a state of wartime can be permanently extended, the powers of the presidency become extremely difficult to curtail. Even the transition from one administration to another, including a shift of control from one party to another, has had little effect upon the willingness of the president to utilize and expand his control over military activities and the importance of those operations to the everyday function of American society. Also, presidential candidates make broad pronouncements about how they will serve as the commander-in-chief should they be elected to the highest office in the land, but when confronted with the full realities of the military and diplomatic situations the nation faces, it becomes much more difficult for a president to radically alter the policies of his predecessor.

A recent case involving the current president demonstrates the point at hand. When Barack Obama campaigned for the presidency in 2008, he made a series of campaign promises that he believed would restore the nation's trust in the military after the scandals following the Afghanistan and Iraq invasions, and build a better international relationship with Middle Eastern nations. In particular, he vowed to fight the wars in Afghanistan and Iraq in a significantly different fashion, especially as pertained to the perceived human rights abuses of his predecessor's administration. On only his second day in office, Obama issued an executive order that called for the closure of the military detention facility at Guantanamo Bay within one year. More than six years after that proclamation, the facility remains in operation, with over 120 enemy captives held within its walls. Further, Obama's announcement that he would place the Guantanamo detainees on trial in civilian courts met the harsh reality that those courts were not equipped to hear the cases with the necessary security apparatus to ensure the safety of the parties involved. The military tribunals that had been promised by President George W. Bush and decried by candidate Obama suddenly became a much more viable option (Kornblut and Finn 2010). Even the promise to give the detainees their day in a military court soon fell by the wayside, as it became evident that much of the evidence that could serve to convict the suspected terrorists had been obtained through covert methods and unsavoury interrogation techniques. Eventually, President Obama had to concede

128   *Paul Springer*

that the Al Qaeda captives at Guantanamo would remain in a form of legal limbo for the time being, as they could not be placed on trial but were far too dangerous to simply be released (Savage 2010).

6.4 The military during domestic crises[3]

The greatest opportunity for the American military to create an existential crisis for the fledgling nation came at the end of the Revolutionary War. George Washington's officers, exhausted by years of fighting and frustrated by broken Congressional promises, met at Newburgh, New York. There, an anonymous letter circulated, suggesting that perhaps the officers should march on Philadelphia and demand satisfaction of their fiduciary claims through force of arms. Washington soon disabused the malcontents of any notion that he would lead, or even condone, such an action. His speech to his veterans cemented the precedent that US military units would forever remain subordinate to their civilian leadership, even if those leaders proved duplicitous and self-interested. The precedent that Washington set held such force that Peter Feaver argues even today, 'Coups are *not* a particularly realistic possibility in this country. There has never been a serious coup attempt, let alone even a temporarily successful coup in the United States' (Feaver 2003, 11).

Despite the lack of the serious threat of a military coup, there were still plenty of challenges to government control in the early republic. Only three years after the Treaty of Paris recognized American independence, farmers in Massachusetts, many of them Revolutionary War veterans, rebelled against what they considered unfair taxation. Their leader, Daniel Shays, called for a march upon Boston and a forceful change of the state leadership. Shays' Rebellion, and the weak state response, demonstrated the need for a stronger central government, one that could maintain a monopoly upon the use of force. The crisis, and the lack of a credible military force to combat it, hastened the production and ratification of the US Constitution. In comparison, just two years after the Constitution went into effect, western Pennsylvania farmers rose in rebellion against the federal Whiskey Tax. President Washington called out the state militias of Maryland, New Jersey, Pennsylvania and Virginia, swore them into federal service, and marched at the head of this temporary army to put down the revolt. In the process, he solidified the assumption that the president, as commander-in-chief, might actually command the US military forces in battle if necessary (Yoo 2009, 68–71; Schaffter and Mathews 1956, 2). On only one other occasion has the US president ever led troops in the field, and the president in question, James Madison, was not a commander of Washington's stature and experience. His short field command during the War of 1812 turned a crisis into a catastrophe, leaving the public buildings of the nation's capital in flames and his army in a mixed state of desertion and mutiny. No subsequent president has taken the role of commander-in-chief in quite so literal a fashion. The more important precedent set by Washington, though, was a decisive use of force to quell any hint of rebellion, or even widespread resistance to federal supremacy. Perhaps such a demonstration was vital to the early republic,

The US military's role in national crises 129

given the new balance of power within the Constitution. However, many of Washington's successors have resorted to military force to solve domestic problems that presented far less danger to the government, the citizenry, or the constitutional system.

After Washington, the next president elected with a significant military background, Andrew Jackson, certainly had few compunctions about using military force to back his executive decisions. In 1832, Vice President John C. Calhoun, an ardent states' rights supporter, offered the legal theory that states had a right to nullify federal laws within the states. The notion that states might simply disregard federal laws certainly created a constitutional crisis, as it flew in the face of the Article Six of the Constitution, often referred to as the Supremacy Clause. In response to a new tariffs bill that established substantially higher taxes, the South Carolina legislature introduced a Nullification Bill that, essentially, rendered the federal tariffs invalid within the state. Jackson wasted no time in calling for Congressional approval to use force, if necessary, to collect the federal tariffs in South Carolina. In response to the mounting discontent, Congress passed a new tariff bill with lower taxes that South Carolina legislators considered acceptable, but at the same time, also approved a Force Bill authorizing the use of federalized militia to compel obedience with the law (Schaffter and Mathews 1956, 3). The Carolina rebels backed down long before any troops could be called up for service, defusing the crisis before it spiralled out of control. However, because no direct confrontation occurred, the issue was not decided so much as delayed, for at least a few decades. When the issue of federal and state competition returned in the 1850s, the Civil War soon followed to settle the concept once and for all.

Jackson is probably most remembered for his decision to forcibly evacuate the 'Five Civilized Tribes' of the southeastern United States, and to transplant them across the Mississippi River to modern-day Oklahoma. When members of the Cherokee, Chickasaw, Choctaw, Creek and Seminole nations refused to depart willingly, Jackson dispatched the US Army to enforce the decree. General-in-chief Winfield Scott personally led the effort, by which most of the tribal members were forced to depart their ancestral lands and move to a completely unknown region. Thousands died along the route, resulting in the horribly accurate title 'The Trail of Tears'. Despite the lack of any evidence that the Five Civilized Tribes represented even a potential threat, the Army acquiesced in this executive action, demonstrating its frequent role as the enforcement arm of the federal government (Remini 1984, vol. 3, 293–314).

As the nation expanded westward, the military's traditional role of defence grew to include frontier constabulary duties. Territory gained from the Mexican War massively expanded the area the Army was tasked to patrol, with almost no increase in the resources or manpower dedicated to the effort. It is little wonder, then, that the Army was completely incapable of responding effectively to the great crises of the 1850s, as the sectional debate over slavery neared an open breach between the North and South. Proponents of both the expansion and the abolition of slavery poured into the western territories and, on a number of occasions, came into open conflict with each other. The only force capable of maintaining order on

130   *Paul Springer*

the frontier, the Army, initially sought to remain neutral, but partisans within its leadership soon began using their commands to intervene on behalf of their preferred side. At best, military forces managed to keep the partisans from killing one another, although a series of raids and reprisals rocked the state of Kansas from 1854 until the outbreak of the Civil War.[4]

It is unsurprising that President Abraham Lincoln, confronted with the secession crisis of 1860–1, feared that he could not trust the Army's leaders to remain loyal, and hence he sought to form a volunteer army to put down the rebellion.[5] He also sought to force states to make their allegiances clear, by demanding that every state loyal to the Union contribute forces to ending the crisis. This provoked the fundamental constitutional crisis of the nation's history, over the question of a state's right to secede from the Union. The question could only be decided by force of arms and, in the four years of brutal conflict, many of the niceties of the republican governmental system were irrevocably changed. Lincoln made the unprecedented decision to suspend the writ of habeas corpus, essentially allowing the government to imprison anyone suspected of disloyalty without the oversight of the judicial branch. Yet, Lincoln is revered as one of the greatest presidents in the nation's history, perhaps in part because he quickly recognized the nature of the emergency and took steps to solve the problem. As Sotirios Barber and James Fleming described his decisions, 'Lincoln's actions were constitutionalist if not constitutional because he sought to restore the conditions of constitutional government' (Barber and Fleming 2005, 240). On the one hand, their explanation seems to be a whitewashing of history, almost going so far as to state that the ends justified the means of this blatantly unconstitutional act. On the other hand, as many scholars have pointed out, the Constitution cannot be expected to clearly lay out the correct action in every circumstance that the nation might face, and an activist executive will often act quickly upon a decision rather than seeking permission, on the grounds that the presidency inherently possesses very broad emergency powers.

In the aftermath of the conflict, it quickly became clear that while the Confederate means to offer military resistance had collapsed, the citizenry had little interest in quietly returning to the Union. Further, Lincoln's 1862 decision to emancipate the slaves of rebel-held territory, expanded by the 13th Amendment in 1865, guaranteed a major socioeconomic upheaval across Southern society. Only a military government might stabilize the situation long enough for tempers to cool, a new administrative organization to arise and the business of the region to resume. The 14th Amendment (1867) exacerbated the situation by extending citizenship, and thus property and voting rights, to freed slaves. It also disqualified former Confederates from holding office, essentially eliminating the entire state and local government bureaucracy, including the judiciary, in a single stroke.[6] Partisans throughout the South responded by sabotaging the railway systems, undermining both the Army's logistics and the states' finances. While this might seem counterproductive, it reduced the legitimacy of newly elected and Republican-controlled state legislatures (Bradley 2009, 178–9).

The federal government quickly moved to restore the economic function of the Southern communities. One of General Grant's first orders was for military forces to expedite cotton shipments along the railways, noting 'The finances of the country demand that all articles of export be gotten to market as speedily as possible' (Schofield 1897, 372–3). In part, this decision might help rebuild the war-torn economy of the South, but it also served to offset some of the costs of occupation. The federal government established military districts to provide security and ensure basic government functions across the former Confederacy. One of the district governors, Major General John Schofield, defended the concept by arguing for, 'Military governments, in the absence of popular civil governments, as being the only lawful substitute, under our system, for a government by the people during their temporary inability, for whatever cause, to govern themselves' (ibid., 376). Another of the district commanders, Major General Dan Sickles, essentially considered himself the dictator of North Carolina for two years, referring to the newly formed state legislature as merely a provisional institution (Bradley 2009, 137).

While the federal government sought to reassert control in the occupied South, it also faced enormous budgetary problems due to the war's cost, and even before formal Confederate resistance ceased, the War Department moved to disband military units, decommission naval ships and massively reduce the government's fiscal outlays. There was little backing for a massive occupation force in the South; instead, the bare minimum necessary to maintain order at polling locations and conduct occasional anti-guerrilla patrols was all that remained. In June of 1865, slightly over 200,000 Union troops stood on Southern soil. By the end of the year, the number was only 88,000, and it fell a further 50,000 troops only a year after Robert E. Lee's surrender. By October of 1866, only 18,000 Union troops remained on hand to control an area of nearly 800,000 square miles (Sefton 1967, 261–2). One of the most reviled men in the Southern occupation, General William T. Sherman, argued in 1865 that military force would constitute a poor means to change minds, and instead could only hope to preserve order and avoid the worst excesses. He noted:

> No matter what change we may desire in the feelings and thoughts of people South, we cannot accomplish it by force. Nor can we afford to maintain there an army large enough to hold them in subjugation. All we can, or should, attempt is to give them rope, to develop in an honest way if possible, preserving in reserve enough military power to check any excesses if they attempt any. But I know they will not attempt any, and you may look for outbreaks in Ohio quicker than in Georgia or Mississippi. You hardly yet realize how completely this country has been devastated, and how completely humbled the man of the South is.
>
> (Sherman 1894, 255–6)

Most historians have judged the Reconstruction of the South a general failure, with anti-equality Democratic Party control reverting to all of the former Confederate states by 1877. Nevertheless, the Army did the best job that might be expected under the circumstances, in large part because it remained content to

132   *Paul Springer*

administer and enforce federal policy, rather than trying to create it. The talent level of the occupation leadership remained remarkably high, with career soldiers shouldering almost the entire command burden of the task. Although the political and social norms of Southern society soon returned to their antebellum status, the Army did manage to minimize the chances of a lingering insurgency, and to create functional institutions to administer the region, all the while operating on a shoestring budget.

The Union's political leadership for Reconstruction changed repeatedly, with President Andrew Johnson essentially at war with Congressional leaders from his own party regarding Reconstruction policies. Johnson's successor, Ulysses S. Grant, certainly had enormous credibility and backing from the military, but he proved far less talented as a politician than as a general, and his administration was tainted by scandals and economic turmoil. The recession of 1873 made paying the occupation troops difficult and led to further reductions in troop strength throughout the former Confederacy. By 1874, only 7,000 occupation troops remained, half of them in Texas performing frontier duties. For all intents, the military pacification campaign had ended, though the last troops were not withdrawn until 1877.

One of the rare opportunities for the Army to use significant amounts of force came as a response to the growing white supremacist movement of the postwar era. Organizations across the South, most prominently the Ku Klux Klan (KKK), sought to intimidate and silence any opposition to white rule. They attacked freedmen's schools, assassinated black political leaders and attacked anyone they thought supported the notion of racial equality. While President Johnson deliberately ignored such activity, and took steps to prevent a substantive military response, President Grant saw the groups as a direct challenge to federal control. When these groups began attacking federal troops and officials, Grant asked Congress for a series of Enforcement Acts to declare strict martial law in places of insurrectionary activity. The KKK and other groups might have continued their tactics for decades, had they not directly challenged the US military and the government it represented. Instead, they invited open conflict with the Army and, within a year, the KKK had been effectively destroyed, as had many groups with a similar vision and ideology (Bradley 2009, 250–1).

One of the key issues of the Election of 1876 was the question of whether Reconstruction should continue. The contest eventually came down to disputed returns in Florida, Louisiana and South Carolina, three states still under a light military occupation. In each state, the returns favoured the Democratic candidate, Samuel Tilden, but allegations of fraud and threats against Republicans caused state election commissions to reverse each of the outcomes. A federal Election Commission eventually decided the issue along strict partisan lines, awarding all of the electoral votes in dispute, and the victory, to Rutherford B. Hayes. As the commission deliberated, President Grant quietly ordered troops to the capital to maintain order in the event of civil unrest. Hayes, a former brigadier general in the Union Army, reportedly promised to end the Reconstruction effort and withdraw the remaining occupying forces in exchange for the presidency, using the Army as a political pawn in the process.[7]

The US military's role in national crises 133

The military resumed its frontier duties in the three decades after the war, once again engaging in a series of conflicts with Native American tribes, many of which give modern scholars pause with respect to their legal and moral aspects. Yet, the Reconstruction era also gave rise to some key controlling mechanisms that limited the Army's role in both war and peace. In 1878, in response to many of the protests against the military's behaviour during Reconstruction, Congress passed the Posse Comitatus Act, which effectively prohibited the Army from acting in a law enforcement capacity. In theory, this law should have clearly defined the explicit limits between law enforcement and military activity (Sievert 2005, 20–2). In practice, the lines remained blurred, and a presidential declaration of crisis typically served to allow Army to engage in limited intervention in domestic affairs. For example, in 1894, President Cleveland dispatched more than 12,000 troops under Major General Nelson A. Miles to put down a railway workers' strike. Cleveland justified the action on the grounds that the strike had shut down the national transportation network and, with it, the delivery of US mail. In his view, this constituted an illegal rebellion against the function of the government. It probably concerned him a great deal more that many of the strikers espoused socialist and anarchist viewpoints, which he considered a dire threat to the safety of the republic, but he had a plausible enough reason to involve the Army. In 1902, President Theodore Roosevelt threatened to send Army soldiers to seize the coal fields of eastern Pennsylvania as an emergency measure to ensure the supply of anthracite coal for the winter. In the end, the threat did not need to be carried out, and perhaps the direct intervention of the president was all that was required to bring the crisis to a peaceful end. Nevertheless, the notion of using the Army in such a fashion produced a great many howls of protest from legal authorities, who pointed out that the president had no authority to order the Army to conduct such an operation. To Roosevelt, the fear of a coal famine, which might cause a humanitarian crisis in the northern cities if it persisted through the winter, far outweighed any constitutional crisis that might be presented by sending the Army to intervene in a labour dispute.

America, a latecomer to World War I who thus avoided most of its costs, emerged as an industrial powerhouse, possessing by far the largest economy in the world during the 1920s. However, when the Great Depression struck, it created an enormous financial crisis for the US government. A few years after the end of World War I, US veterans had been promised a cash bonus for their service, to be paid in 1945. With unemployment skyrocketing, many of the veterans dubbed themselves the 'Bonus Army' and began to demand immediate payment of the bonus. President Herbert Hoover refused to consider such an early payout, on the grounds that it would require substantial tax increases to fund such an expenditure. After a minor clash between police and the protesting veterans, Hoover ordered General Douglas MacArthur and the Army to remove the protestors from a shantytown they had constructed on the outskirts of the nation's capital. MacArthur ordered a regiment of infantry, backed up by tanks, to assault the protestors' shacks with bayonets and tear gas. Once they had been evicted, MacArthur ordered the buildings burned. Militarily, the operation was a success,

134   *Paul Springer*

but from a political standpoint, it was an utter disaster. A young baby died in the chaos, provoking a massive condemnation of Hoover, MacArthur and the entire Army. When the Army so visibly turned upon its own veterans, it signified the absolute enormity of the financial crisis at hand, and the massive effects the Depression could have upon the civil–military relationship.

As in the previous conflict, the US entered World War II later than most belligerents, and fought the war on foreign soil, using American industrial might as a key resource in the conflict. The United States emerged from the conflict as one of two victorious superpowers, cautiously eyeing its erstwhile ally, the Soviet Union, while struggling to gain worldwide economic and cultural hegemony. Although the US and USSR never engaged in open conflict, for nearly five decades, a Cold War between the rival nations overshadowed the international and domestic politics of both countries. In the United States, the Cold War led to an unprecedented peacetime buildup of military force, as well as the constant deployment of garrisons around the world to keep an eye on the Soviets. Essentially, the American government sought to remain on a wartime footing, ready for the expected showdown to commence at any moment. At the same time, significant domestic changes began to dominate American society. In particular, a burgeoning civil rights movement and a push for racial equality emerged in the postwar United States. The military soon became a locus of the movement, when President Harry S. Truman ordered the desegregation of the military in 1948 via Executive Order 9981. Through this action, the military became not just the enforcement mechanism for presidential policy, but also the experimental laboratory for social change.

In the Deep South, where segregation had been the norm since the end of Reconstruction, any push to enforce social change by the US government was almost guaranteed to trigger a backlash at the state level. Southern states ruthlessly enforced segregation rules, cloaked under the guise that segregated facilities and services were 'separate but equal'.[8] When the Supreme Court finally ruled in *Brown v. Board of Education of Topeka* (1954) that segregated public schools were inherently unequal, the stage was set for a major social crisis. President Dwight Eisenhower had little interest in the school desegregation effort, but he refused to allow Southern states to openly defy federal law and the Supreme Court's ruling. His effort to enlist the assistance of Southern law enforcement agencies, judicial systems and even elements of the National Guard within those states that most heavily practised segregation fell on deaf ears. As a result, Eisenhower decided to deploy elements of the 101st Airborne Division to enforce the Supreme Court ruling and escort African-American children to school in Little Rock, Arkansas. The sight of battle-hardened veterans of the Korean War, wearing US military uniforms and marching into an American public school, shocked the citizenry and drew massive amounts of opprobrium down upon Eisenhower's Administration. Eisenhower's personal popularity, as well as his military credibility as the former Supreme Allied Commander of World War II, helped him weather the controversy and enforce his position on the segregation issue. The use of troops, which could have easily escalated the crisis, instead served as a buffer

The US military's role in national crises 135

between the fighting sides, allowing a gradual relaxation of the tempers on each side of the crisis.

The military remained one of the most trusted and respected institutions in the United States throughout the 1950s, due in large part to the sheer number of veterans within the US population. During the 1960s, though, the perception of the military gradually shifted due to its involvement and behaviour in Vietnam. Not only did the public gradually begin to question the necessity of entering the Vietnam War, it also began to push back in reaction to images of atrocities and misbehaviours committed by American troops against Vietnamese civilians. As the popularity of the war declined, resistance to conscription for the war rose, particularly on college campuses. The growing rivalry between uniformed personnel and campus radicals came to a head on 4 May 1970, when members of the Ohio National Guard opened fire upon protestors marching at Kent State University. Four American youths died in the incident, and an iconic photo of a student crying over the body of a fallen comrade swept the nation. The perception of the military had reached its modern nadir, just as the situation in Vietnam began to collapse. Conditions of military service for the remainder of the 1970s were simply terrible, with enormous discipline problems, drug habits and extremely low pay for service members. Under Presidents Ronald Reagan and George H.W. Bush, the military slowly rebuilt its credibility through a series of small deployments, followed by the overwhelmingly successful Persian Gulf War. At the same time, the rewards for military service, and the resources devoted to its members, steadily grew.

In 1992, President William Clinton defeated Bush's re-election effort, despite his personal lack of a military background. According to some accounts, Clinton burned his Vietnam-era draft card, a fact that became a significant campaign issue for many voters. To offset his perceived weaknesses on military affairs, Clinton sought retired officers who would endorse his candidacy. In so doing, Clinton blatantly increased the growing politicization within the officer corps (Stevenson 2006, 212). He held a tumultuous professional relationship with service personnel during his presidency. Kurt Campbell and Michael O'Hanlon summed up his administration's civil–military partnership by stating 'During the Clinton admin- istration in particular, many Democrats seemed intimidated by the military brass' (Campbell and O'Hanlon 2006, 77). Clinton's election led many naysayers to predict that the military might openly defy his orders as commander-in-chief. This fear was exacerbated when Clinton's first initiative upon taking office was to consider the possibility of allowing homosexual service members to serve openly in uniform. After a lengthy public debate that, at times, turned ugly, the president backed down from issuing an executive order opening military service to gay and lesbian volunteers, and instead compromised on the completely unworkable and somewhat capricious 'Don't Ask, Don't Tell' policy. Under this system, recruiters and commanders could not enquire about a service member's sexuality. However, those uniformed members who were caught in any form of homosexual activity faced immediate dismissal via court-martial, including the loss of any accrued retirement benefits. The policy remained in place for two

136 *Paul Springer*

decades, infuriating partisans on both sides of the issue (Langston 2003, 1–2; Herspring 2005, 412–13). His very public need to back down in the face of military opposition to his policies set a precedent for his relationship with the military, leading Peter Feaver to pronounce 'It is hard to imagine a president with a weaker hand vis-à-vis the senior military leadership than President Clinton; that weakness translated into extremely low expectations of punishment and consequently, strong incentives for shirking' (Feaver 2003, 288). Given that enlisted personnel tend to take their cues from officers, when military leaders condemned the commander-in-chief, a general reduction of order and discipline permeated the entire force.

6.5 The military and modern crises

There are many different types of crisis that might confront the United States and for which the military might be proposed as a logical element of the national response. First and foremost, of course, is the possibility of a major war and, in such an event, the military is the obvious primary mechanism for the management of the crisis. While a traditional invasion of the continental United States is currently unlikely, that is no longer the sole, or even the most common, form of aggression between nation-states. Rather, in the twenty-first century, warfare is far more likely to involve sub-state groups, possibly on all sides of a conflict. The American military is well equipped and trained to engage in a conventional conflict, and has demonstrated its prowess in such operations for much of the post-Cold War period. It is the type of conflict most preferred by American strategists, who can focus upon the conquest of a well-defined geographic area, or the annihilation of a uniformed foe. At the same time, they can set clear delineations between enemy civilians and military forces. If the 1991 and 2003 invasions of Iraq proved anything, it was that the US military is unmatched in this type of conflict. Unfortunately, potential enemies and rivals internalized this lesson far better than did the US military and political leadership, both of which seemed to give little thought to the practical long-term ramifications of displaying such a powerful conventional warfighting dominance.

The September 11 attacks rocked the nation, and shocked the military from its general stupor towards non-state threats.[9] Not since the Pearl Harbor attacks had thousands of American citizens died on American soil. On 20 September 2001, President George W. Bush first used the term 'War on Terror' to explain the military's new and most pressing role in world affairs. Essentially, he wished to convey that the conflict was not simply the United States against Al Qaeda, but, rather, that the United States and its allies would consider any nation or group that utilized terrorism to be a dire enemy. It soon became evident that the United States was engaged in a new type of conflict, one that challenged not only military planners and operators, but also many of the underpinning assumptions about the use of military force, the relationship of civilian and military leaders and the nature of the US constitutional system. The enemy, far from agreeing to engage in a conventional fight with the American forces in-theatre, instead withdrew

The US military's role in national crises 137

from most engagements and splintered into regional affiliates that launched renewed terror campaigns in a myriad of locations. The invasion of Afghanistan eliminated one Al Qaeda sanctuary, but probably accelerated the franchising of the terrorist organization into other locations. American frustrations with the inability to bring the campaign in Afghanistan to a close led to a raft of poor decision-making regarding the treatment of enemies, particularly those captured in the conflict.

Within a few weeks of the initial engagement, the Bush Administration recognised that it did not have a satisfactory location to hold the most dangerous enemy combatants. Bringing them to the United States might raise constitutional issues, and the administration certainly did not wish to see them represented by lawyers in US courtrooms, particularly as it attempted to wring useful intelligence information out of them. Leaving them in the theatre of operations created a significant security problem, particularly when a series of mass escapes demonstrated the difficulty of keeping a close watch on a large enemy population under austere circumstances. The Bush Administration had little choice about getting quickly involved in the war in Afghanistan, but it gave little thought to how to handle captured enemies. It is possible that this important consideration simply fell by the wayside, or that most leaders assumed that Al Qaeda was comprised entirely of fanatics who would not consider surrendering. Nevertheless, within a few months, the United States possessed hundreds of prisoners and had little idea of where to put them. After a lengthy debate, a compound at Guantanamo Bay, Cuba, was determined to be the 'least worst place' for the prisoners (Greenberg 2009, 4–5). This location offered a secure facility far from the area of operations, and at the same time, completely divorced from any media scrutiny. Because it was outside of the United States, internees could not hope to claim any constitutional protections and, at the same time, they did not qualify for the protections of the Geneva Convention. Conditions at the compound were initially very rough, and the first images to emerge from the prison showed shackled and prostrate prisoners in stress positions, undergoing harsh interrogations and generally appearing to be mistreated by the government. When word of water-boarding began to slip out of the compound, human rights activists immediately protested that the government was engaged in torture. Intelligence agencies remained largely silent on the issue, although a number of officials speaking off the record suggested that the techniques were being used to prevent another major attack (Strasser 2004, 32–3; Danner 2004, 199–204; Greenberg and Dratel 2005, 1239).

While still engaged in Afghanistan, the administration began to build a case for engaging in a second war in Iraq. The initial attacks went well, with a small, highly mobile army quickly reaching Baghdad and toppling the Hussein regime. Unfortunately, the situation quickly soured, as Iraqi President Saddam Hussein evaded capture for nearly nine months and launched a massive insurgency against American occupation. Poor planning on the US side added fuel to the fire, as there was little advance thought given to how to handle thousands of Iraqi surrenders; an enormous number of the captives were thoughtlessly placed in the infamous Abu Ghraib prison compound. There, a minimal US guard staff subjected the

138 *Paul Springer*

prisoners to a wide variety of abuses, all captured in photographs and shared via the internet. As the horrors of Abu Ghraib became common knowledge, they also served as a massive recruitment tool for the Iraqi insurgency and a major stain on American honour. Further reports of prisoner abuse at the Guantanamo complex continued to surface, reinforcing the perception that the United States had lost its moral compass and was out of control in its desire for world domination. Not only were service personnel subjected to greater danger due to the failings at Abu Ghraib and Guantanamo, the abuses also caused a rift between the military and the broader American society in domestic politics. Yet, the military struggled to hold any senior personnel accountable for the abuses under their command, choosing only to prosecute the junior-most individuals involved in the controversies. Major General Antonio Taguba was assigned to investigate the abuses at Abu Ghraib, and called for the entire chain of command to be held accountable, including senior members of the Bush Administration. Instead, Taguba was forced to retire, almost certainly for levelling his criticisms at higher-ranking officers and administration officials (Hansen and Friedman 2009, 81; Hersh 2007).

6.6 The military's role in future crises

The military, as one of the most important institutions in American society, and one of the most capable organizations regarding emergency response and logistical operations, will naturally be a key aspect of any crisis response in the twenty-first century. This section addresses a number of potential crises that might confront the nation, and examines how the military might react to each situation. The five forms of crisis that are presented for examination are a presidential succession controversy; an environmental disaster requiring a much greater relief effort than civil authorities can provide; a domestic insurrection; a disease epidemic; and a fiscal meltdown. While historians are naturally hesitant to offer substantive predictions about future behaviour, in part out of the fear we might write our way out of a job, these scenarios are presented as ways to envision the likely roles played by the military during periods of domestic stress in the near future.

6.6.1 A succession crisis

One of the failures of the Constitution's original design was in addressing how to handle the death, disability, or criminal activity of a president. Although it is clear that if the president dies, the vice president should assume the office, it is not so obvious whether that individual should be considered president, or merely the acting president while a new election can be held. In the first few presidencies, the distinction was more than academic, given that the vice presidency was held by the runner-up in the presidential election. Thus, had President John Adams died in office, not only would the presidency have fallen to Thomas Jefferson, it also would have included a complete shift in the ruling party. The 12th Amendment addressed the issue by making the vice presidency a separately elected office, and did so before any presidents actually died in office.

The US military's role in national crises 139

The first president to do so, William Henry Harrison, had only been in place for a month when he died of pneumonia. His successor, Vice President John Tyler, chose to act in the full capacity of the presidency and made no effort to arrange for an out-of-cycle election. Congress acquiesced in this behaviour, and the nation's business continued without a hitch, albeit with a vacant vice presidency. By setting this precedent, though, Tyler made it extremely difficult for a vice president to temporarily assume the duties of the presidency, should that office-holder be incapacitated. When James Garfield was shot in 1881, he lingered for three months before succumbing to the wound. Although he was incapable of conducting the nation's business, there was no mechanism to turn the presidency over to Vice President Chester A. Arthur while Garfield still lived.

Most presidents are succeeded by the winner of a presidential election and, in most contests, there is a clear-cut victor. In 2000, a close-run presidential election ended in controversy. The electoral votes of Florida could not be immediately allocated to either Vice President Albert Gore or Governor George W. Bush, as there were irregularities in the paper ballot system that required a hand-recount of votes in several counties. Not content to simply await the outcome of the election, Bush sued Gore in a case that quickly rose to the Supreme Court, where it was decided along strict partisan lines, 5–4, awarding Bush the presidency. The decision came down before President Clinton was due to leave office, meaning that it did not necessarily rise to the level of constitutional crisis, but it certainly led to a great deal of discord within political circles.

To its credit, the military remained aloof from the machinations that went into deciding the outcome, but it is not difficult to envision a different outcome in a future contested election. Given the highly partisan nature of the current officer corps, it is plausible, albeit unlikely, that the military could refuse to accept the outcome of an election. Egypt offers a recent example of military intervention in the domestic civil affairs of a key US ally. In 2011, President Hosni Mubarak resigned from the presidency amid the turmoil of the Arab Spring uprisings, and transferred power to the Egyptian Armed Forces as the only institution in the nation that might maintain order. The military oversaw the establishment of elections, which resulted in Mohamed Morsi assuming the presidency on 30 June 2012. His administration lasted barely a year before he was removed by the military that had overseen his election; in 2015 he was convicted of ordering the torture and murder of political opponents (Wedeman *et al.* 2013; Robinson 2015). Brian Kalt argues that while the military choosing a president in the United States would be intolerable in peacetime, doing nothing during wartime would also be unacceptable. The worst response from the military, of course, would be a split along partisan divides, with the US armed forces essentially choosing both sides of the contest and setting the conditions for a second civil war (Kalt 2012, 164–72). A partisan military split of this nature might seem far-fetched, and yet the recent history of the world is filled with governments toppled and replaced by the military. In just the past two decades, direct military intervention in domestic politics has been integral to the creation of the current governments of Cambodia, the Democratic Republic of Congo, Egypt, Fiji, Mali, Mauritania, Myanmar, North Korea, Pakistan, Russia,

140 *Paul Springer*

Thailand and Yemen. Each of these interventions was, in part, triggered by internal crisis, including economic collapses. It is dangerous to assume that the United States is somehow immune to such an apparently common event.

A future election or secession crisis is not an impossibility. As states increasingly move towards voting mechanisms that are designed to make electoral participation as easy as possible for citizens, they show little evidence of maintaining an adequate security posture towards the sanctity of the vote. Online voting, which has been tried in a number of nations around the globe, has received little traction in the United States, largely due to fears of a cyber-attack that might disrupt the results, despite the number of voting irregularities that have been discovered over the history of American elections (Gross 2011). When the federal government tested a system to allow deployed military to vote electronically, it issued an open invitation to hackers to test the system's security. It took a group of University of Michigan graduate students less than two days to hack into the network and change the votes (Wheaton 2010). Given that the system was established to allow military voters to participate in elections, it is not hard to imagine that the military might be hesitant to accept the results of an election conducted via the internet. Further, unlike the old paper ballot system, there is no guaranteed mechanism for a recount in the event of a corrupted election. Should such a contested election occur during a larger crisis, the results might prove disastrous.

Likewise, a terror attack, or a strike from a peer competitor nation, could theoretically kill or incapacitate a substantial portion of the nation's leadership, particularly if it was launched during a State of the Union presidential address, or under similar circumstances in which the majority of the civilian leadership is gathered in a single location. Although the military is especially vigilant about any threats at such key times, no amount of security can guarantee that an attack will fail. As a matter of policy, a handful of representatives of each branch of government, including at least one Supreme Court justice, one cabinet member and a few members of the Senate and House of Representatives, are kept at alternate locations during these events. This precaution prevents the complete decapitation of the government in a single strike, but there is no guarantee that the military would be inclined to follow the orders of a presidential appointee, should the office of the presidency fall to a lower-ranking cabinet member with no military expertise.

6.6.2 An environmental crisis

The military has long played a role in domestic disaster relief, particularly in response to environmental catastrophes. While the Posse Comitatus Act generally prohibits the use of military forces in civilian law enforcement situations, there are exemptions to those regulations under dire emergencies. In particular, the Department of Defense (DOD) reserves the right to engage in:

> Actions that are taken under the inherent right of the US government, a sovereign national entity under the US Constitution, to ensure the preservation

The US military's role in national crises   141

of public order and to carry out governmental operations within its territorial limits, or otherwise in accordance with applicable law, by force, if necessary.
(US Department of Defense 1989, Encl. 4)

The DOD's position largely rests upon the provisions of the Robert T. Stafford Disaster Relief and Emergency Assistance Act, first passed in 1988 and substantially amended in 2000, 2006 and 2013. This act facilitated the ability of state and local authorities to request federal assistance in the event of a major disaster, to include both environmental and man-made events. As one of the largest and most logistically capable organizations, the military is naturally considered a significant resource in emergency situations, and may be tasked with: debris removal; search and rescue; medical care; supply of food and shelter; and supplying technical advice on disaster management and control. Interestingly, the military is still banned from directly providing law enforcement services except on a temporary basis, and is required to cede control back to civilian authorities at the earliest possible opportunity (Stafford 2013).

One of the most dangerous potential environmental disasters is presented by the nuclear power generating stations located across the United States. The reactors, which have all operated for three decades or longer, provide an important percentage of the nation's energy supply, but do so at the risk of a catastrophic failure. Although the United States has never had a complete reactor meltdown, two cases from other nuclear powers are illustrative of the risks. In 1986, a reactor at the Ukrainian Chernobyl plant exploded, flinging radioactive debris into the environment. Dozens of first-responders died in the initial attempts to battle the fire. Eventually, a 20-mile exclusion zone had to be declared around the plant, requiring the evacuation of 350,000 residents. International efforts are still being launched in the hopes of containing the remaining radioactive material, which continues to leach into the surrounding environment. In 2011, the Fukushima Daiichi nuclear power plant was hit by a tsunami, rupturing the reactor and releasing a massive amount of radioactive material; 300,000 Japanese civilians had to be temporarily evacuated from the region and the cleanup is expected to require decades. In both cases, as would be the case in a potential nuclear disaster in the United States, the military supplied much of the expertise regarding nuclear technology. In particular, the US Navy, which has more practical experience with nuclear reactor designs and operations than any other agency in the United States, would be invaluable in a nuclear catastrophe. The US military actually supplied robots to move into the Fukushima reactor and examine the damage, sparing the risks to human first-responders (McPherson 2011).

6.6.3 An insurrection crisis

Although a foreign invasion might not be highly likely, a domestic insurgency is an entirely possible scenario. Insurgencies require several elements to maximize their chances of success. First and foremost is an identifiable cause that can draw enough adherents to make the insurgency viable. There are a number of such

142 *Paul Springer*

causes within the United States that give the federal government cause for concern. Each year, the Federal Bureau of Investigation reports on the possibilities of a domestic insurrection, and lists the types of groups most likely to create such a campaign. In 2002, just five months after the September 11 terror attacks, Dale L. Watson, one of the top counterterrorism officials in the FBI, reported to Congress:

> Domestic right-wing terrorist groups often adhere to the principles of racial supremacy and embrace antigovernment, antiregulatory beliefs ... The second category of domestic terrorists, left-wing groups, generally profess a revolutionary socialist doctrine and view themselves as protectors of the people against the 'dehumanizing effects' of capitalism and imperialism.
>
> (Watson 2002)

Although insurrection is not chief among the worries of the US government, it does present one potential constitutional crisis in which the military's proper response has already been established. In 1807, Congress passed the Insurrection Act, a set of laws that specifically authorized the president to deploy troops in domestic areas to combat rebellion and general lawlessness. For nearly 200 years, the law remained in force, unchanged and largely unused, although it was occasionally cited as justification for minor uses of troops. The most prominent exception was putting down the Southern rebellion against federal authority in 1861. Under the Insurrection Act, the president can employ active duty, reserve and National Guard units in federal service to restore law and order under extreme circumstances. The most common cause of such deployments since 1945 has come from urban rioting. In 1965, race riots in the Watts district of Los Angeles triggered the activation of troops from the California National Guard. Similar riots in Detroit two years later also provoked a federal troop deployment. During the aftermath of the 1992 Rodney King verdict, riots erupted throughout Los Angeles. Governor Pete Wilson, realizing that the local authorities could not control the situation, requested federal assistance, and soon more than 13,000 soldiers from the 7th and 40th Infantry Divisions and the 1st Marine Division began to patrol the streets of Los Angeles (Globalsecurity.org 2011; Jones 2011).

For a brief period from 2006–8, it became far easier for the president to invoke the provisions of the Insurrection Act. The 2007 Defense Authorization Bill included substantial revisions to the Insurrection Act, allowing the president to call out military forces to restore order in cases of natural disasters, epidemics and terrorist attacks. By broadening the Insurrection Act to include these categories, the law essentially weakened the Posse Comitatus Act, a move that incited a number of conspiracy theorists to pronounce a federal plan to institute martial law. However, the relaxed wording was repealed in 2008, reverting the law back to the 1807 verbiage. When protestors against income inequality began to gather in New York's Zuccotti Park, a national movement entitled 'Occupy Wall Street' quickly spread to other locales. State and national authorities carefully monitored the situation and, although, in the end, they did not call for any military assistance in responding to the generally peaceful protests, allegations of federal coordination of

The US military's role in national crises   143

the efforts to undermine the protests soon emerged (Wolf 2012; Moynihan 2014). Should any future protest movement of this type erupt, particularly if its organizers call for acts of violence, it is entirely likely that the military would be called upon to supply personnel and equipment for restoring order.

6.6.4 An epidemic crisis

Given that the military has in some ways been transformed into the president's organization of choice for solving both domestic and global problems, perhaps it is unsurprising that President Obama ordered the deployment of up to 3,500 American military personnel to the West Africa nations of Liberia and Senegal to help provide security for health care workers combatting the spread of the Ebola virus. These troops, almost none of whom were trained medical personnel, theoretically could help to contain the spread of the deadly disease in the hope of preventing a massive outbreak in the United States. They were designated to supervise the construction of Ebola treatment units, operate a staff training course in the region to teach health care workers how to prevent the transmission of the disease, and distribute supplies to the stricken region (White House 2014). This venture evokes comparisons to the Somalia deployment of 1992–3, and demonstrates the myriad of ways in which the president can utilize the military as a primary response to crises, even those that have not yet had a direct effect upon the homeland. The military role in future pandemics will largely depend upon how the current Ebola crisis response fares, as any contamination of American service personnel with Ebola might curtail future deployments for similar purposes. If the international efforts to halt the spread of Ebola succeed, though, particularly if they manage to maintain domestic order in the affected nations at the same time, it is entirely likely that the military will be called upon for similar activities in the future. Should a pandemic reach American shores, it is likely to quickly overwhelm the ability of local and even state authorities to maintain order, making it almost a certainty that military forces will be called upon for domestic service.

6.6.5 A fiscal crisis

A fiscal meltdown would create an enormous set of obstacles for the US government as a whole and, in particular, for the US military. In 2013, austerity measures referred to as 'sequestration' called for a mandatory cut of government spending, half of which was taken out of the military budget. Although it amounted to only a 10 per cent reduction in military finances, the lack of advanced warning meant that a heavy burden of the cuts fell upon the personnel working for the military, with a corresponding drop in morale. The military's response to sequestration was not to simply grin and bear it, but rather to make the cuts as visible and painful as possible, essentially engaging in a domestic political struggle to rally public support for the military over other spending priorities. No major weapons systems acquisition programmes were eliminated; instead, the majority of cost reductions

144 *Paul Springer*

came from personnel systems, including a system of unpaid furloughs for DOD employees.

Given that approximately half of all global military spending is done by the United States, there is certainly a case to be made for reducing the size of the US military budget. However, that reduction should be done through deliberate, well-planned action rather than drastic slashes across the entire budget. Further, those reductions should also have a corresponding understanding that the military will not be able to perform all of the same functions that it has been asked to undertake in the recent past. With the sequestration plan in place, if a massive depression struck the United States, the government might find itself unable to pay its bills, including those associated with the military. Likewise, if the US debt limit is reached without some mechanism to keep the government solvent, the paycheques of military personnel could be halted. On previous occasions when this was a possibility, the personnel were informed that they should continue to perform their duties, including those in war zones, even if they might never be repaid for the time served. Such a solution is untenable even in the short-term, and is likely to create increased friction between the military and the society it serves if they become a regular occurrence.

The massive increase in the US defence budget since 1945 is largely tied to the approach the Department of Defense has adopted for conducting warfare on behalf of the nation. It rests upon a few fundamental assumptions. The first, and most important, is that the nation's wars should be conducted as far from the national soil as possible. The contiguous United States have not seen a substantial amount of military conflict for more than a century, even though American troops have been deployed to engage in dozens of conflicts around the globe. The US military chose, in the Cold War era, to place a premium upon the quality of technology, equipment and training of its personnel, rather than relying upon a large quantity of troops. Although this reduced the size of the military as a whole, it also meant that each individual unit would be substantially more expensive, as each soldier might be needed to have the combat efficiency of several soldiers from an enemy's force. Finally, in 1973 the US military embraced the notion that it should be composed entirely of volunteers. Although this certainly reduced any social tensions created by a draft, it also made the fiscal costs associated with recruiting and retaining personnel quickly rise, particularly in periods of economic health when potential recruits have more options. There has also been an unintended effect, in that the military bears less resemblance to the society that it represents than had previously been the case. The officer corps is overwhelmingly drawn from the middle class, while the enlisted ranks are primarily the product of lower-income households. The military has a higher percentage of rural recruits than the population as a whole, and a much higher percentage of service personnel are drawn from the South than from other regions. This lack of a resemblance may, in time, cause greater friction between uniformed service members and civilians, particularly if the budgetary battles increase (Dempsey 2010, 187–9). While the different backgrounds of officers and enlisted personnel might appear to be a source of friction, the upward mobility of enlisted personnel

The US military's role in national crises 145

into the officer ranks, as well as the strong emphasis upon discipline and team-building, tends to reinforce the notion of a monolithic entity united to face all challengers.

Of course, a general fiscal crisis creates all kinds of tension within the nation, not solely within the government and military sectors. The incidence rate of property crime tends to rise in direct relation to rising unemployment, and if state and local governments are forced to reduce the size of their law enforcement expenditures, it is entirely plausible that the military might be called upon to fill some of the gaps that it can legally fill under Posse Comitatus. In particular, National Guard units might be called upon by the state governors to serve an auxiliary police function. Naturally, that would reduce the availability of military units for any form of overseas activities, which, in turn, creates a trickle-down effect of a gradual withdrawal from international interventions. As the 2014 *Quadrennial Defense Review* stated:

> Under continued sequestration-level cuts, the Department would maintain its priority focus on homeland defense – albeit at heightened risk. Decreased levels of readiness and capacity would challenge the Department's ability to maintain air, missile, and maritime defenses over time, particularly if we faced a large-scale conflict overseas, while also negatively affecting our ability to support domestic homeland security agencies and catastrophic disaster response support to civil authorities.
>
> (US Department of Defense 2014, 54)

Although some might consider such a reduction of deployments a positive development that might raise the general perception of the United States in the world, it would also come into conflict with the DOD's assumptions about modern conflicts and, theoretically, put the homeland at greater risk of attack by sub-state actors, particularly terrorist organizations. Also, this emphasis upon the fiscal problems of the United States offers credence to the idea that attacks targeting the financial health of the nation might prove the most effective means to undermine American military dominance.

6.7 Conclusion

Over its nearly 250-year history, the United States has continually relied upon its military forces as an effective means to counter the negative effects of a wide variety of crises. Although the military's fundamental purpose is to fight and win the nation's wars, there is no reason to believe that it will not continue to have a secondary function as an emergency services provider and a stable influence upon society in periods of crisis. In many ways, this serves both the military and society exceedingly well. The military, which for several decades has been the most trusted institution of the federal government, is able to regularly demonstrate its continuing value to the nation, and hence to justify its admittedly enormous annual budget (Gallup 2014).

146   *Paul Springer*

US society naturally benefits by knowing there is a large and extremely capable organization that has repeatedly proven its willingness and ability to serve the nation through periods of crisis during both war and peace. As long as the military continues to reflect the society that produces and supports it, and avoids becoming an overtly politicized organization, this symbiotic relationship is likely to function as a stabilizing force in curtailing the future constitutional crises that may confront the republic. If, however, one side or the other should feel betrayed in the relationship, the US military, like every democratic nation's armed forces, contains within it the ability to trigger a major crisis that could shake the very foundations of the republic. Thus, it is in the best interests of both the military and American society as a whole to maintain a close vigilance over the ways and means by which the military is asked and allowed to assist with crisis responses, and to remain aware of the military's fundamental role of conducting violent operations in the nation's defence.

Notes

1 The Civil War, which lasted from 1861–5, included 600,000 dead from the combined Union and Confederate Armies. US involvement in World War II, from 1941–5, resulted in 400,000 US dead.

2 Despite the lack of a declaration of war against an enemy nation, presidents have felt little compunction about declaring war upon a variety of 'opponents', none of them military in nature. For example, President Lyndon B. Johnson declared a 'War on Poverty' during his 1964 state of the union address, despite the confusion as to what military action might be undertaken to destroy poverty. Ronald Reagan's 'War on Drugs' presented at least the possibility of targeting international narcotics traffickers and their state sponsors, which led to US military action in a number of locations, including the 1989 invasion of Panama under Reagan's successor, George H.W. Bush. In 2001, George W. Bush declared a 'War on Terror', suggesting that the military might attack any enemy that engaged in a specific activity, terrorism, but actually signifying a decision to attack Al Qaeda. Conveniently, Al Qaeda's leader, Osama bin Laden, had declared war against the United States in 1996, offering a certain symmetry to the Bush declaration.

3 For the purpose of this discussion, 'peacetime' will be considered to include any period prior to World War II when the United States was not involved in a declared war, and any time after World War II that did not involve the engagement of substantial numbers of American combat troops. Thus, the Korean War, Vietnam War, Persian Gulf War and the invasions of Afghanistan (2001) and Iraq (2003) will be considered wartime, despite the obvious attempts of the government not to place American society and industry on a wartime footing.

4 One of the worst incidents came on 21 May 1856, when a pro-slavery posse attacked the abolitionist presses in Lawrence, destroying dozens of private properties. Just three days later, John Brown and a handful of fervent abolitionists attacked the homesteads of pro-slavery activists, hacking five to death with broadswords. Shortly after the killings, Brown and his sons left Kansas, evading the federal troops searching for them, and fled into the shelter of abolitionists in New England. Brown later re-emerged to attack the federal arsenal in the hopes of inciting and arming a general slave uprising, but was defeated by a party of US Marines and elements of the Virginia militia, all under the command of Robert E. Lee.

5 Lincoln was right to be nervous, as nearly half of the regular Army officers resigned their commission to fight for the Confederacy, including a particularly large percentage of the highest-ranking officers. His first choice to lead the force destined to put down

The US military's role in national crises 147

the rebellion was none other than Robert E. Lee, who declined the position upon the secession of his home state of Virginia on 17 April 1861.

6 A similar move in the 2003 occupation of Iraq, dubbed 'debaathification', put hundreds of thousands of Iraqi government employees out of work, including virtually the entire Iraqi military, creating an enormous recruiting pool for the burgeoning insurgency.

7 From the election of Ulysses S. Grant in 1868 until the death of William McKinley in 1901, every president but Grover Cleveland was a veteran of the Union Army. For nearly four decades, the status of Union veteran was almost as strong a prerequisite for the office as being an American citizen. Virtually all of the presidents in question managed to fairly high rank, with most wearing a general's stars by 1865. At one point, one future president commanded another, with Private William McKinley taking orders from Major Rutherford B. Hayes. Not surprisingly, there are a large number of monuments to the heroism of future presidents sprinkled throughout the National Park System's Civil War battlefields. Visitors to Antietam National Historic Site might notice an enormous monument to McKinley's service in the battle. Among his acts of valour during the battle was the heroic delivery of hot coffee and doughnuts to the Union troops engaged above Burnside's Bridge. The only Democrat elected in this period was Grover Cleveland, who had paid a substitute to assume his position in the Union ranks. This might account for the origins of a prevailing notion in the twentieth century that Republican presidents are inherently stronger in military and foreign affairs than their Democratic counterparts.

8 The wording refers to the Supreme Court ruling in *Plessy v. Ferguson*, which found that segregation was permissible so long as there was no discernible difference in the quality of services or opportunities being offered. Needless to say, in the Southern states in particular, there was a very broad interpretation of the term 'equal', but no dissembling whatsoever on the concept of 'separate'.

9 Most citizens had never heard of Al Qaeda, despite its attempt to destroy the World Trade Center in 1993 and its leader's declaration of war against America and the west in 1996. Clinton, of course, was privy to the latest intelligence reports on the growing danger of the group, and, in 1998, rescinded portions of the series of executive orders banning assassinations, essentially declaring open season on the leaders of terror organizations that targeted the United States.

References

Barber, Sortirios A., and James E. Fleming. 'War, Crisis, and the Constitution'. In Mark Tushnet, ed., *The Constitution in Wartime: Beyond Alarmism and Complacency*. Durham, NC: Duke University Press, 2005, pp. 232–48.

Bradley, Mark K. *Blue Coats and Tar Heels: Soldiers and Civilians in Reconstruction North Carolina*. Lexington: University Press of Kentucky, 2009.

Campbell, Kurt M., and Michael E. O'Hanlon. *Hard Power: The New Politics of National Security*. New York: Basic Books, 2006.

Danner, Mark, ed. *Torture and Truth: America, Abu Ghraib, and the War on Terror*. New York: New York Review of Books, 2004.

Dempsey, Jason K. *Our Army: Soldiers, Politics, and American Civil-Military Relations*. Princeton, NJ: Princeton University Press, 2010.

Edelson, Chris. *Emergency Presidential Power: From the Drafting of the Constitution to the War on Terror*. Madison: University of Wisconsin Press, 2013.

Egerton, Douglas R. *The Wars of Reconstruction: The Brief, Violent History of America's Most Progressive Era*. New York: Bloomsbury Press, 2014.

Feaver, Peter D. *Armed Servants: Agency, Oversight, and Civil–Military Relations*. Cambridge, MA: Harvard University Press, 2003.

148   *Paul Springer*

Gallup. 'Confidence in Institutions'. *In Depth: Topics A to Z.* 2014. http://www.gallup.com/poll/1597/confidence-institutions.aspx

Gardner, Lloyd C. *Killing Machine: The American Presidency in the Age of Drone Warfare.* New York: The New Press, 2013.

Globalsecurity.org. 'Operation Garden Plot: JTF-LA Joint Task Force Los Angeles'. *Military.* 2011. http://www.globalsecurity.org/military/ops/jtf-la.htm

Greenberg, Karen. *The Least Worst Place: Guantanamo's First 100 Days.* Oxford: Oxford University Press, 2009.

Greenberg, Karen J., and Joshua L. Dratel, eds. *The Torture Papers: The Road to Abu Ghraib.* Cambridge, UK: Cambridge University Press, 2005.

Griffin, Stephen M. *Long Wars and the Constitution.* Cambridge, MA: Harvard University Press, 2013.

Gross, Doug. 'Why Can't Americans Vote Online?' *CNN,* 8 November 2011. http://www.cnn.com/2011/11/08/tech/web/online-voting

Hansen, Victor M., and Lawrence Friedman. *The Case for Congress: Separation of Powers and the War on Terror.* Surrey, UK: Ashgate, 2009.

Hersh, Seymour M. 'The General's Report'. *The New Yorker,* 25 June 2007. http://www.newyorker.com/magazine/2007/06/25/the-generals-report

Herspring, Dale R. *The Pentagon and the Presidency: Civil–Military Relations from FDR to George W. Bush.* Lawrence: University Press of Kansas, 2005.

Jones, Nate. '"Garden Plot:" The Army's Emergency Plan to Restore "Law and Order" to America'. *NSA Archive,* 12 August 2011. https://nsarchive.wordpress.com/2011/08/12/document-friday-garden-plot-the-armys-emergency-plan-to-restore-law-and-order-to-america

Kalt, Brian C. *Constitutional Cliffhangers: A Legal Guide for Presidents and Their Enemies.* New Haven: Yale University Press, 2012.

Kornblut, Anne E., and Peter Finn. 'Obama Advisers Set to Recommend Military Tribunals for Alleged 9/11 Plotters'. *Washington Post,* 5 March 2010. http://www.washingtonpost.com/wp-dyn/content/article/2010/03/04/AR2010030405209.html

Langston, Thomas S. *Uneasy Balance: Civil–Military Relations in Peacetime America since 1783.* Baltimore: Johns Hopkins University Press, 2003.

Madison, James. *The Writings of James Madison,* ed. Gaillard Hunt. New York: G.P. Putnam's Sons, 1900–10.

Marshall, Tyrone C., Jr. 'Debt is Biggest Threat to National Security, Chairman Says'. *DoD News,* 22 September 2011. http://archive.defense.gov/news/newsarticle.aspx?id=65432

McPherson, Stephanie M. 'How Battle-Tested Robots Are Helping Out at Fukushima'. *Popular Mechanics,* 18 April 2011. http://www.popularmechanics.com/military/a6656/how-battle-tested-robots-are-helping-out-at-fukushima-5586925

Moynihan, Colin. 'Officials Cast Wide Net in Monitoring Occupy Protests'. *The New York Times,* 22 May 2014. http://www.nytimes.com/2014/05/23/us/officials-cast-wide-net-in-monitoring-occupy-protests.html

Posner, Eric A., and Adrian Vermeule. *The Executive Unbound: After the Madisonian Republic.* Oxford: Oxford University Press, 2010.

Remini, Robert V. *Andrew Jackson,* 3 vols. New York: Harper & Row, 1984.

Robinson, Julian. 'Egypt's Former President Mohammed Morsi is Sentenced to 20 Years for Ordering the Arrest and Torture of Protestors in 2012'. *Daily Mail* (London), 21 April 2015. http://www.dailymail.co.uk/news/article-3048223/Egypts-Morsi-faces-likely-death-penalty-verdict.html

The US military's role in national crises   149

Savage, Charlie. 'Detainees Will Still Be Held, but Not Tried, Official Says'. *The New York Times*, 22 January 2010. http://www.nytimes.com/2010/01/22/us/22gitmo.html

Schaffter, Dorothy, and Dorothy M. Mathews. *The Powers of the President as Commander in Chief of the Army and Navy of the United States*. Washington, DC: Government Printing Office. 84th Congress, 2nd Session, H. Doc. 443, 1956.

Schofield, John M. *Forty-Six Years in the Army*. New York: The Century Company, 1897.

Sefton, James E. *The United States Army and Reconstruction, 1865–1877*. Baton Rouge: Louisiana State University Press, 1967.

Sherman, William T. *The Sherman Letters*, ed. Rachel Sherman Thorndike. New York: Charles Scribner's Sons, 1894.

Sievert, Ronald J. *Defense, Liberty, and the Constitution: Exploring the Critical National Security Issues of Our Time*. Getzville, NY: William S. Hein, 2005.

Stafford, Robert T. *The Stafford Act: The Robert T. Stafford Disaster Relief and Emergency Assistance Act of 2013*. US Code 42 (2013), § § 5121 et seq. http://www.fema.gov/media-library-data/1383153669955-21f970b19e8eaa67087b7da9f4af706e/stafford_act_booklet_042213_508e.pdf

Stevenson, Charles A. *Warriors and Politicians: US Civil–Military Relations under Stress*. New York: Routledge, 2006.

Strasser, Steven, ed. *The Abu Ghraib Investigations: The Official Reports of the Independent Panel and the Pentagon on the Shocking Prisoner Abuse in Iraq*. New York: Public Affairs, 2004.

US Department of Defense. 'Department of Defense Cooperation with Civilian Law Enforcement Officials'. Directive 5525.5. 1989.

US Department of Defense. *Quadrennial Defense Review 2014*. 2014. http://archive.defense.gov/pubs/2014_Quadrennial_Defense_Review.pdf

Watson, Dale L. 'Testimony before the Senate Select Committee on Intelligence'. Washington, DC, 6 February 2002. https://www.fbi.gov/news/testimony/the-terrorist-threat-confronting-the-united-states

Wedeman, Ben, Reza Sayah and Matt Smith. 'Coup Topples Egypt's Morsy; Deposed President Under "House Arrest".' *CNN*, 4 July 2013. http://edition.cnn.com/2013/07/03/world/meast/egypt-protests

Wheaton, Sarah. 'Voting Test Falls Victim to Hackers'. *The New York Times*, 8 October 2010. http://www.nytimes.com/2010/10/09/us/politics/09vote.html

White House. 'Fact Sheet: The US Response to the Ebola Epidemic in West Africa'. 6 October 2014. https://www.whitehouse.gov/the-press-office/2014/10/06/fact-sheet-us-response-ebola-epidemic-west-africa

Whiting, William. *War Powers under the Constitution of the United States*. 10th edn. New York: Little, Brown & Company, 1864.

Wolf, Naomi. 'Revealed: How the FBI Coordinated the Crackdown on Occupy'. *Guardian* (London), 29 December 2012. http://www.theguardian.com/commentisfree/2012/dec/29/fbi-coordinated-crackdown-occupy

Yoo, John. *Crisis and Command: A History of Executive Power from George Washington to George W. Bush*. New York: Kaplan, 2009.

7 The dark side of modernity
Existential threats to life as we know it

Tevi Troy

7.1 Introduction

Presidents and top government officials plan for a wide variety of possible disasters, but rarely contemplate the possibility of a complete collapse of the US government. It is true that the US government has some continuity of government protocols, but it is not clear how or whether they would be adhered to if things became so bad that they necessitated the use of such protocols. If such a systemic disaster were ever to take place, the immediate and longer-term responses by America's leadership class would have profound implications both for the entire US citizenry and the prospect of human freedom worldwide. While this type of collapse may not be a likely scenario, it would be so devastating that it requires at least some serious thought and planning.

There are a number of ways in which this could happen. External, 'black swan'-type events could, of course, take policy-makers and citizens by surprise; by definition, they would come without warning. But, whatever happens, the most likely source of such an event – as well as an inevitable consequence – would be an economic collapse. An economic collapse would not only devastate our country and our way life, but could also lead to some of the second-order effects discussed in this chapter, such as a collapse of our electronic systems, or a pandemic that spiralled out of control, without any governmental bodies able to hold it in check.

In addition, these other effects, such as a mass pandemic or a grid collapse, would themselves almost certainly lead to an economic collapse. The inextricable linkage of an economic collapse to other sorts of disasters makes coping with such an event a necessary part of disaster planning. Whatever happens in the disaster world is sure to have significant economic implications, which means that policy-makers need to see an economic response as an integrated element of any kind of crisis preparation. The engine that makes the US run is its strong economy. Without it, we begin to face dangers to all aspects of our way of life.

This chapter will examine US thinking on the problem of systemic economic collapse, and make recommendations to policy planners for how to prevent some of the gravest dangers – whatever the cause – and how to prepare should the worst happen.

7.2 Economic collapse

One thing that connects every American to one another is the US economy. You can be a banker in New York or a farmer in Nebraska – the state of the US economy will have a tangible impact on you and your well-being. This interconnected and well-integrated US economic system is, and has long been, the envy of the world. For generations, it has contributed to bringing millions of people out of poverty, not just in America, but around the world. This success makes many people around the world dependent on the vitality of the US economic engine. As the saying goes, America sneezes and the world catches a cold.

For the most part, the primacy of the US economy has been a good thing, for Americans and for the world alike. For the past two centuries, the spread of working market economies has generated untold wealth and brought up living standards for hundreds of millions of the people. In the period following World War II, US leadership and innovation has improved the destiny of billions of people all the way into the twenty-first century.

It is important to recognize just how significant and far-reaching the increase in economic opportunity and living standards has been. The development of free markets and the rule of law, especially in Western countries and the freer parts of Asia, has reshaped international relations and the prospects of peace. Largely as a result of economic and technological improvements, the millennia-long quest for food and water is no longer a daily and life-threatening challenge in the modern world. One of the primary reasons for the lifting of that burden is the development of modern economic systems that allow for civilization-changing improvements in the production and distribution of food. Food is apparently so little of a concern in the US these days that the US throws away about 141 trillion calories annually, about 1,249 calories per person per day. This is the equivalent of $161.6 billion worth of food, about 31 per cent of our overall food supply (Barclay 2014). This abundance (and waste), combined with the fact that Americans spend only about a tenth of their incomes on food, is mind-boggling (Sturm and An 2014). Even more extraordinary is that the vast majority of Americans do almost nothing when it comes to the production of that food, freeing people to pursue other opportunities and develop new ideas and innovations (American Farm Bureau Federation 2015).

The apparent end of the quest for food, however, is only one component of the free market revolution. The development of comfortable living quarters, sanitation systems, hospitals, safe transportation and extensive trade means that the lifestyles of the average American are far more comfortable than even members of the royalty from previous eras. In twenty-first-century America, for example, 99.7 per cent of poor households have a refrigerator, 97.9 per cent have a TV, 95.2 per cent have a stove and oven and 74.7 per cent have air conditioning. And these figures are for Americans at the lowest end of the economic scale. For average Americans, the numbers are even higher, although it is difficult to get higher than figures like 99.7 per cent (US Energy Information Administration 2005). The flip side of having these modern conveniences, however, is that we have become utterly dependent on them.

152   *Tevi Troy*

Free markets and the rule of law enable the human innovation and investment that create these material blessings and put them in the hands of more and more citizens. It is no exaggeration to say that the story of the post-war era in America has, for the most part, been consistent periods of growth punctuated by brief recessions that bring increasing waves of opportunity and comfort. The most significant recent break in this cycle was the housing collapse and recession of 2008. Before that, there appears to have been a far-reaching trust that policy-makers either knew how to create fairly regular economic growth, or knew enough to get out of the way enough to let economic growth take place. Either way, growth was the key. Growth rates of 3–5 per cent kept the US population largely well off – recognizing, of course, certain large and inexcusable pockets of poverty – kept the US military well equipped and allowed policy-makers to avoid difficult questions regarding competing spending priorities.[1]

US economic growth did more than just raise living standards in both the US and the world. Steady US growth also contributed to global stability. Other countries, many of which had less developed political systems and were rife with more intense ethnic rivalries, could be made placid in circumstances of economic growth. In periods when US economic growth ground to a halt, the odds of bad things happening internationally significantly increased.

The linkage of material well-being and stability goes back centuries. Think back to the French Revolution. When the masses have food, political systems can manage strife. When basic necessities are lacking, it becomes much harder for governments to contain disagreements and class or ethnic hatred. Furthermore, as Washington descends further and further into gridlock, and class warfare makes at least a rhetorical resurgence, there arises the question of whether the constitutional bonds that once tied us are no longer as strong as they once were. In normal circumstances, the republic remains fairly safe, but in times of economic strife, both America and other countries could see their societal ties fray. As *The Wall Street Journal*'s Dan Henninger (2014) put it, 'If the American economic engine slows permanently to about 2%, you're going to see more fires around the world like Ukraine and Venezuela. At the margin, the world's weakest, most misgoverned countries will pop, and violently.'

For all of these reasons, and more, the most important job of the government is to keep the US economy humming. Under a growing economy, the population is happy, foreign conflicts are less likely, the deficits remain manageable. Without a growing economy, there is the very real potential for very bad things to happen.

One problem with facing this challenge is that policy-makers typically do not know when an economic collapse will occur, nor how to prevent it. The 2008 catastrophe, for example, was caused at least in part by a housing bubble, yet government policy-makers – on the left and on the right, in Congress and in the executive branch – had been steadily focused on increasing homeownership, even among those who could not afford it. Furthermore, once a crisis happens, the options for stopping or ending a collapse are limited. As recent experience shows, it can take a long time to right the economic ship after things go horribly wrong.

The dark side of modernity 153

Even in the case of 2008, in which some people did warn that there was a housing bubble, or that Wall Street was overleveraged with debt instruments, those people were not in the right places at the right times to do something about it (Bartlett 2009). The president, as powerful as he may be, does not have control over all of the levers of economic policy-making. The Federal Reserve arguably holds more cards than the president. And even in the case of Fannie Mae and Freddie Mac, which the George W. Bush Administration worried about and tried to reform, bipartisan Congressional resistance prevented any of the proposed reforms from being enacted (Jefferson 2008). For good or for ill, our system is designed in such a way that it would be extremely difficult for policy-makers to effectuate rapid changes that could prevent a collapse, *even if the policy-makers knew that a collapse was coming and knew what steps were necessary to prevent that collapse.*

For these reasons, economic catastrophes, while rare, will often come as a surprise. That said, there is at least one looming economic disaster that cannot be considered a surprise, namely the massive and unsustainable deficits that the US is carrying. This figure, in excess of $18 trillion and expected to hit $21 trillion by 2024, is exacerbated by the long-term liabilities that the US entitlement programmes face (McSherry 2013; Samuelson 2014). The Medicare programme, which provides health coverage for America's growing 65 and older population, faces a short-term deficit larger than that of Greece, and long-term unfunded liabilities in excess of $35 trillion (Sasse 2015). All told, long-term US debt obligations are in the range of $80 to $100 trillion (Cox and Archer 2012; Congressional Budget Office 2014). By 2039, interest payments alone will cost 4.5 per cent of GDP, potentially crippling the government's ability to spend money on anything else. Our long-term unfunded obligations are a big number, but not a cause for immediate panic. After all, these obligations are long-term promises, not already-incurred debts. The words 'long term' mean exactly that, taking place over a 75-year period. And slight changes in growth rates, demographic trends, or policies can make big changes in what those long-term obligations will mean at the end of the 75-year window (Thompson 2012).

Even though we should not have to worry about paying this debt tomorrow, these long-term obligations remain a concern. Just as these numbers can change for the better, they can also change for the worse. And even if they don't change at all, they would constitute an unmanageable obligation. Recent behaviour by the US government does not inspire confidence regarding the ability of the US to reduce its long-term obligations. In fact, if recent behaviour is a guide, the problem is likely to worsen.

The debt problem is not only a problem for the United States, but it is also a problem for the world, and the world is noticing. In 2011, Standard & Poor's downgraded the US governments AAA credit rating (Peralta 2011). Large holders of US debt, including Russia and China, are both increasingly nervous about being stuck with these obligations. They can hardly be expected to risk their own interests. This could carry severe consequences for America. The irresponsibility of accruing these trillions of dollars in obligations constitutes behaviour that would not be tolerated elsewhere. As the financial analyst Peter Schiff has

154   *Tevi Troy*

written, 'We owe trillions. Look at our budget deficit; look at the debt to GDP ratio, the unfunded liabilities. If we were in the Eurozone, they would kick us out' (Hill 2015).

The accumulation of debt has thus far not caused an economic collapse, but that does not mean it won't happen. It only means that it has not happened yet. When it does happen, if it does happen, it will happen very fast. Our new globalized world, with instantaneous financial transactions and information alike, will mean that a financial crisis is far less likely to be localized and much more likely to be global. As former Treasury Secretary Larry Summers has observed (Ramo 2009, 57–8), 'The problem of global financial markets is that they are like modern jet planes. They get you where you need to go faster, but the crashes are far, far worse.' This is even truer if the crisis begins in the US, where the ripple effects will be felt more keenly.

There is no guarantee that the US debt will be the cause of the next economic collapse, but it clearly is a likely culprit. For this reason, the only rational response would be to take serious steps to get our debt situation under control. This would include some unpopular measures, which would focus on reducing the size of our long-term obligations by adjusting inflation rates, means-testing benefits and increasing the retirement age. Thus far, the US government has been unwilling to take such steps, but if they fail to do so before a debt-fuelled crisis hits, the government's inaction will be revealed to have been extremely short-sighted.

This is not to say that steps to alleviate the debt crisis won't be painful. They will. But not preventing a debt-fuelled economic collapse will be far more painful. In fact, one of the reasons given for the reluctance to trim back unrealistic entitlement promises is that such steps could harm the poor. If our looming debt crisis does, indeed, create an economic collapse, it will be a disaster for our nation and our way of life. In such an economic catastrophe, those living at the low end of the economic ladder will be the first to suffer because they have so little to fall back on.

First, the loss of economic dynamism will mean the loss of economic opportunity for those who aspire to rise from poverty. Loss of jobs also means that low-skill, low-wage jobs will be the first to go. Even now, France's anaemic state-heavy economy hires only the most productive and well educated, while the poorly educated or those without social connections are left behind (Organization for Economic Co-operation and Development [OECD] n.d.). In such cases of 'Eurosclerosis', the highly educated often seek government positions and pensions to protect them from economic displacement caused by excessive government.

In addition, if we don't trim our entitlement programmes, they will collapse. In an economic crisis, programmes for the poor will be eviscerated; they will not be sustained, as liberals want, and they will not be reformed, like conservatives want. They will be cut indiscriminately because we will have no choice.

Finally, the poor will be disproportionately affected because they have no savings to fall back on. According to Bricker *et al.* (2012), families in the bottom income quintile had a median net worth of $8,500 in 2007; in 2010 the median net worth of the bottom quintile was $6,200, a decline of 27 per cent. The recession reduced the holding of the poor by a quarter of its value. If a complete economic collapse takes place, it will not only be a human tragedy, but it will also be a civic disaster, as the disproportionately affected poor could be a source of major civil and possibly global unrest. As disaster chronicler Joshua Cooper Ramo (2009, 57–8) has noted, 'every once in a while the physics come along and munch away decades of civilized life, the way the 1929 stock market crash tightened Europe's downward economic spiral, helping to elevate Hitler and the whole horrible historical train wreck that came afterward'.

Fortunately, disaster is not destiny, and it is far from too late to take steps to prevent one from happening. There is even historical precedent for getting our debt under control by taking a series of measured, non-radical steps to control spending and maintain revenue levels. According to former head of the Council of Economic Advisers, Martin Feldstein (2011), 'It is worth remembering that after World War II we brought our national debt down from 109 percent of GDP to 46 percent of GDP in 1960.' According to Feldstein, the US accomplished this without major tax hikes or spending cuts, but by keeping spending steady while the economy grew. Such an event is not just doable, though, it is also necessary. Our economic future is dependent on the ability of our elected officials to manage our spending priorities responsibly and make the hard choices. Thus far they have not been up to the task, but better policies in the future could lead to better results.

Another possible solution to our debt and deficit troubles could come from renewed economic growth. Naysayers of previous eras have suggested that the American moment might be over, only to be surprised by the manufacturing boom of the 1950s, corporate restructuring in the 1980s and the internet revolution in the 1990s. American innovation has defeated the nattering nabobs of negativism in the past, and could do so again. Former White House speechwriter David Frum (2012) has even identified three likely sources of an American economic resurgence: the discovery of new energy sources, renewed innovation in pharmaceuticals and biologics and the revitalization of America's inner cities.

Frum may be right, but there are a host of other possibilities as yet not thought of as well. Economic changes often come from unanticipated places. Policy-makers must therefore understand that we do not and cannot know which innovations will prove to be transformative. Despite the importance of innovation, we need policies that prepare for disasters by enabling the investment and innovation that allow for human beings to create new products and processes without the government putting its thumb on the scale in favour of one kind of innovation or another.

7.3 The viral danger

At one point in the recent Ebola crisis in West Africa, the situation was so dire that Liberia's defence minister declared the pandemic a 'serious threat' to Liberia's very existence. Such a pronouncement was not unwarranted. Still, most Americans probably think the defence minister was guilty of hyperbole. This American cultural prejudice stems, in large part, from the belief that an affluent America's health and social institutions are more stable than those of Liberia and other developing nations. And, of course, there are some good reasons for thinking that, as

156   *Tevi Troy*

long as America remains affluent. But this relative stability does not mean that America, and particularly America's leaders, can afford to ignore the concept of potential existential threats to the US and to developed countries as a whole.

Ebola is a legitimate concern, but it is far from the only viral threat the US faces. In fact, it is worth remembering that the Spanish Influenza of 1918–19 killed approximately 50 million people, including 675,000 Americans (Vergano 2014; US Department of Health and Human Services [HHS] n.d.). It infected more than a quarter of the US population and even reduced US life expectancy by an entire decade. It even ravaged the battlefields and encampments of World War I, where it was responsible for 43,000 of America's 116,000 deaths in that war (Taubenberger 2006). Even more sobering is the realization that flu is not a tropical exotic. It comes every year, in different strains. Fortunately, none of the strains over the past century have been as deadly as the 1918 flu, but flu remains a real danger (Doshi 2008).

As recently as the 1990s, the US could count on an average of 36,000 deaths annually from flu (Thompson *et al.* 2003, 179–86). That number has gone down in recent years, in large part due to widespread use of the annual flu vaccine (Center for Disease Control and Prevention [CDC] 2010). But the vaccine itself, while a life-saver, is far from perfect. In the 2014–15 flu season, the vaccine effectiveness – the percentage by which a vaccine reduces the risk of getting the disease – was as low at 18 per cent (Shapiro 2015). Even in a so-called good year, the vaccine effectiveness rate is in the 60–90 per cent range, so the possibility of vaccine failure remains a constant, if low-grade threat (Healthline 2014).

Other worrisome pathogens include MERS – the Middle East Respiratory Syndrome – and SARS. MERS emerged in 2012 and infected more than 700 people (Fox 2014). The disease, which appeared to originate in Saudi Arabia, was particularly worrisome because of the Hajj, the annual pilgrimage of 2 million Muslim worshippers to the holy city of Mecca (Carrington 2014). This annual event worried public-health officials as it threatened to carry MERS to all corners of the globe. SARS, a related coronavirus, killed about 800 people and cost the world economy about $50 billion in 2002–3 (Wagner 2013; Cooper and Kirton 2013).

In addition to these naturally occurring diseases, there is also the concern of bio-terror, a deadly man-made pathogen that could spread far and wide and overwhelm our public-health capabilities (Center for Disease Control and Prevention [CDC] 2007). US intelligence officials know that there are people who wish to do us harm and are actively looking at ways to use bioweapons against the US. ISIS, for example, has been looking at ways to weaponize the Bubonic plague (Thornhill 2014). In addition to all of the threats that we know about are the unknown threats. A new and deadly disease is a possibility. Only 30 years ago few had heard of or understood HIV-AIDS (Fader 2014).

Fortunately, modern medicine has made great strides in dealing with deadly diseases. A century ago, a mere infection posed a mortal threat to humans, and now antibiotics have given humankind the capacity to detect and defeat once-deadly infections (Jones *et al.* 2012). But there are limits to what modernity can

The dark side of modernity 157

accomplish, and modernity brings with it its own dangers. While we have solved many medical puzzles, far more remain unsolved, without vaccines or cures to address them. Modern air travel, so beneficial to the spread of commerce and of ideas, also brings with it vulnerability to the spread of deadly diseases. Diseases that would once stay in only one remote corner of the world, or, if they spread, spread very slowly, can now ricochet around the globe in real time.

When it comes to deadly diseases, technology is a two-way street. While we now have greater tools to combat diseases, the dangers are now greater as well. Technology allows bad actors to develop bio-terror weapons that can wreak untold horrors anywhere around the world. It would be relatively simple for a competent scientist to create and distribute a deadly pathogen. Even if such a pathogen did not cause mass casualties, it could cause mass panic, with news of an outbreak spread immediately throughout the world via both the traditional and social media. In addition, modern transportation networks would not only allow the disease to spread, but would also allow the perpetrator to escape quickly to anywhere around the world within 48 hours.

In such a scenario, though, technology would be our friend as well. Both private and public sector actors have the capacity to identify emerging disease in real time. Existing stockpiles of countermeasures mean that there is a good probability that the vaccine or treatment for the new pathogen already exists. And if no counter-measure existed, there is a good chance that one could be created and brought to market in a relatively short time. The modern transportation system could be an ally as well, allowing for rapid transport of disease samples to the relevant labo-ratories and quick distribution of an existing countermeasure, should one exist. Modern law-enforcement tools would also make it hard for the assailant to escape the long arm of the technologically enhanced law.

The threat of deadly diseases rising to pandemic proportions highlights the need to expand US efforts to prevent their spread – and if they occur, to stop them. Doing so requires a number of key steps. First, we must revisit our existing capabilities and make sure we can do what we say we can do. In the run-up to the Ebola outbreak, US health officials were overly optimistic about the US health system's ability to control Ebola within the United States. When the first US Ebola patient arrived at a Dallas hospital, it quickly became clear that not every US hospital was prepared to deal with such a deadly contagion. The hospital misdiagnosed the patient, then sent him home, where he could, potentially, have infected others (US Energy and Commerce Committee 2014). After his readmis-sion a few days later, when it was obvious that he had Ebola, the patient infected two health care workers at the hospital. The patient, Thomas Eric Duncan, died, but the two health care workers survived (ibid.). Following this incident, the Center for Disease Control changed its protocols for dealing with Ebola and later released a more limited list of hospitals that were equipped to handle Ebola patients (Park 2014).

We also need to improve our detection capabilities. The World Health Organization was slow to recognize what was happening with Ebola in West Africa, just as PAHO – the Pan American Health Organization – tarried in picking

158   *Tevi Troy*

up the H1N1 'Swine Flu' in Mexico in 2009 (Roland 2015; Brown 2009). US officials need to improve their detection capabilities by using private-sector technology and innovation to counter the slowness and siloed nature of government bureaucracies.

Third, we need to accelerate the development of countermeasures, which is a painfully slow process. The US already has existing programmes to address this issue, such as 2004's Project Bioshield to finance and promote medical counter-measures, but they have proven to be insufficient (Russell 2005). Just to take one example, the National Institutes of Health (NIH) reported promising research on an Ebola vaccine for monkeys in 2000, yet the 2014 outbreak occurred without a vaccine available for human use (Sullivan *et al.* 2000; World Health Organization [WHO] 2015). Congress needs to improve the incentives and processes for countermeasure development.

All of these will face resistance from entrenched bureaucracies. Public-health officials do not want to hear that their protocols are insufficient or ineffective. There will be internal resistance to relying on private-sector detection methods rather than existing government systems. And Congress will be reluctant to spend more money on countermeasure development. Indeed, funding for the Strategic National Stockpile has been dropping in recent years (Hayden 2013).

Despite these challenges, it is important that the US government persists in developing contingency plans for potentially deadly disease outbreaks. Recent evidence shows that our existing systems are inadequate and need to be bolstered, if not overhauled (Levi *et al.* 2014). Since 9/11, we have made great strides in improving our capabilities in this area, against both natural and man-made threats. But the job is clearly not yet done. More work remains if we are going to keep the American people safe from the viral threats we face. If we fail, and a killer disease of the magnitude of the 1918 Spanish Flu, or worse, takes hold, our entire interdependent global economy could grind to a halt, taking government systems with it as well.

7.4 Grid collapse

Another worrisome threat that can potentially wreak havoc and devastation on our system of government and our way of life is threats to our electric grid. The hack of Sony over the movie *The Interview*, likely done by North Korea, underscores how vulnerable companies are to some kind of cyber-attack (Altman and Fitzpatrick 2014). Companies differ from government, of course, but government is highly vulnerable as well: the government revealed, in the spring of 2015, that hackers had compromised the data of approximately 4 million past and present federal workers. For these reasons, concerns about a collapse of our computer-based systems continually remain high in the public consciousness. As Peggy Noonan wrote in *The Wall Street Journal* (2014),

> all our essentials and most of our diversions are dependent in some way on this: You plug the device into the wall and it gets electrical power and this makes your life, and the nation's life, work. Without it, darkness descends.

The dark side of modernity 159

That darkness could strain the bonds of civilization relatively quickly. According to the Brookings Institution's Joseph Kramek, writing in 2013, 'Utilities provide services which, if disrupted for long periods of time, may result in economic chaos and may even lead to social unrest.'

The author John Steele Gordon (2014) encapsulated our level of dependence on computers in the following 'thought experiment':

> Imagine it's 1970 and someone pushes a button causing every computer in the world to stop working. The average man on the street won't have noticed anything amiss until his bank statement failed to come in at the end of the month. Push that button today and *civilization collapses in seconds*.
>
> (Emphasis added)

The starkness of our dependence happened, Gordon explained, 'because the microprocessor is now found in everything more complex than a pencil'.

These fears have lately been manifesting in the realm of popular culture. Some kind of attack that takes out power, utilities and our entire computer-based system remains a constant concern in movies, TV and popular books. In *Die Hard 4: Live Free or Die Hard*, cyberterrorists attack multiple pieces of the web-based grid in order to pull off a massive heist. In the remake of *Red Dawn*, our nation becomes vulnerable to outside attack when an electromagnetic pulse (EMP) disrupts all of our advanced weaponry, taking out the electricity in the process. In a host of recent TV shows, including the *Walking Dead, Revolution, Dark Angel, Falling Skies* and *The Last Ship* – not to be confused with the similarly themed *The Last Man* – humanity must cope with a world in which most if not all of our pre-existing systems are no longer available (IMDB various). And the 2009 book *One Second After*, specifically designed to scare Americans about the prospects of a successful EMP attack, became a bestseller (Forstchen 2011). Wikipedia even has an entry dedicated to 'Electromagnetic pulse in fiction and popular culture'.[2] Clearly there is a growing fear in the collective consciousness of the nation regarding the devastating impact such an attack could have on our way of life.

Beyond the pop culture concerns, though, there is some evidence that we do face a very real threat. In the winter of 2014, it emerged that there had been a systematic effort to disrupt the power supply in the area of Silicon Valley. Some unknown assailant or assailants cut fibre-optic cables and fired bullets from an AK-47 into 17 of 23 transformers at the Metcalf power substation in San Jose, California. Other than the damage it caused – which took a month to repair – the general public knows little about this attack (Smith 2014); the upper echelons of government may know more.

There were a number of worrisome elements to this attack. First, it appears to have been well planned, well targeted and strategically executed. Attacking Silicon Valley, the home of so much of our cyber-intellectual capital, would have a disproportionately large impact on our nation as a whole. Effects of a coordinated attack on our power systems could have national implications. According to *The Wall Street Journal*'s Rebecca Smith (ibid.), disabling as few as nine of the 55,000

160　*Tevi Troy*

electric-transmission substations in the US on a high-usage day could lead to 'a coast-to-coast blackout'.

While this particular attack appeared focused on a single area, the attackers seem to have known what they were doing, and planned the attack to inflict the maximum possible damage. As Former Federal Energy Regulatory Commission head Jon Welinghoff said, it was a 'purposeful attack, extremely well planned and executed by professionals who had expert training'. Compounding all of this was the fact that the attack happened in April of 2013, and the general public did not even find out about it until February of 2014. And yet, despite that enormous time lag, the FBI still does not appear to have any idea who had carried out the attack and, at the time, were unwilling to characterize it as terrorism (Crovitz 2014).

Beyond this mysterious assault on one of our physical power stations, we also face the constant threat of cyber-attacks, against our power supply, against weapons systems and against our information systems. Cybercrime alone costs the US $100 billion annually and $575 billion worldwide (Lewis and Baker 2013). Another estimate, by the Center for Strategic and International Studies, found that cybercrime and economic espionage combined cost the world economy some $445 billion annually (Nakashima and Peterson 2014). Whichever number you pick, the sheer scale of cyber assaults is staggering. According to *Politico*'s Tal Kopan (2014), 'if cybercrime were a country, it would have the 27th largest economy in the world'. While cybercrime itself does not rise to the level of disaster, its existence speaks to the prevalence of hacking, which is the method by which an attack on the grid could happen.

Government officials are seriously concerned about this problem. The 2008 Obama presidential campaign was hit by a significant cyber-attack, so top campaign officials knew about the danger even before they knew they'd be serving in government (Glendinning 2008). Furthermore, according to *The New York Times*'s Peter Baker (2013), the outgoing George W. Bush Administration provided contingency plans to the incoming Obama Administration on about a dozen possible scenarios that the new administration might face in its early days, among them 'a cyber-attack on American computer systems'. (Although that did not happen at the start of the administration, one of the other possible scenarios, renewed instability in the Middle East, did take place in Obama's first term.)

In addition to the problems of espionage and theft, there is also the certainty that the US would come under cyber assault in any future military action. This is especially so if the dispute were to be against Russia or China, or against their interests or allies, as both nations have active cyber warfare units (Thomas 2014). In the case of any attack by the US, or against the US, it could count on the fact that its opponents would use cyber-attacks to harass and frustrate both its economic and military capabilities.

This is no longer in the realm of theory; it is a reality of modern warfare. Israel, for example, regularly experiences attempted cyber disruptions during flare-ups in conflicts with terror groups like Hamas. During 2014's Operation Protective Edge, Palestinian hackers, with an assist from Iran, attempted what Israel characterized as 'a major attack' on Israeli operations. That attack, which aimed to disable Israeli

The dark side of modernity 161

websites, failed. But Israeli security forces now recognize that cyber defence is a standard part of modern warfare. The Israeli Defense Forces even have a division specifically dedicated to cyber defence. According to the unnamed head of that division, in this latest war, 'For the first time, there was an organized cyber defense effort alongside combat operations in the field. This was a new reality.' The Israeli official expected the cyber struggle to intensify over time. 'I won't be surprised if, next time, we meet [terrorists] in the cyber dimension,' he warned (Israel Defense Forces 2014). Going forward, the US must be prepared to deal with this challenge as well.

In addition to the certainty that we are already facing – and will continue to face – a variety of cyber threats, there is also the problem that the US government does not seem prepared to work together to address these perils. The entire US government seemed caught off guard by the Sony hack, but there had been warnings about this problem for years. Former US Secretary of Defense Bob Gates recalled, in his memoir (2014, 449–51), that the nation was 'dangerously vulnerable' to cyber-attack. He even mentions that there were warnings of 'a major cyber-attack' planned against the US in the autumn of 2010. Despite this obvious weakness, Gates saw 'a deep division within the government – in both the executive branch and Congress – over who should be in charge of our domestic cyber defense'. Compounding the problem was the fact that multiple players thought that it was in their bailiwick: 'government or business, the Defense Department national security agency, the department of homeland security, or some other entity'. In addition, Gates found, the government could not agree on what the strategic priority should be, national security or civil liberties. According to Gates, '[t]he result was paralysis'.

These intra-governmental divisions were not just an abstract concern. They had real-world ramifications. Gates says that he specifically requested an opinion from the DOD General Counsel's office on the question of what level of cyber-attack would prompt military retaliation. According to Gates, in a somewhat chilling passage (ibid., 450–1): 'I was still waiting for a good answer to that question three years later.' What this means is that, separate and apart from our capacity to mitigate or rectify such an attack, the security establishment was unable or unwilling to grapple with the question of how we should respond militarily if hit with a crippling cyber-attack. And, although Gates included some obligatory language about having seen 'considerable progress' on his watch, the overall picture he paints of our cyber-preparedness was not remotely comforting.

One of the most obvious, but no less devastating dangers would be to our power systems. One reason for the potential devastation is that such attacks are theoretically multipronged. The primary threats to America's electrical grid come from three very different sources – cyber warfare over the net, a physical assault, or an EMP from above. This diversity of threats indicates how difficult it is for the president, or anyone, to prepare for this challenge. But the difficulty of the challenge is no excuse for failing to address – or at least better understand – it. In fact, the ability of the threat to come from so many different directions increases the likelihood that it could happen.

The first thing the US needs to do to prepare for a possible assault on its electric grid is to undertake a realistic assessment of the threat so they are not caught

162 *Tevi Troy*

unawares, as in the Sony hack. Such an assessment will reveal vulnerabilities that need to be addressed, vulnerabilities of both a physical and a cyber nature. Discovery of these vulnerabilities, however, is not enough. The US needs to make a concerted effort to shore up the weaknesses – both physical and cyber – in its existing systems. In addition, the US needs to respect the potential of our federal system in building a more resilient social structure by leveraging the leadership and strengths of state and local resources, not just rely on Washington prerogatives.

Beyond assessing and fixing vulnerabilities, the US also needs to develop a doctrine of war for infrastructure attacks. As Secretary Gates noted, the US does not know how it could or should respond to an attack on its infrastructure, and the bureaucracy has been resistant to determining that doctrine. This is not surprising. Determining how to respond to new and asymmetric attacks is not a job for the bureaucracy. But is important to do so, in coordination with appropriate cabinet-level officials – State, Defense, Justice, Treasury and Homeland Security – as well as with our diplomatic partners.

Article 51 of the United Nations charter does grant states the ability to respond to a nation's cyberspace, but it does not and cannot determine the level of the response (Valeriano and Maness 2012). This determination needs to include some kind of scale of intensity for figuring out which attacks warrant hitting back. This review should also create a risk benefit scale for opposing targets that the US identifies in response. Cyber warfare differs from conventional warfare in that counterattacks can have many more unexpected ripple effects. Taking out an electrical station that powers a military base could also affect hospitals or schools in the same grid. In addition, America's use of offensive cyber capabilities can bring about their own retaliatory efforts, and can also break down standards of restraint that currently do exist between nation-states and even criminal enterprises. These kinds of decisions cannot be made by military personnel on the ground, but need to be considered by senior military and political officials (Lewis 2013).

Another problem with these kinds of new and difficult question is that traditional defence and political officials will almost certainly not have experience with these questions. For this reason, the president needs to consider a designated office to cope with these questions and to lead our cybersecurity efforts. Such an office could be modelled on the Department of Homeland Security (DHS) in its effort to have a crosscutting overview of US government agencies, but would need to avoid the cumbersome and bureaucratic aspects of DHS as it has come to be.

This is not a call for useless rearrangement of deck chairs. Changes in doctrine, tactics and organization must be made with security, not politics, egos, or committee jurisdictions in mind. Furthermore, empty government declarations will not do the trick. As Secretary Gates recalled about the various and periodic national strategy directive documents that emerge from the bureaucracy (2014, 144),

> I don't recall ever reading the president's National Security Strategy when preparing to become secretary of defense. Nor did I read any of the previous National Defense Strategy documents when I became secretary. I never felt disadvantaged by not having read the Scriptures.

The dark side of modernity 163

Obviously, some new document that goes unread by senior officials will do little to prepare the US government for the very real threats it faces to its electronic infrastructure and, ultimately, to its way of life.

Of course, these dangers are not mutually exclusive, but can, in fact, be interrelated. Each of the three crisis scenarios described above can either precede or follow the others, as first-order consequences lead to secondary-level disasters as well. For example, an economic collapse could lead to a grid collapse or prevent us from countering the spread of a deadly disease, while a loss of the power grid would almost surely lead to a massive economic dislocation. In our interrelated system, a disaster in one area would be unlikely to remain contained in that one area alone.

7.5 The dangers unchecked

All of the dangers listed are addressable, through smart and long-term policy improvements. A large part of addressing the problem is by maintaining America's economic viability as essential to staving off many of the most frightful possible scenarios. Yet Washington in recent years has shown relatively little ability to engage in smart or long-term policy planning. This raises the question: what if one of the dangers outlined above does occur, and what if the government fails to prevent it – the ideal – or address it once it happens? If there were a disease, a grid meltdown or economic catastrophe so severe that it led to a complete collapse of the US government, what would happen then? The answers to these questions may be terrifying to contemplate, but better to address them now, while we still have a relatively stable and secure government, economy and society.

The first and most basic collapse would be in the form of the rule of law. Forget about the thousands of pages of government regulations about drug safety, egg size, or the provision of employment benefits such as health care. In this scenario, government would not perform even basic law-enforcement functions. Streets would not be safe to walk. Stores and homes would be looted and border enforcement would be even worse than it is now. In this initial phase, the strong would prey on the weak, good people would stay off the streets and commerce would grind to a halt. Resorting to Hobbes again, we would face a situation of *bellum omnium contra omnes* – a war of all against all. As a result, basic necessities would not make it to the market, and people would die from lack of access to food and medicine. Furthermore, the nation would be vulnerable to foreign invasion with no army to stop it.

As dire as this sounds – and it would, indeed, be dire – it is likely that this phase would not last indefinitely. Individuals would band together to create informal associations to provide protection, associations that would likely evolve into more formal groupings, in the form of proto-police forces. These groupings would do little to prevent the possibility of foreign invasion, but the fact of the matter is that whatever catastrophe disabled the US government would probably have destroyed foreign military forces as well. (If this is not the case, then an invading foreign force would solve the problem of no ruling entity, although it

164　*Tevi Troy*

would, of course, raise many other problems beyond the scope of this study.) Even if these forces were relatively successful at keeping some measure of peace, and assuming foreign invasion did not happen for whatever reason, the proto-police forces would likely be callous and indiscriminate. There is little to no chance they would be mindful of our current constitutional protections, and they would be erratic and unreliable. With democratic elections having become a luxury of the pre-crisis era, these forces would be largely unaccountable to the body politic.

In addition to the public safety aspects of a governmental collapse, there is also the issue of the myriad government functions beyond those of keeping the peace. Approximately two-thirds of federal government spending is directed towards transfer payments of one kind or another: social security, Medicare, disability payments, welfare assistance, food stamps, farm subsidies and so much more. The disappearance of these payments would mean that millions of Americans who rely on government cheques would no longer be receiving those cheques. If businesses could not maintain operations, millions more Americans reliant on paycheques from their employers would also suddenly find themselves without regular income. Even those with at least some measure of wealth might no longer have purchasing power, as most people maintain their holdings in stocks, bonds, bank accounts, or real estate, none of which would be readily available during a system-wide collapse.

Without the United States government backing the dollar, cash itself might turn into nothing more than soft green pieces of paper. Given that toilet paper is a required and high demand commodity during times of crisis – witness the recent toilet paper shortage in Venezuela – there is the strong possibility that the most valuable use of the dollar in such a scenario would be as toilet paper. How the mighty dollar would have fallen, indeed.

If the dollar was no longer an instrument of value, then we would have returned to a basic barter economy. Goods would be exchangeable for other goods or services rather than currency. The relative value of goods and services would also change in a significant way. Services that command large dollar amounts today – legal services, accounting, financial advice – would lose most of their value (as would, ahem, policy analysis and writing). The practice of medicine would retain or perhaps even increase in value, and the cost of other services – farmers, mechanics and carpenters – would skyrocket. Similarly, currently valuable items such as gems, precious metals and electronic devices would lose value relative to non-perishable necessities – canned foods, water bottles, weapons, medications and, yes, toilet paper.

The collapse of government would also have tremendous implications for the ability to transport goods and services. Government would no longer be able to maintain the quality of the roads or guarantee the safety of those travelling on those roads. The concept of travel could return to the medieval period, when night-time sojourns were too dangerous to undertake and individuals sought the shelter of walled cities – think gated communities – when the sun went down. International travel, so dependent on government-maintained air traffic control,

The dark side of modernity 165

or government-protected shipping lanes would be almost nonexistent. Given that the US currently imports 15 per cent of its food (including 50 per cent of fresh fruit, 20 per cent of fresh vegetables and 80 per cent of seafood), the loss of imports itself would drive up the cost and reduce the availability of food. Domestic travel, already made difficult by the inability of government to maintain roads or protect safety, would be further curtailed by unmanaged traffic snarl-ups as well as the lack of availability of petrol. These problems are only a microcosm of the full spectrum of devastating changes to our everyday lives, all of which will require a re-conception of the role of the individual in society.

Returning to a medieval system on both the governmental and technological front is a frightening prospect. The reality may even be worse, though. Mankind in a pre-technological era had the skills to take care of itself, knowing how to hunt, fish, till and store food, as well as how to fashion primitive tools. Post-modern individuals for the most part do not have these skills, and have become overly reliant on modern technologies for their everyday necessities. A generation trained on iPhones would do poorly in a world where iPhones no longer worked.

As damaging as a catastrophic collapse would be in the US, there is the distinct possibility that things would be even worse outside the US. First, the US already exerts pressure around the world on many countries to maintain democratic systems and practices. This pressure is, to be sure, not always effective, but things would be even worse without it. Without such pressure, the descent into tyranny would be even more rapid. In addition, the American citizenry is used to democratic systems and practices. Many others, especially non-Western nations, do not have such traditions and would have little compunction about resorting to tyranny. A catastrophic, systemic collapse would be a devastating blow to human freedom around the globe.

As for solutions, they are hard to come by. It is impossible to make policy suggestions for governments for how to behave in a world in which governments do not exist. The best policy advice is for the government to take steps to try and prevent such crises from happening. With respect to the economy, policy-makers should take care not to interfere with the engine of economic growth, and should take active steps to resolve our looming debt situation. In terms of disease prevention, we need to improve our detection capabilities and accelerate the development of disease countermeasures. To protect our electric grid and other computer systems, both the public and the private sector must bolster their cyber defences and the government must determine a doctrine of war for cyber-attacks.

Beyond these ideas, though, advice is best geared for individuals. In the world of a government collapse, individuals would have to take steps to protect themselves and their communities, but also to rebuild shattered societies. Most of the preparedness strategies recommended today – have excess food and water, purchase a generator, keep cash on hand – would be effective for only a short period until those supplies ran out. Longer-term strategies would require individuals to develop skills that have long been thought unnecessary in urban environments. Public policy could play a role here as well. Perhaps education, as a matter of course, should give each citizen at least one practical skill that would be needed

166   *Tevi Troy*

if the normal workings of the economy ceased. In this way, it would not just be those relegated to 'shop class' who had the skills necessary to survive in a post-catastrophe environment, and the nation as a whole would be more resilient in facing a crisis.

We would also need individuals prepared to rebuild society not only physically, but from a political standpoint as well. Dangerous strains of thought that are counter to individual freedom would gain in popularity. Resilient individuals would have to have both physical skills and mental and philosophical fortitude in order to rebuild America into the shining city on a hill it has been for centuries.

The unfortunate bottom line is we can't fully prepare for such a scenario, as we can't know with certainty what would bring it about. We can, however, recognize that we don't have the answers and that we do require more serious thought and planning than has been done thus far. In the absence of taking steps to prepare for catastrophic collapse, we face real dangers to our systems, our way of life and to the cause of human freedom around the world.

Notes

1 As US government spending patterns over this period indicate, when forced to confront the choice between A and B, Congress has consistently chosen both.
2 Many of the works are eBooks, but the fact remains that EMP is a lively plot source for dystopian novels.

References

Altman, Alex, and Alex Fitzpatrick. 'Everything We Know About Sony, *The Interview* and North Korea'. *TIME*, 17 December 2014. http://time.com/3639275/the-interview-sony-hack-north-korea
American Farm Bureau Federation. 'Fast Facts about Agriculture'. 2015. http://www.fb.org/newsroom/fastfacts
Baker, Peter. *Days of Fire: Bush and Cheney in the White House*. New York: Doubleday, 2013.
Barclay, Eliza. 'US Lets 141 Trillion Calories of Food Go To Waste Each Year'. *National Public Radio*, 27 February 2014. http://www.npr.org/sections/thesalt/2014/02/27/283071610/u-s-lets-141-trillion-calories-of-food-go-to-waste-each-year
Bartlett, Bruce. 'Who Saw The Housing Bubble Coming?'. *Forbes*, 2 January 2009. http://www.forbes.com/2008/12/31/housing-bubble-crash-oped-cx_bb_0102bartlett.html
Bricker, Jesse, Arthur B. Kennickell, Kevin B. Moore and John Sabelhaus. 'Changes in US Family Finances from 2007 to 2010: Evidence from the Survey of Consumer Finances'. *Federal Reserve Bulletin* 98, no. 2 (June 2012): 1–80. http://www.federalreserve.gov/pubs/bulletin/2012/pdf/scf12.pdf
Brown, David. 'System Set Up After SARS Epidemic Was Slow to Alert Global Authorities'. *Washington Post*, 30 April 2009. http://www.washingtonpost.com/wp-dyn/content/article/2009/04/29/AR2009042904911.html
Carrington, Daisy. 'How Saudi Arabia Goes Hi-tech to Manage Millions during the Hajj'. CNN. Cable News Network, 8 October 2014. http://www.cnn.com/2014/10/08/world/meast/how-hi-tech-manages-millions-during-the-hajj/

The dark side of modernity 167

Center for Disease Control and Prevention (CDC). 'Bioterrorism Overview'. 12 February 2007. http://emergency.cdc.gov/bioterrorism/overview.asp

Center for Disease Control and Prevention (CDC). 'Estimates of Deaths Associated with Seasonal Influenza – United States, 1976–2007'. *Morbidity and Mortality Weekly Report* 59, no. 33 (27 August 2010): 1057–62. http://www.cdc.gov/mmwr/preview/mmwrhtml/mm5933a1.htm

Center for Disease Control and Prevention (CDC). 'CDC Tightened Guidance for US Healthcare Workers on Personal Protective Equipment for Ebola'. *CDC Newsroom*, 20 October 2015. http://www.cdc.gov/media/releases/2014/fs1020-ebola-personal-protective-equipment.html

Congressional Budget Office. 'The 2014 Long-Term Budget Outlook'. 25 July 2014. https://www.cbo.gov/publication/45471

Cox, Chris, and Bill Archer. 'Why $16 Trillion Only Hints at the True US Debt'. *The Wall Street Journal*, 28 November 2012. http://www.wsj.com/articles/SB100014241278873233532045781273740390087636

Crovitz, L. Gordon. 'The Power Grid: Our Achilles' Hill'. *The Wall Street Journal*, 10 February 2014: A11.

Doshi, Peter. 'Trends in Recorded Influenza Mortality: United States, 1900–2004'. *American Journal of Public Health* 98, no. 5 (May 2008): 939–45. http://www.ncbi.nlm.nih.gov/pmc/articles/PMC2374803

Dosso, Zoom. 'Ebola "Overwhelming" Health Services in West Africa'. *Business Insider*, 10 September 2014. http://www.businessinsider.com/afp-ebola-overwhelming-health-services-in-west-africa-2014-9

Fader, Lainna. 'Newsweek Rewind: 30 Years Ago, Scientists Discovered the Cause of AIDS'. *Newsweek*, 24 April 2014. http://www.newsweek.com/newsweek-rewind-30-years-ago-scientists-discovered-cause-hiv-248566?piano_t=1

Feldstein, Martin. 'America's Challenge'. *AEI Annual Dinner Address* 2011. 3 May 2011. https://www.aei.org/wp-content/uploads/2011/10/Feldstein-speech-2011-Kristol.pdf

Forstchen, William R. *One Second After*. New York: Forge, 2011.

Fox, Maggie. 'MERS Outbreak Could Spread With Annual Pilgrimage: Officials'. *NBC News*, 17 June 2014. http://www.nbcnews.com/storyline/mers-mystery/mers-outbreak-could-spread-annual-pilgrimage-officials-n132866

Frum. David. 'Three Seeds for America's Future Economic Boom'. *CNN*, 18 June 2012. http://www.cnn.com/2012/06/18/opinion/frum-three-leaps-ahead

Gates, Robert. *Duty: Memoirs of a Secretary at War*. New York: Knopf, 2014.

Glendinning, Lee. 'Obama, McCain Computers "Hacked" During Election Campaign'. *Guardian*, 7 November 2008. http://www.theguardian.com/global/2008/nov/07/obama-white-house-usa

Gordon, John Steel. 'The Little Miracle Spurring Inequality'. *The Wall Street Journal*, 3 June 2014: A13.

Hamburg, Margaret A. 'Food Safety Modernization Act: Putting the Focus on Prevention'. *US Department of Health & Human Services*. http://www.foodsafety.gov/news/fsma.html

Hayden, Erika Check. 'Budget Forces Tough Look at Biodefence'. *Nature News*, 10 April 2013. http://www.nature.com/news/budget-forces-tough-look-at-biodefence-1.12766

Henninger, Daniel. 'The Growth Revolutions Erupt'. *The Wall Street Journal*, 26 February 2014. http://www.wsj.com/articles/SB10001424052702304255604579407270835417610

Hill, Christian. 'US Economy Will Implode, Helpless in Face of "Financial Pearl Harbor"'. *News Max*, 27 May 2015. http://www.newsmax.com/Finance/MKTNews/americas-economic-pearl-harbor/2013/02/14/id/490495

168   Tevi Troy

IDF Blog. 'The Attack Against Israel You Haven't Heard About'. *Israel Defense Forces*, 22 August 2014. http://www.idfblog.com/blog/2014/08/22/attack-israel-havent-heard

IMDB. *The Last Man*. 2000. http://www.imdb.com/title/tt0231956/?ref_=nv_sr_4

IMDB. *Dark Angel*. 2000–2. http://www.imdb.com/title/tt0204993/?ref_=nv_sr_1

IMDB. *Die Hard 4: Live Free or Die Hard*. 2007. http://www.imdb.com/title/tt0337978

IMDB. *Falling Skies*. 2011–present. http://www.imdb.com/title/tt1462059/?ref_=nv_sr_1

IMDB. *Red Dawn*. 2012a. http://www.imdb.com/title/tt1234719/?ref_=nv_sr_1

IMDB. *Walking Dead*. 2012b. http://www.imdb.com/title/tt1234719/?ref_=nv_sr_1

IMDB. *The Last Ship*. 2014–present. http://www.imdb.com/title/tt2402207/?ref_=nv_sr_1

Jefferson, T. 'White House Warned About Fannie and Freddie'. *Glenn Beck*, 23 September 2008. http://www.glennbeck.com/content/articles/article/198/15484

Jones, David S., Scott H. Podolsky and Jeremy A. Greene. 'The Burden of Disease and the Changing Task of Medicine'. *New England Journal of Medicine* 366 (2012): 2333–8. http://www.nejm.org/doi/full/10.1056/NEJMp1113569?query=featured_home&

Kirton, John J. *Moving Health Sovereignty in Africa: Disease, Governance, Climate Change*. Burlington, VT: Ashgate, 2014.

Kirton, John J., and Andrew F. Cooper. *Innovation in Global Health Governance*. Burlington, VT: Ashgate, 2013, p. 135. https://books.google.com/books?id=0ZfpKVVC8NMC&print sec=frontcover&source=gbs_ge_summary_r&cad=0#v=onepage&q&f=false

Kopan, Tal. 'Cybercrime Costs $575 Billion a Year, $100 Billion to US'. *Politico*, 9 June 2014. http://www.politico.com/story/2014/06/cybercrime-yearly-costs-107601

Kramek, Joseph. 'The Critical Infrastructure Gap: US Port Facilities and Cyber Vulnerabilities'. *Brookings Institution*, 3 July 2013. http://www.brookings.edu/research/papers/2013/07/03-cyber-ports-security-kramek

Krucik, George. 'Flu: Prevention'. *Healthline*, 23 July 2014. http://www.healthline.com/health/flu-prevention#Overview1

Levi, Jeffrey, Laura M. Segal, Dara Alpert Lieberman, Kendra May and Rebecca St Laurent. 'Outbreaks: Protecting Americans from Infectious Diseases 2014'. *Trust for America's Health and Robert Wood Johnson Foundation Issue Report*. December 2014. http://healthyamericans.org/assets/files/Final%20Outbreaks%202014%20Report.pdf

Lewis, James Andrew. 'Truly Damaging Cyberattacks Are Rare'. *Washington Post*, 10 October 2013. http://www.washingtonpost.com/postlive/truly-damaging-cyberattacks-are-rare/2013/10/09/ae628656-2d00-11e3-b139-029811dbb57f_story.html

Lewis, James Andrew, and Stewart Baker. 'The Economic Impact of Cybercrime and Cyber Espionage'. *Center for Strategic and International Studies and McAfee*, July 2013. http://csis.org/files/publication/60396rpt_cybercrime-cost_0713_ph4_0.pdf

Lupkin, Sidney. '2nd Dallas Nurse Ebola-Free, Thanks Hospital, Family and God'. *ABC News*, 28 October 2014. http://abcnews.go.com/Health/dallas-nurse-discharged-ebola-treatment/story?id=26495682

McSherry, Mark. 'Why Your Tax Dollars Don't Reduce the $17 Trillion Debt'. *Forbes*, 15 October 2013. http://www.forbes.com/sites/markmcsherry/2013/10/15/how-your-tax-dollars-dont-reduce-the-17-trillion-debt

Nakashima, Ellen, and Andrea Peterson. 'Report: Cybercrime and Espionage Costs $445 Billion Annually'. *Washington Post*, 9 June 2014. http://www.washingtonpost.com/world/national-security/report-cybercrime-and-espionage-costs-445-billion-annually/2014/06/08/8995291c-ecce-11e3-9f5c-9075d5508f0a_story.html

Noonan, Peggy. 'America's Power is Under Threat'. *The Wall Street Journal*, 6 February 2014. http://online.wsj.com/news/articles/SB10001424052702304680904579365412479 18511

The dark side of modernity 169

Organization for Economic Co-operation and Development (OECD). n.d. 'Better Life Index: France'. http://www.oecdbetterlifeindex.org/countries/france

Park, Alice. 'Here Are the 35 US Hospitals Approved to Treat Ebola'. *TIME*, 2 December 2014. http://time.com/3614047/ebola-hospitals-cdc

Peralta, Eyder. 'Standard & Poor's Downgrades US Credit Rating'. *NPR*, 5 August 2011. http://www.npr.org/sections/thetwo-way/2011/08/06/139038762/s-p-lowers-united-states-long-term-rating

Ramo, Joshua C. *The Age of the Unthinkable: Why the New World Disorder Constantly Surprises Us and What We Can Do About It*. New York: Little Brown, 2009.

Roland, Denise. 'Experts Criticize World Health Organization's "Slow" Ebola Outbreak Response'. *The Wall Street Journal*, 12 May 2015. http://www.wsj.com/articles/experts-criticize-world-health-organizations-slow-ebola-outbreak-response-1431344306

Russell, Philip K. 'Project BioShield: What It Is, Why It Is Needed, and Its Accomplishments So Far'. *Oxford Journals*. Oxford: Oxford University Press, 2005. http://cid.oxfordjournals.org/content/45/Supplement_1/S68.full

Samuelson, Robert.J. 'The Budget Stalemate Continues'. *Washington Post*, 17 December 2014. http://www.washingtonpost.com/opinions/robert-samuelson-the-budget-stalemate-continues/2014/12/17/f579aa7e-860a-11e4-b9b7-b8632ae73d25_story.html

Sasse, Ben. 'House Should Reject Medicare Change'. *POLITCO Magazine*, 26 March 2015. http://www.politico.com/magazine/story/2015/03/medicare-change-gop-116416.html#.VWehRfl4pcR

Shapiro, Emily. 'Flu Vaccine Less Effective Than Expected: CDC'. *ABC News*, 28 February 2015. http://abcnews.go.com/Health/flu-vaccine-effective-expected-cdc/story?id=29293197

Smith, Rebecca. 'Assault on California Power Station Raises Alarm on Potential for Terrorism'. *The Wall Street Journal*, 5 February 2014. http://www.wsj.com/articles/SB10001424052702304851104579359141941621778

Sturm, Roland, and Ruopeng An. 'Obesity and Economic Environments'. *CA: A Cancer Journal for Clinicians* 64 (2014): 337–50. http://www.ncbi.nlm.nih.gov/pubmed/11117750

Sullivan, Nancy J., Anthony Sanchez, Pierre E. Rollin, Zhi-yong Yang and Gary J. Nabel. 'Development of a Preventative Vaccine for Ebola Virus Infection in Primate'. *Nature* 408, no. 6812 (30 November 2000): 605–9. http://www.ncbi.nlm.nih.gov/pubmed/11117750

Taubenberger, Jeffery K. 'The Origin and Virulence of the 1918 "Spanish" Influenza Virus'. *Proceedings of the American Philosophical Society* 150, no. 1 (March 2006): 86–112. http://www.ncbi.nlm.nih.gov/pmc/articles/PMC2720273/pdf/nihms123030.pdf

Thomas, Timothy L. 2014. 'Nation-State Cyber Strategies: Examples from China and Russia'. In Franklin D. Kramer, Stuart H. Starr and Larry K. Wentz, eds, *Cyberpower and National Security*. Washington, DC: Potomac, 2009, pp. 465–88. http://ctnsp.dodlive.mil/files/2014/03/Cyberpower-I-Chap-20.pdf

Thompson, Derek. 'Is Our Debt Burden Really $100 Trillion?'. *The Atlantic*, 28 November 2012. http://www.theatlantic.com/business/archive/2012/11/is-our-debt-burden-really-100-trillion/265644

Thompson, William W., David K. Shay, Eric Weintraub, Lynnette Brammer, Nancy Cox, Larry J. Anderson and Keiji Fukuda. 'Mortality Associated with Influenza And Respiratory Syncytial Virus in the United States'. *The Journal of the American Medical Association* 289, no. 2 (2003): 179–86. http://jama.jamanetwork.com/article.aspx?articleid=195750

Thornhill, Ted. 'Is ISIS Trying to Develop Biological Weapons?'. *Daily Mail*, 29 August 2014. http://www.dailymail.co.uk/news/article-2737639/ISIS-laptop-reveals-terror-group-working-biological-weapon-spread-bubonic-plague.html

170   *Tevi Troy*

US Department of Health and Human Services (HHS). n.d. 'The Great Pandemic: The United States in 1918–1919'. http://www.flu.gov/pandemic/history/1918/the_pandemic/index.html

US Energy and Commerce Committee. 'Notable Elements of Mr Duncan's Initial Emergency Room Visit'. 16 October 2014. http://energycommerce.house.gov/sites/republicans.energycommerce.house.gov/files/Hearings/OI/20141016/Timeline2.pdf

US Energy Information Administration. 'Residential Energy Consumption Survey'. 2005. http://www.eia.gov/consumption/residential/data/2005

Valeriano, Brandon, and Ryan Maness. 'The Fog of Cyberwar: Why the Threat Doesn't Live Up to the Hype'. *Foreign Affairs*, 21 November 2012. https://www.foreignaffairs.com/articles/2012-11-21/fog-cyberwar

Vergano, Dan. '1918 Flu Pandemic That Killed 50 Million Originated in China, Historians Say'. *National Geographic*, 24 January 2014. http://news.nationalgeographic.com/news/2014/01/140123-spanish-flu-1918-china-origins-pandemic-science-health

Wagner, David. 'There's Good News and Bad News About This New SARS-Like Virus'. *The Wire*. The Atlantic Monthly Group, 19 February 2013. http://www.thewire.com/global/2013/02/theres-good-news-and-bad-news-about-new-sars-virus/62300/

Wikipedia.'Electromagnetic Pulse in Fiction and Popular Culture'. Last updated 16 March 2016. http://en.wikipedia.org/wiki/Electromagnetic_pulse_in_fiction_and_popular_culture

World Health Organization (WHO). 'Ebola Vaccines, Therapies, and Diagnostics'. *Programmes: Essential Medicines and Health Products*. 26 May 2015. http://www.who.int/medicines/emp_ebola_q_as/en

Index

Page numbers in italic refer to figures and tables.

Abu Ghraib prison 137–8
accidental outcomes: constitutional crises
    49–50
Acharya, Viral V. 45
Adams, John 138
adherence to rule of law: during a crisis
    7–8, 39–48, 52
Affordable Care Act *see* Patient Protection
    and Affordable Care Act (ACA)
Afghanistan 126, 127, 137
Africa 6
Age of Revolution (1776-1815) 2
agencies: crises and new 27
aggregate household debt 79–80
Agricultural Adjustment Act (1933) 18
Agricultural Adjustment Administration 27
AIDS 6
air travel 157
Al Qaeda 136, 137, 147n9
American Civil Liberties Union 22
Ancien Régime 2
Anglo-American political tradition 7
antibiotics 6, 156
Arab Spring 139
Arkansas 114, 134
Armistice (1918) 24
Army (US) 126, 129–30, 131, 132, 133,
    134, 147n7
Arthur, Chester A. 139
Article 6 (US Constitution) 129
Article 51 (UN Charter) 162
Ashcroft, John 28
austerity measures 143–4
auto bailouts 41, 42, 48, 55, 60
auto bankruptcy 64
autonomy (presidential) 21
auxiliary precautions (constitutional) 37, 39

bad weather 6
Bailey curve 98
bailouts: auto 41, 42, 48, 55, 60; banks 41,
    43, 45, 48, 49–50, 54–5, 60, 62; fund
    allocation 42–3
Baker, Peter 160
balance of power 49, 129
balanced budget amendment 8, 63, 108
Balasubramanian, Bhanu 45
bank reserves: Federal Reserve interest
    payments on 27, 97, 104
banking crises 8
banking panics 51, 55, 58, 114
bankruptcy: default and 108; of the Fed
    104–5; Hospital Insurance trust fund
    96; Lehman Brothers 48; Whig Party
    proposed national legislation 115
Bankruptcy Code 64
banks: bailouts 41, 43, 45, 48, 49–50,
    54–5, 60, 62; costs of Dodd-Frank
    legislation 44–5; political influence and
    TARP fund distribution 43; response
    to Durbin Amendment 47; *see also*
    commercial banks; investment banks;
    state-chartered banks
Barber, Sotirios A. 130
barter economy 164
Bastiat, Frédéric 30
Bear Stearns 41, 54
bellum omnium contra omnes 163
Bennett, James 79
Bernanke, Ben 57
Bernstein, David 38
bicameralism 38
big box retailers 46–7
Bill of Rights 37, 49
bio-terror 156, 157

172 *Index*

Black, Lamont K. 48
'black swan'-type events 150
Blankfein, Lloyd 45
Blau, Benjamin. 43
Bologna, Jamie 8
bond illusion 110
Bonus Army 133–4
boom towns 82
'Bootleggers and Baptists' law 38
borrowing ability (government) 108–9
Brains Trust 20
Bricker, Jesse 154
British investors 116
Brown, John 146n4
Brown v. Board of Education of Topeka (1954) 134
Bryan, William Jennings 52
Buber, Martin 89
Buchanan, James 63, 73, 76, 77, 81
budget deficits (US) 153; constitutional rules prohibiting 63; lack of effort to reduce 73; persistence of 84; as a way of life 62
budget tragedy (democratic) 80–2, 84
budgeting complexity 84
bureaucracy: resistance to viral countermeasure development 158; theory of 81
Burns, Scott 73, 77
Bush, George H.W. 135, 146n2
Bush, George W. 13, 49, 50, 60, 95, 127, 136, 137, 138, 139, 146n2, 153, 160
business failures 62
Byrd-Grassley legislation 73

Calhoun, John C. 129
California 48, 82, 92, 142, 159
Cambodia 139
campaign contributions: allocation of bailout funds 42–3
Campbell, Kurt 135
canal boom 114
Capital Purchase Program (CPP) 43
care: giving government credit for 30
Carter, Jimmy 21
Center for Disease Control 157
Center for Strategic and International Studies 160
central banks 97
centrally planned economies 32
change: crisis and real 1; *see also* ideological change; reform; regime change/collapse
checks and balances (constitutional) 37

Chernobyl power plant explosion 141
China 3, 4, 32, 105, 111, 153, 160
Chrysler 42, 60, 64
Citizen United 60
citizenship 51, 130
civic education 8, 64, 165–6
civil order: reconstitution of 84
Civil War 37–8, 49, 63, 97, 102, 129, 130, 146n1
civil-military partnership 135
Clay, Henry 114, 115
Cleveland, Grover 52, 133, 147n7
Clinton, Hilary 92
Clinton, William (Bill) 61, 95, 135–6, 139
closed-end funds *104*, 105, 107
closed-group unfunded liability 112
coalitional politics 81
codification: short-term suspensions of the rule of law 43–7
Cold War 134, 144
collective action 56, 59, 77
collusive federalism 91
combative debating tactics 22
commercial banks 27, 104, 105, 107
commercial corporations 86
commercial and industrial (C&I) loans 48
common property budgeting 81
commons tragedy 80–1
community banks 44
competition 37, 74, 82, 84, 87, 129
complexity in budgeting 84
computer-based systems: concerns about a collapse of 158–9
Confederates 130
Congress 49, 57, 90, 125, 158
Congress as Santa Claus 77–8
Congressional Budget Office (CBO) 95, 98, 101–2
consensual democracy: public debt within a system of 77–9
Constitution (US) 49; amendments *see individual amendments*; Article Six 129; collusive federalism and the turning upside-down of 91; a failure in original design 138; federalist feature of original 90; general welfare clause 77–8; institutional protections 31; morphing into a democratic oligarchy 74; purpose 36–7; Shays Rebellion and production and ratification of 128; turning right-side up 92; *see also* state constitutions
constitutional bonds 152
constitutional crises: (1787 and 1865) 50–1; constitutional opportunity 36–9;

Index 173

determination of good or bad outcomes 49–61; Nullification Bill 129; secession (1860-1) 130
constitutional opportunity 36–9
constitutional reconciliation 89–91
constitutional revolutions 28
contagion (financial) 58
contingency plans 158, 160
contingent liabilities 83, 103
contractual mythology: public debt and 75–7
Coolidge, Calvin 39
coronavirus 156
Couch, Jim F. 42
counter-elites 3
countermeasures (viral) 157, 158
court decisions: crises and new 28
credence goods 82
credit markets 75, 78, 85, 86, 108
credit rating 153
credit reports 75
credit transactions 75
creditors 109
crises: military role *see* military; normality versus 16–18; US and possibility of a not too distant 1; *see also* constitutional crises; environmental crises; financial crises; fiscal crises; national emergencies; regime collapse; systemic collapse
crisis opportunism 1, 15–16; creation of a ratchet effect 18–25; need to guard against 32–3; priority list of options 25–8
crony capitalism 9, 60, 61, 62
cyber attack 140, 158, 160–1, 165
cyber defence 161, 165
cyber warfare 162
cybercrime 160
cybersecurity 162
Cyree, Ken 45

de jure formal rules 50
deadly diseases 6, 156, 157–8
debaathification 147n6
debit card intercharge fees 46, 47
debt-to-GDP ratio 101–2, 155
debtor-creditor relationships 75
debtor-in-possession financing 42
debtors 109
decision-making: slowness in 126
default: cascade into 100–2; historical case study 113–16; long-run consequences 108–13; prediction of 8; reasons for

likelihood 96, 97–100; short-run consequences 102–8
defence budget (US) 144
Defense Authorization Bill (2007) 142
defensive war 126
defined benefit programmes 83
deflation 51, 113, 114, 116
democracy 74, 77, 89; liberty and 89–91; time and political capital accounts 84–7; *see also* consensual democracy; progressivism; representative democracy
Democracy in America 91–2
democratic budget tragedy 80–2, 84
democratic despotism 92
democratic oligarchy 74, 75, 84, 87–9
Democratic Party 52, 62, 131
Democratic Republic of Congo 139
Department of Agriculture (US) 27
Department of Defense (US) 124, 140–1, 144, 145, 161
Department of Energy (US) 27
Department of Health and Human Services (US) 156
Department of Homeland Security (US) 162
depression(s) 3, 52, 114–15; *see also* Great Depression
desegregation 134
despotism (democratic) 92
detainees (Guantanamo) 127–8
detection capabilities (disease) 157–8
Detroit 142
Die Hard 4: Live Free or Die Hard 159
Dimon, Jamie 45
disaster relief 140–1
Disaster Relief and Emergency Assistance Acts 141
discrepancy: in unfunded liabilities 83
discretion (government) 40, 41, 47–8; *see also* executive discretion; presidential discretion
disease(s) 6, 156, 157–8
disequilibrium 22
dissent 28
do nothing 17, 29
do something 17, 18, 20, 30
Dodd-Frank legislation 41, 44–5, 46, 47, 65n11
dollar-denominated financial securities 113
dollars 113
domestic holders: Treasury debt *104*, 105, 107, 111
domestic politics: military interventions 139–40

174 *Index*

'Don't Ask, Don't Tell' policy 135–6
Dorgan, Byron 21
Dorsch, Michael 43
double contingency 83
double-entry accounting 79
Duchin, Ran 43, 48
Duncan, Thomas Eric 157
Durbin Amendment (Dodd-Frank) 46, 47

Eastern European countries 32
Ebola outbreak 6, 143, 155, 157
Ebola vaccine 158
economic analysis 30
economic benefits: of a default 109
economic collapse 151–5, 163
economic crises 5–6; rule of law during
   see rule of law; *see also* depression(s);
   recessions
economic dislocations 4, 36, 40, 163
economic dynamism 38, 62, 154
economic espionage 160
economic freedom 8–9, 32
economic growth 40, 109, 116, 152, 155
economic prosperity 40, 53, 114, 116
economic recovery 40–1, 51
economic resurgence 155
economic-privilege seekers 15
economies of scale 87
economy: primacy of US 151
Edelson, Chris 127
Egypt 139
Eisenhower, Dwight D. 134
Election (1876) 132
Electoral College 37
electrical grid collapse 161–2
electromagnet pulse (EMP): weaponry
   disruption 159
elites: conflict between public opinion and
   54; constitutional crisis outcomes 50–2;
   degraded state of, in policing overreach
   61; power 54; and regime change 3; and
   the rule of law 8, 53
Elmendorf, Doug 102
Emanuel, Rahm 1, 15
emergency agencies 25
Emergency Fleet Corporation 24
emergency plans and programmes 18, 22,
   23, 24, 31
emergency presidential power 127
energy resources 100
Enforcement Acts 132
entitlement programmes: debt and
   probably collapse 154; *see also*
   unfunded liabilities

environmental crises 6, 140–1
epidemic crises 6, 143
Epstein, Richard 74, 91
Erie canal 114
espionage 160
Europe 2, 3, 32, 116; *see also individual*
   countries
Eurosclerosis 154
excessive resource exploitation 80, 81
exchange-traded funds *104*, 105, *107*
executive: advantage during crises 20–1
executive authority 57, 59, 61
executive departments 13
executive discretion 31, 39, 57
Executive Order (9981) 134
expansion (governmental) 18, 20, 23, 31, 37
experience goods 82
external shocks 74
extraordinary tax 78, 79

factional democracy 78, 79–80, 81
famine 6
Fannie Mae 103, 153
favour-seeking 42
Feaver, Peter 128, 136
federal bonds 79
Federal Bureau of Investigation (FBI)
   142, 160
Federal Energy Administration 27
Federal Energy Office 27
federal government (US) 37; assets 100;
   borrowing ability after a default 109;
   challenges to 128; as containing seeds
   of its own destruction 31; course
   reversal 32; crisis mode 124–5; division/
   disagreement about cyber defence 161;
   early 90–1; executive departments 13;
   expenditure 8, 14–15, 115; growing
   routine lawlessness 7; indebtedness
   see US public debt; intervention, auto
   bankruptcies 64; preventing/moderating
   harms caused by 28–32; regulatory
   agencies 13–14; response to financial
   crises 8, 39, 41, 49, 51–3, 54–5,
   108; response to public outcries 18;
   unpreparedness for collapse 161
federal judiciary 37, 38
federal power 15, 18, 37–8, 39
Federal Reserve 43, 44, 91, 153; foreign
   securities 111; interest payments on
   bank reserves 27, 97, 104; monetary
   contraction and exacerbation of crisis
   (1929) 5; response/approach to 2008
   financial crisis 16, 57, 58; Treasury debt

owned by 103–4, *107*; unlikelihood of eliminating funding shortfall 97

federal tariffs: nullification of 129

federalism 31, 37, 38, 39, 90–1

Federalist No. 10 37, 62

Feldstein, Martin 155

feudalism 91

Fiat 42, 64

fiat money 97, 101, 104, 113

Fifth amendment 91

Fiji 139

films (apocalyptic) 7, 159

financial crises: and economic freedom 8–9; and reform 8; *see also* banking panics; economic crises

financial crisis (2008): causes 152; government response 15–16, 39, 41, 49, 57; trend towards lower seigniorage 97

financial firewalls 100–1

financial institutions: campaign contributions and allocation of bailout funds 42–3; indirect support of government debt 104; lobbying and firm performance 43; risk profiles 45; Treasury security holdings 105; *see also* banks

financial intermediaries 77, 78, 107, 108

financial markets (global) 154

firm performance: lobbying and 43

firms: impact of default on 108

First Amendment 22, 60

fiscal collapse 3, 4

fiscal commons 80

fiscal crises 5–6; fiscal gap and future US 95; military role in 143–5; pragmatic regime change as possible solution to 7; as a quality of progressivist democracy 73–92; recognition/prediction of a future US 8; undermining of the rule of law 8

fiscal discipline 56, 117

fiscal domination 77

fiscal gap 95–6, 98–100, 108

fiscal history 97

fiscal illusion 110, 112

fiscal reforms 115

fiscal trajectories 73–4

Five Civilized Tribes 129

Fleming, James 130

flexible price adjustments 51

Florida 114, 132, 139

flu 156, 158

Foldvary, Fred 80

food 6, 151

Force Bill 129

foreign currency assets 113

foreign holdings: Treasury securities *104*, 105, *106*, 110–11

foreign invasion 163–4

foreign investors 116

formal legal restraints 59, 60

Fourteenth Amendment 38, 63, 102, 130

Framers (constitutional) 37, 39

France 2, 154

Freddie Mac 103, 153

free competition 87

free markets 151, 152

freed slaves 38, 51, 130

French Revolution 2, 4, 152

Friedman, David D. 108

Friedman, Milton 1, 116

frontier duties (military) 129–30, 133

Frum, David 155

Fukushima Daiichi power plant 141

future payments: debt and obligation to make 76–7, 82–3, 85, 113

Garfield, James 139

Gates, Bob 161, 162

GDP: federal outlays and receipts as a per cent of (1940-2012) 98–9; government spending as a per cent of (1903-2012) 14; *see also* debt-to-GDP ratio

General Motors 42, 48, 60, 65n10

general welfare clause 77–8

generational accounting 95

Germany 2, 4

global economy 40, 158

global stability 152

globalization 97, 98, 154

Glorious Revolution (1688) 2

GNP per capita (1893) 52

Gokhale, Jagadeesh 95

gold holdings 100

gold standard 102

Gordon, John Steele 159

Gordon, Scott 80

Gore, Albert 139

government(s): ability to generate fiscal crises 74; course reversal 32; crisis-driven growth *see* ratchet effect; defaults and borrowing ability 108–9; limiting/reining in overreach 29, 30; perceived as first resort in solving problems 17; United States *see* federal government (US); local governments (US); state governments (US)

Government Accountability Office 45

government action: crises and belief in necessity of 57; crises and new

176 *Index*

precedents in 26; emergencies and justification for quicker 31; and socio-economic emergencies 29
government policies: crises due to inept/bad 5, 29; crisis-driven 26–7, 30; emergency *see* emergency plans and programmes; in response to public outcries 18; unpredictability and moral hazard 41
government size: banking crises 8; commonly used index of 14; and implosion 31; and intensifying democratic oligarchy 87–9; national emergencies and 15
government statements 29
government-sponsored enterprises (GSEs) 42, 103, *104*, 105, 107, 153
Grant, James 52, 53
Grant, Ulysses S. 130–1, 132, 147n7
Great Depression 14, 38, 39, 41, 49, 51–2, 102, 116, 133
Great Inflation 97, 98
Greece 4, 110, 153
Greek debt crisis 101
green cars 42
greenbacks 63, 97, 101
Greve, Michael 38, 91
grid collapse 6, 158–63
gridlock 31
Grinath, Arthur 116
Guantanamo Bay 127–8, 137, 138

H1N1 Swine flu 158
Haan, Jakob de 8
hacking 140, 160–1
Hamas 160
Harding, Warren G. 23, 39, 52–3
Harrison, William Henry 139
hasty action 21, 31
Hayek, Friedrich 40, 117
Hayes, Rutherford B. 132, 147n7
Hazelwood, Lieu N. 48
Hazlitt, Henry 30
hedge funds 105
Henninger, Dan 152
Higgs, Robert 5, 52, 54
Hitler, Adolf 4
Hobbes 163
homestead principle 115
Hoover, Herbert 53, 133, 134
Hospital Insurance trust fund 96, 100–1
House of Representatives 37, 140
household debt 79–80
household sector: Treasury securities holdings *104*, 105, 107, 111

housing collapse 152
housing GSEs 42, 103, 153
human capital 108, 110, 111
Human Rights Watch 22
Hummel, Jeffrey Rogers 8, 52
100 per cent threshold: debt-to-GDP ratio 101–2
Hussein, Saddam 137
hyperinflation(s) 4, 97, 98, 101

ideological change 30, 32
ideological competition 82
ideological entrepreneurs 19, 20
ideological learning 25
ideologues 15
ideology: complementarity of liberty and democracy 89, 90; constitutional crisis outcomes and popular 53–6; political life 17; revolutionary regime change 3
Igan, Deniz 43
Illinois 114
impeachment 60, 61
imperial executive 126
imperial presidency 21
income inequality protests 142–3
income tax burdens 81
income tax legislation 52
India 8, 32
Indiana 114
individual liberty *see* liberty
inevitability of executive authority: crises and 57
inflation 97, 98; *see also* deflation; hyperinflation(s)
informal constraints 57, 59, 60
information-shaping 54
innovation 152, 155
Institute for Energy research 100
institutional protections 31, 37, 38
institutionalization 27
insurance companies *104*, 105, *107*
insurance prices 45
insurgency 3, 137, 138, 141
Insurrection Act (1807) 142
insurrection crisis: military role 141–3
inter arma enim silent leges 28
intercharge fees (debit card) 46, 47
interest groups 18, 19, 20, 37, 39, 62
interest payments: on commercial bank reserves 27, 97, *104*; US debt obligations 153
intergenerational transfers 109, 113
International Monetary Fund (IMF) 45
Interstate Commerce Commission 13

intertemporal transfers 109
The Interview 158
invasion foreign force 163–4
investment 152
investment banks 44, 105; *see also* Bear
  Stearns; Lehman Brothers
Iraq 28, 127, 136, 137–8, 147n6
Ireland 8, 32
iron triangles 23–4
Israel 160–1
issuers of asset-backed securities *104, 107*
Italy 2

Jackson, Andrew 26, 129
Japan 105, 111, 141
Jefferson, Thomas 13, 17, 138
Johnson, Andrew 49, 132
Johnson, Lyndon B. 146n2
Jouvenal, Bertrand de 77, 89
judiciary 37, 38, 59

Kalt, Brian 139
Kansas 130
Kelly, Brian Y. 45
Kennedy School of Government 44
Kent State University 135
King, Rodney 142
Knight, Frank 80
Knox, Frank 26
Kopan, Tal 160
Korean War 14, 99, 126, 134, 146n3
Kotlikoff, Lawrence J. 73, 77, 95
Kovacevich, Richard 58
Kramek, Joseph 159
Krugman, Paul 102, 103
Ku Klux Klan (KKK) 132

Laffer curve 98
laissez faire 117
large banks 44, 45, 46, 63
Latin America 2, 3
law enforcement 61, 123, 133, 134, 140,
  141, 145, 157, 163
lawlessness (government) 7
leadership: and regime change 4
Lee, Robert E. 131
left-wing terrorists 142
legal constraints: constitutional crisis
  outcomes 56–61
legal tender law 63
legislation: crises and new 27; theory of
  states' right to nullify federal 129;
  see also individual acts; rule of law
Lehman Brothers 41, 48, 58

lenders 85, 109
Lenin 4
leviathan 7, 9
liability: for public debt 76–7; *see also*
  personal liabilities; tax, liabilities;
  unfunded liabilities
liberal legalism 57–8, 59
Liberia 143, 155
liberty 7, 9, 33, 36, 37, 38, 39, 89–91
life expectancy 156
lifestyle evolution 6
Lincoln, Abraham 49, 130, 146n5
literature (apocalpytic) 7, 159
living standards 151, 152
loan transactions 85, 109
lobbying: and firm performance 43
local governments (US): expansion of
  activities 13; expenditure to GDP
  ratio 14; financing 86; indebtedness
  73; ownership value associated with
  politically managed enterprises 86;
  Treasury security holdings *104,*
  105, 107; as unsuccessful in reining
  in excessive obligations of pension
  programmes 62
Lochner v. New York 38
log roll 18
logjams 17, 18, 19, 23
Los Angeles 142
Louisiana 114, 132

MacArthur, Douglas 133, 134
MacCallum, Spencer H. 80
McClellan, George 7
McKinley, William 147n7
Madison, James 37, 125, 128
Mali 139
market liberalization 8
market-oriented reform 8
Maryland 114, 128
mass privation 3
Massachusetts 82, 92, 128
material well-being 152
maturity phase 18, 22–3
Mauritania 139
media 28, 29, 56, 61, 123
Medicaid 46, 95, 98, 100, 101, 111, 112, 116
Medicare 1, 56, 73, 82, 83, 96, 98, 100,
  101, 103, 111, 112, 116, 117, 153, 164
medicine 6
medieval period: governmental collapse
  and return to 164–5
Mellon, Andrew 53
Mercatus Center study 44–5

178   *Index*

Merchant Fleet Corporation 24
MERS – Middle East Respiratory
 syndrome 156
Metcalf power substation 159
Mexican War 129
Mexico 110, 158
Meyer, Eugene 24
Michigan 114
middle-class interest-group politics 62
Miles, Nelson A. 133
military: and crisis opportunism 15; as
 enforcement mechanism of choice for
 civilian leaders 123–4; interventions,
 domestic politics 139–40; *see also* US
 military
military districts 131
military government 7, 131
Mises: Ludwig von 117
Mississippi 114
Mitchell, Broadus 27
mixed economy 117
Moberg, Lotta 86
modern conveniences: reliance on 151
Moley, Raymond 20, 21
monarchs' debt 79
monetary constitution 63
monetary contraction 5, 116
monetary expansion 51, 97, 105, 113
monetary policy 90–1, 105
money market funds *104*, 105, 107
Monroe, James 51, 65n6
moral hazard 40, 41, 46, 47–8, 58, 61
Morsi, Mohamed 139
mortality (flu-related) 156
Mubarak, Hosni 139
Mullen, Mike 124
Murphy, Liam 90
mutual funds *104*, 105, 107
Myanmar 139

Nagel, Thomas 90
national bankruptcy legislation 115
national emergencies 26; and government
 spending 14–15; preventing harms
 caused by government responses 28–32;
 and the ratcheting loss of economic and
 social liberties 33
National Guard 134, 135, 142, 145
National Institutes of health (NIH) 158
national markets 38
national security emergency(ies) 39,
 40–1, 49
National Socialism 4
Native American tribes 129, 133

Navy (US) 126, 141
Nazism 3
nearly full-employment deflation 51, 116
networks 88
New Deal 30, 39, 49, 53, 60
New Jersey 128
New York 114, 115, 128, 142
New Zealand 8, 31, 32
news censorship 28
news media reports 29
Niskanen, William 74, 81
Nixon, Richard 27, 60, 61, 102
non-financial corporations: Treasury
 security holdings *104*, 105
non-profit sector: Treasury securities
 holdings 105, 107
Noonan, Peggy 158–9
normality versus crisis 16–18
North Carolina 131
North Korea 139, 158
nuclear power plants 141
Nullification Bill 129

Obama, Barack 21, 41, 46, 48, 50, 55, 59,
 60, 64, 127–8, 143, 160
Obamacare *see* Patient Protection and
 Affordable Care Act (ACA)
obligation to make future payments 76–7,
 82–3, 85, 113
Occupy Movement 9, 142–3
Office of the Comptroller of the Currency 13
O'Hanlon, Michael 135
Ohio 114
Ohio National Guard 135
oligarchic democracy 74, 75, 84, 87–9
Olson, Mancur 39, 56, 59, 62
One Second After 159
online voting 140
open competition 87
open-ended contractual relationships 75
open-group unfunded liability 112
Operation Protective Edge 160
opponents: intimidation of, during crises 21–2
opportunism *see* crisis opportunism;
 political opportunism; post-contractual
 opportunism
organized insurgency 3
organized interest groups 19
Ostrom, Elinor 80
Ostrom, Vincent 90
ownership 80, 85, 86

Pakistan 139
Palestinian hackers 160–1

Pan American Health Organization (PAHO) 157–8
pandemics 143, 157
paper money 63, 97, 101
Pareto, Vilfredo 81–2, 90
path dependency 25
Patient Protection and Affordable Care Act (ACA) 22, 46, 96
Paulson, Henry (Hank) 57, 58, 62, 65n10
pay-as-you-go social insurance 109, 112, 116, 117
peacetime: military role in 126
'pen and phone' lawmaking 50, 53
Pennsylvania 114, 128, 133
personal debt 75–6, 80
personal liabilities 78, 92
personal responsibility 7
personnel: crises and new government 26; US military 124, 143, 144–5
pharmaceutical companies 46
piggybacking: special interests 40, 42
Pitlik, Hans 8
Plessy v. Ferguson 147n8
Pogo 62
policy education 30
political benefit: of a default 108–9
political competition 82, 84
political connections: and receipt of bailout funds 43
political crises 2
'political economy of crisis opportunism' 15
political favouritism 39
political incentives: tax limitations and 92
political influence: and TARP fund distribution 43
political opportunism 15, 40, 41, 46, 51, 61
political tradition (Anglo-American) 7
political uncertainty 41
the poor: impact of economic collapse on 154–5
popular culture: and grid collapse 159
popular ideology: constitutional crisis outcomes 53–6
Posner, Eric 56–61
Posse Comitatus Act (1878) 133, 140, 142, 145
post-contractual opportunism 75
post-crisis period 18, 43–4
post-petition financing 42
power grid collapse/disruption 6, 159–60
power plant disasters 141
power(s): congressional 49; democratic 77; elites 54; fiscal crisis as competition for 74; governmental *see* federal power;

presidential power; the military as a major instrument of American 126; opportunists' management of new 28; US Constitution and frustration of factional 36; *see also* balance of power; separation of powers
pragmatic regime change 2, 3, 7, 8
pre-crisis normality 18, 19–20
pre-emption 115
pre-technological skills 165
preparedness strategies 165–6
presidential discretion 21, 44, 50
presidential elections 139
presidential power 21, 126–7
presidents: army veterans 147n7; informal constraints 57, 59; question of constitutional privileges when a state of war has not been declared 125; two-term limit 49; in wartime 126–8; *see also individual presidents*; vice presidency
Primo, David 73
private debt 63, 78, 85, 109
private pension funds *104*, 105, 107
private property 80–1, 84, 85, 86, 89, 90, 91, 92; *see also* property crime; property rights; taking property
private sector: economic crises in 5; impact of repudiation on 105
privately ordered credit markets 85
pro-slavery activists 146n4
Progressive era 38, 39, 84
progressivism 89–90, 91; fiscal crisis as a quality of 73–92; perception of government as first resort to solve problems 17, 19; unsustainable public spending 8
Project Bioshield 158
propaganda 21, 25, 29
property crime 145
property rights 52, 53, 59, 90, 130
protectionism 37, 38
proto-police forces 163, 164
public accommodation: government's enlarged role 23
public debt: contingent liability 83; and contractual mythology 75–7; as fiscal domination 77; as a global problem 153; and obligation to make future payments 76–7, 82–3, 85, 113; theory of 74–5; time, democracy and 84–7; United States *see* US public debt; within a system of consensual democracy 77–9; within a system of factional democracy 79–80

180 *Index*

public disorder 3
public health officials 158
'public interest' policies 22
public land: sale of 115
public opinion 52, 53, 54, 55, 58, 59, 60
public policy: crisis preparedness 165–6
public safety: governmental collapse and 163–4
public support: crisis policy-making 29–30

Quadrennial Defense Review 2014 124, 145
quantitative easing 104

race riots (1965) 142
radical regime change 2, 3
railway workers' strike 133
railways 115–16
Rajagopalan, Shruti 90
Ramo, Joshua Cooper 155
random networks 88
rapid reform: system design and difficulty of 153
ratchet effect 15, 18–25, 33, 40
Reagan, Ronald 27, 39, 135, 146n2
real assets 100, 108, 110, 113
recessions 8, 55, 108, 113, 132, 152
Reconstruction of the South 130–2, 133
Red Dawn 159
reform: financial crises and 8; system design and difficulty of rapid 153
regime change/collapse 2–4, 6, 7, 44
regime instability 6
regulatory compliance costs (Dodd-Frank) 44–5
regulatory offices and agencies 13–14
Reinhart, Carmen H. 101, 103
rent-extraction 46
rent-seekers 15
rent-seeking 38, 46, 51, 54, 61, 62
rent-seeking legislation 38, 39, 47
representative democracy 16, 89
Republican Party 55, 56
repudiation(s) 8, 64, 96, 97–100, 101, 102, 104, 105, 108, 109, 115
residual claimancy 85
retirement funds *104*, 105, 107
retrenchment 8, 14, 18–19, 23–5, 29
revolutionary regime change 2–3
Revolutionary War 101, 102, 128
Ricardian equivalence 86, 110
right-wing terrorists 142
risk profiles: US financial institutions 45
risk ratings: commercial and industrial (C&I) loans 48

risk-adjusted crash insurance prices 45
risk-taking 43, 46, 48
Roberts, Owen J. 20
Rogoff, Kenneth S. 101, 103
Roosevelt, Franklin D. 20, 21, 26, 30, 49, 60
Roosevelt, Theodore 13, 133
rule of law 7, 151, 152; attack on argument for adhering to, during crises 56–7; civic education for understanding and support for 64; codifying short-term suspensions of 43–7; collapse in 163–4; economic recovery 40–1; elite lack of respect/ hostility to 8, 53; judiciary intervention to uphold 59; maintaining during times of crisis 7–8, 39–48, 52; moral hazard 47–8; and the next crisis 61–4; role of elites in sustaining 50–1; Tea Party Movement support for 55
Russia 2, 3, 4, 101, 113, 139, 153, 160

Sargent, Thomas J. 115
SARS – Severe Acute Respiratory Syndrome 156
scale-free networks 88
Schiff, Peter 153–4
Schofield, John 131
Scott, Winfield 129
secession crisis (1860-1) 130
Section 4 (14th Amendment) 102
security brokers/dealers and holding companies *104, 107*
segregation 134
seigniorage 97, 98
self-governance 50, 77, 89
Senate 37, 90, 140
senators 37
Senegal 143
separation of powers 31, 37, 39, 57, 125
September 11 attacks 22, 136
sequestration 143–4
Seventeenth Amendment 37, 38
Shays, Daniel 128
Sherman, William T. 131
Sibelius v. NFIB 60
Sickles, Dan 131
Siegan, Bernard 38
Silicon Valley 159
Sixteenth Amendment 38
Slaughter-House Cases 38
slavery 37, 129
small(er) banks 44–5
Smetters, Kent A. 95
Smith, Rebecca 159–60

social insurance 109, 112, 116, 117
Social Security 1, 56, 62, 73, 82, 83, 96, 98, 101, 103, 111, 112, 116
social unrest 159
socialism 4, 117
socio-economic emergencies 29
Somalia 143
Sony hack 158, 161
Sosyura, Denis 43, 48
South Carolina 129, 132
Southern states 130–2, 133, 134
Soviet Union 31, 101, 134
Spanish Influenza (1918-19) 156
special interests 30, 31; benefits, securing of 62; favour-seeking 42; government overreach 29; need for adherence to rule of law during times of crisis 40; piggybacking 40, 42; protectionism 38; as winners in suspensions of rule of law 44
spoils system 26
spot transactions 75
Springer, Paul 6
stability 152
Stafford, Robert T. 141
Standard & Poor 153
state constitutions 115
state governments (US): defaults 114, 115; expansion of activities 13; expenditure to GDP ratio 14; federal government refusal to bail out 52; fiscal reform 115; indebtedness 73, 114; right to nullify federal laws 129; Treasury security holdings *104*, 105, 107; as unsuccessful in reining in excessive obligations of pension programmes 62
state of nature 7
state protectionism 37, 38
state of war 125
state-chartered banks 114, 116
Stevenson, Charles 125
stewardship land and heritage assets 100
Stimson, Henry 26
stock market 5, 105, 108, 155
Strategic National Stockpile 158
student loans 100
Sturm, Jan-Egbert 8
subsidy (TBTF) 45–6
succession crisis: role of military in a 138–40
Summers, Larry 154
sunset provisions: emergency measures 31
Supremacy Clause 129
Supreme Court 37, 39; crises and new court decisions 28; and government

intervention in auto bankruptcies 64; legal tender laws 63; limiting of range of action available to political actors 53; nullification of executive overreach 59; presidential attacks 60; relenting of opposition to New Deal 60; revolution (1937) 20; ruling against segregated public schools 134; striking down of income tax legislation 52; upholding of the rule of law 51
surveillance 22
survival skills 6–7, 165–6
Swift v. Tyson 37
Swine Flu 158
Switzerland 88
Sylla, Richard 116
systemic collapse 150–66; addressability 163; dangers unchecked 163–6; economic 151–5; grid collapse 158–63; policy advice 165; possibilities of military government following 7; viral danger 155–8
systemic lying: unfunded liabilities as a form of 84

Taguba, Antonio 138
taking property 91
tax: closure of fiscal gap 98–100; financing 78, 79; liabilities 80, 109, 111; limitations 92; *see also* income tax
Taylor, John 58
'Tea Party' movement 9, 54–6
technology: and disease 157
terror attack 140; *see also* bio-terror; cyber attack; September 11 attacks
terrorist groups 6, 142, 145, 160
Thailand 140
Thatcher, Margaret 32
theft 160
Thirteenth Amendment 130
Three Little Pigs 85
Tilden, Samuel 132
time: debtor-creditor relationships 75, 77; democracy and political capital accounts 84–7; importance during crises 20–1
time preference 85
Tocqueville, Alexis de 92
'too big to fail' 45–6
torture 137, 138, 139
tragedy of the commons 80–1
Trail of Tears 129
transfer payments: systemic collapse and disappearance of 164
transportation system 157

182   Index

travel 157, 164–5
Treasury: approach to 2008 financial crisis 57, 58; consequences of a default 95–117; financial report (2015) 100, 112
Treaty of Paris 128
Troubled Asset Relief Program (TARP) 42, 43, 48, 50, 58, 60, 97
Troy, Tevi 6
Truman, Harry S. 134
trust funds 96, 100–1, 103, 105; *see also* Hospital Insurance trust fund; Medicare; Social Security
Tsarist regime 4
TV shows (apocalyptic) 159
Twelfth Amendment 138
two-term limit (presidential) 49
Tyler, John 139
tyrannophobia 58, 60
Tytler, Alexander 74

Ukraine 152
UN Charter (Article 51) 162
unemployment 52, 116, 133, 145
unfunded liabilities 82–4; elimination 92; estimations 62, 73; financial firewall 100–1; as a form of systemic lying 84; major sources 73; and the possibility of not too distant crisis 1; time, democracy and 84–7; unsustainable 7; *see also* Medicare; Social Security
United Auto Workers 42, 64
United Kingdom 2, 32, 102
United States: economic crises and the rule of law *see* rule of law; government *see* federal government (US); local governments (US); state governments (US); possibility of a not too distant crisis 1; primacy of the economy 151; scale of governance and democratic oligarchy 88–9; Treasury default *see* default
upside-down constitution 91, 92
US military: budget 144; Cold War and peacetime buildup 134; conscription 23; desegregation (1948) 134; 'Don't Ask, Don't Tell' policy 135–6; embedding of reporters in units 28; inter-service rivalry in budgeting 23; intervention, Latin America 110; as a major instrument of American power 126; and modern crises 136–8; officer oaths 124; personnel 124, 143, 144–5; politicization of officer corps 135; possibility of cyber-assault 160;

proposed tribunals for Guantanamo detainees 127; question of constitutional privileges when a state of war has not been declared 125; respect for 7; role in domestic crises 6, 128–36; role in future crises 138–45; role in national crises 123–47; role in war and peace 125–6; small size of 126; spending 111; subordinate to civilian leadership 128; three strategic pillars 124; twenty-first century challenges 124; *see also* Army (US); Navy (US)
US public debt 7; (1946-82) 98; accumulation 84; current 73, 76, 153–4; depression-generated (1837) 115; financial firewall 101–2; government unwillingness to address 154; interest on Revolutionary War 102; and the possibility of a not too distant crisis 1; possible solution to 155; restructuring 113; unfunded liability as an unseen component of 73; validity of 63–4, 102; *see also* debt-to-GDP ratio
utility services disruption 159

vaccines 156, 158
Van Buren, Martin 51, 115
Venezuela 152, 164
Vermeule, Adrian 56–61
vested interests 26–7
vice presidency 138–9
Vietnam War 28, 126, 135, 146n3
viral danger 6, 143, 155–8
Virginia 128
volunteers (military) 144
voting mechanisms 140
voting rights 130
vulnerability: to attack 161, 162

Wagner, Richard E. 8, 73, 74, 77, 80, 86, 90
Walgreen 46–7
Wall Street Journal 16, 27, 46, 152, 158–9, 159
Wallis, John Joseph 115, 116
Walters, Stephen 82, 92
War of 1812 51, 114, 128
war: congressional prerogative to declare 125; growth in government spending 14; presidency in time of 126–8; role of military during 125–6; *see also* *individual wars*
'war of all against all' 163
War on Drugs 146n2
War Finance Corporation (US) 24

Index 183

War Industries Board (US) 27
War on Poverty 146n2
War on Terror 39, 49, 136–7
warfare: twenty-first century 136
Warren, Charles 77, 86
Warren, Elizabeth 62
Washington, George 7, 49, 102, 128
water-boarding 137
Watson, Dale L. 142
weaponry disruption 159
Weaver, Carolyn 83
Weimar Republic 2, 4
welfare state 32, 36, 96, 117
Welinghof, Jon 160
Western Europe 32
Whig Party 114–15
white supremacist movement 132

Whiting, William 125
Wikipedia 159
Wilson, Pete 142
Wilson, Woodrow 27
winners and losers: in new regimes 44
Wirth, Steffen 8
World Health Organization (WHO) 157
World War I 4, 38, 52, 126, 133, 156
World War II 3, 28, 49, 97, 99, 102, 126, 134, 155

Yemen 140
Young, Andrew 8

Zandberg, Eelco 8
Zimbabwe 97, 101
Zywicki, Todd J. 7–8

# Taylor & Francis eBooks

Helping you to choose the right eBooks for your Library

Add Routledge titles to your library's digital collection today. Taylor and Francis ebooks contains over 50,000 titles in the Humanities, Social Sciences, Behavioural Sciences, Built Environment and Law.

Choose from a range of subject packages or create your own!

Benefits for you
- » Free MARC records
- » COUNTER-compliant usage statistics
- » Flexible purchase and pricing options
- » All titles DRM-free.

Benefits for your user
- » Off-site, anytime access via Athens or referring URL
- » Print or copy pages or chapters
- » Full content search
- » Bookmark, highlight and annotate text
- » Access to thousands of pages of quality research at the click of a button.

 Free Trials Available
We offer free trials to qualifying academic, corporate and government customers.

eCollections – Choose from over 30 subject eCollections, including:

Archaeology	Language Learning
Architecture	Law
Asian Studies	Literature
Business & Management	Media & Communication
Classical Studies	Middle East Studies
Construction	Music
Creative & Media Arts	Philosophy
Criminology & Criminal Justice	Planning
Economics	Politics
Education	Psychology & Mental Health
Energy	Religion
Engineering	Security
English Language & Linguistics	Social Work
Environment & Sustainability	Sociology
Geography	Sport
Health Studies	Theatre & Performance
History	Tourism, Hospitality & Events

For more information, pricing enquiries or to order a free trial, please contact your local sales team:
www.tandfebooks.com/page/sales

 The home of Routledge books

www.tandfebooks.com